'*Against Decolonisation* launches a trench war. Its flaming arrows hit all, sparing no axiom of reflex decolonisation. This is a *bólèkájà* (come-down-let-us-slug-it-out) critique in its most consequential form. If you are not provoked by its argument, *you sabe nothing*.'

Adélékè Adéèkó, Humanities Distinguished Professor, Ohio State University

'With characteristic cogency, lucidity and audacity, Táíwò shows that "decolonisation" has become an idea promoting indiscriminate hostility to forms of thought and practice wrongly tarred with malign colonial auspices. The ironic result is a rhetoric that gives short shrift to African agency. It's time to drop the erroneous conflations and recognise our right to inventive appropriation of the human commons.'

Ato Sekyi-Otu, Emeritus Professor of Social and Political Thought, York University, Toronto, and author of *Left Universalism, Africacentric Essays*

'Táíwò has written an indispensable book. To sloganise for cultural and ideological decolonisation is to deny history and agency to Africa. He makes his point through a thorough analysis of politics, economics and debates around language and philosophy.'

Gayatri Chakravorty Spivak, Columbia University, author of *A Critique of Postcolonial Reason*

'A bracing and much-needed riposte to contemporary efforts to "decolonise" culture, language and politics in the Global South. Elegantly demonstrating the ignorance and violence of such aims, Táíwò inaugurates a new way of thinking about the persistence of empire as one of the great intellectual and political themes of our times.'

Faisal Devji, Director of the Asian Studies Centre, University of Oxford

'This is a book whose time has come. Basing his arguments principally on philosophy and language, Táíwò demonstrates how "decolonisers" reject as inauthentically African the works of even the most gifted and influential African scholars, thinkers and writers. Consistently cogent, commonsensical, powerful and wise, this book will not be the last word on decolonisation—but it is close to it.'

Biodun Jeyifo, Professor of African and African American Studies and of Comparativ

'A highly important and deeply argued book. Táíwò asks us not to succumb to the simplistic siren song of the word "decolonisation". A vague word, an easy trope does not help to create the modern African with complicated agency amidst complex historical and twenty-first-century demands.'

Stephen Chan OBE, SOAS University of London, author of *African Political Thought*

'With immense brio and a generous dose of common sense, Táíwò exposes the weaknesses of an over-extended notion of decolonisation and offers a convincing alternative. This highly readable, engaging and challenging book is a must for everyone interested in modern Africa.'

Dame Karin Barber, Emeritus Professor of African Cultural Anthropology, University of Birmingham

AGAINST DECOLONISATION

/ AFRICAN
/ ARGUMENTS

African Arguments is a series of short books about contemporary Africa and the critical issues and debates surrounding the continent. The books are scholarly and engaged, substantive and topical. They focus on questions of justice, rights and citizenship; politics, protests and revolutions; the environment, land, oil and other resources; health and disease; economy: growth, aid, taxation, debt and capital flight; and both Africa's international relations and country case studies.

Managing Editor, Stephanie Kitchen

Series editors

Adam Branch
Alex de Waal
Alcinda Honwana
Ebenezer Obadare
Carlos Oya
Nicholas Westcott

OLÚFẸ́MI TÁÍWÒ

Against Decolonisation

Taking African Agency Seriously

HURST & COMPANY, LONDON

IAI   International African Institute

Published in collaboration with the International African Institute.
First published in the United Kingdom in 2022 by
C. Hurst & Co. (Publishers) Ltd.,
New Wing, Somerset House, Strand, London, WC2R 1LA
Copyright © Olúfẹ́mi Táíwò, 2022
All rights reserved.

Printed in Great Britain by Bell and Bain Ltd, Glasgow

The right of Olúfẹ́mi Táíwò to be identified as the author of
this publication is asserted by him in accordance with the
Copyright, Designs and Patents Act, 1988.

Distributed in the United States, Canada and Latin America by
Oxford University Press, 198 Madison Avenue, New York, NY 10016,
United States of America.

A Cataloguing-in-Publication data record for this book
is available from the British Library.

ISBN: 9781787386921

This book is printed using paper from registered sustainable
and managed sources.

www.hurstpublishers.com

In loving memory
of
Tejumola Olaniyan
Friend, brother, interlocutor, collaborator, leader, benefactor, in-law, and
just an embodiment of decent humanity.
I will never stop missing you. Rest well.

CONTENTS

ACKNOWLEDGEMENTS

After the initial mix of emotions towards the lockdown necessitated by the Covid-19 pandemic in 2020 passed, I resolved to pound my frustrations out on the blank page. I could not have adopted a better and more productive stance towards this historical contingency in light of what has come out of it. This book is one of the products of this lockdown and my reaction to it. Simultaneously, having access to many interlocutors who willingly took my long calls, consented to reading bits and whole pieces of the manuscript, patiently hearing me out on those numerous occasions when ranting took the place of sedate expressions, and, on the whole, never refrained from checking my rhetorical excesses, even unreasoning enthusiasm, ultimately made all the difference in the production of this work. I can never repay their many kindnesses, but I remain forever grateful to them for being my friends and interlocutors.

I would like to be very clear. In a very real sense, this is Ebenezer Obadare's book. It was he who, in a series of phone calls after the original essay that inspired this work was published, first called my attention to the possibility that there might be a book lurking there. More than that, the structure that emerged from our conversation forms the division of the book as it stands. I have recounted this here to demonstrate the many ways in which the business of knowledge production always involves, or even requires, conversations, disagreements, honesty and, most importantly, respect, all geared to ensuring that friends never let friends advertise their stupidity to an uncaring, sometimes unkind, world.

I am blessed to have Zeyad El Nabolsy, an Africana graduate student like no other who, it was my good fortune, got assigned to me as my research assistant at the time when I was accelerating research to expand the original material. As I have told him and other associates, the principal reason this book materialised so quickly owes a whole lot to his diligence and brilliance in aiding my research with his astute summaries of materials and, especially in our weekly meetings, his reflections, commentaries, criticisms and, finally, meticulous documentation of the work. He has been more of a junior colleague than a student.

Naminata Diabate, colleague and now very dear friend, constant interlocutor on the phone and during long walks, by the force of her queries and objections forced a lot more clarity than I would otherwise have attained.

Many others have contributed their time, attention, commentaries and even twitter-ing to the emergence of this book. Professor Sheila Walker invited me to present a part of it to Scripps College before the pandemic sadly put paid to the idea. Molara Wood has been generous with comments and excerpting on Twitter! Kunle Ajibade never fails to encourage me and remind me of why we do what we do as denizens of a life of the mind. Siba Grovogui, Gerard Aching, Akin Adéṣọkàn and Adéléké Adéèkọ́, dear friends, colleagues and collaborators, have forced more nuance on my writing than they realise with their ongoing reactions to my work and my language.

The Cornell Political Theory Workshop curated during the lockdown by William Cameron invited me to contribute to its sessions. I thank Will for his kind invitation and the audience of the workshop for a very rewarding session. I extend my gratitude to my colleagues, Professor Thomas Pepinsky and Professor

ACKNOWLEDGEMENTS

Cathy Caruth, who both shared with me in conversations afterwards their reactions to the presentation.

My graduate students, Lauren Siegel, Enoch Aboi, Renatta Fordyce, Radwa Saad and Enongene Nkumbe, have all been invaluable travellers with me on this journey, having been exposed to the material in class and in conversations beyond the classroom.

The front office staff at Africana—Treva Levine, Donna Pinnisi and Renée Milligan, and the Work Study Assistants who work with them—remain invaluable in enabling our work in the department. They do their work with good humour and a cheerful disposition.

The staff at the John Henrik Clarke Africana Library, especially Saah Nue Quigee, as well as the unseen staff of the InterLibrary Loan division of the Cornell University Library have been absolutely indispensable in securing materials often and on time which have contributed to the success of this venture.

I would also like to remark on the extraordinary help of Stephanie Kitchen and the rest of the editorial team at African Arguments, as well as the many anonymous reviewers who worked on the manuscript. I am convinced that this is a much less flawed book thanks to their interventions and insistence. I have benefited from both.

The team at Hurst led by Alice Clarke has been wonderful to work with and I am grateful to them.

Adéyínká Táíwò remains the critic and interlocutor who often is the first to listen to many of my ideas when they are still unbaked, and is ever gentle but firm in letting me know when she thinks they might not fly.

I remain blessed by all of my interlocutors and can only hope that this book rewards their confidence. A ò ní bàjẹ́ lọ́wọ́ ara wa. Mo dúpẹ́.

Olúfẹ̀mi Táíwò
April 2022

PREFACE

It was only as I finished writing this book that it occurred to me that it might be useful to situate it in the broader context of my ongoing research. I hope that this helps my audience to appreciate the much larger set of challenges that face scholarship on Africa, towards the illumination of which my book is a modest contribution.

I am one of the few scholars from the continent who still argues in favour of the relevance of the so-called 'Enlightenment Project' to the advancement of Africa and the progress of its peoples. I have already argued my case in a no-holds-barred, full-throated defence of 'modernity' and why it offers Africa the most promising path for getting out of the 'misery corner' of the globe. This book was *Africa Must Be Modern: A Manifesto*, and it was originally published, by design, in Nigeria, because I hoped to reach an audience of young, educated (though not necessarily university-educated) Africans. My research had led me to believe that if colonialism had not pre-empted modernity in Africa, and turned it into an object of revulsion for most African intellectuals, a lot of what many people think is 'wrong' with the continent today may have been averted.

My work on philosophy and the history of ideas has left me troubled by the persistent but erroneous belief of many African scholars that modernity is a 'European', 'Western' or 'white' arte-fact. While I continue to fight against this misconception, unfor-tunately 'anti-modernity' scholars have rarely considered it worth their while to engage with the alternative point of view. But this is not the main problem. The issue is that the literature which came out of these historical errors continues to be dominant in scholarship about the continent by both Africans and non-Afri-cans today. It is within this context that I originally wrote the paper which has become the present book.[1] Because modernity is conflated with Westernism and with 'whiteness'—and all three with colonialism—decolonisation (the negation of colonialism) has become a catch-all idea to tackle anything with any, even minor, association with the 'West'. This is not only problematic as a matter of theory and history, but it is incorrect, too.

Because subscribers to this all-encompassing 'decolonisation' pay no mind to those of us who argue for the oneness of human-ity and against the racialisation of modernity, I prefer to leave them to their designs. Instead, this book is addressed to those who seek, or can be persuaded, to consider alternative paths to making sense of reality. As the Yorùbá saying goes, there are many roads that enter a market. I offer this book as one road to improving our understanding of Africa's position in the world of ideas and events. To this end, *Against Decolonisation* seeks to (1) identify blind spots in current scholarship and direct our atten-tion to how they might be redressed; and (2) show how and why those alternative paths may actually lead to more insights than the existing, dominant orientations. In doing so, I call attention to themes, thinkers, ideas, movements, programmes and writings which are hardly ever referenced in discussions on 'decolonisa-tion'. My hope is that expanding our horizons in this way may lead to more robust and, importantly, more accurate explanations of the challenges facing contemporary Africa.

I address *Against Decolonisation* to people who are still unsure about the worth of the decolonising trope, and who can use my

PREFACE

intervention to help them make a productive decision; to people who already embrace 'decolonisation' (because everybody does and no-one has yet shown them where it may be wrong), so that they can work out if they truly agree; and to others, especially students and young scholars, who may be uncomfortable with the indiscriminate application of this idea to all aspects of life, but don't yet feel informed enough to take it on.

I limit myself in this work to discussing 'decolonisation', and have refrained from addressing the different concept of 'decoloniality'. This is for the simple reason that while the term 'decoloniality' has its roots in a particular movement in philosophy centred around Latin America, as a philosopher myself, I remain unimpressed about its claims and what it really adds to our understanding. Decoloniality, as anthropologist Arjun Appadurai explains, 'is not a successor to colonialism and coloniality ....
Instead, [it] offers an alternative, one that is rooted in Indigenous thought and practice about nature, community, and solidarity.' But this alternative, as Appadurai assesses (and with which I agree) 'rests on a reversal of the historical impact of capitalism and colonialism. It seeks to return us to an earlier period of precolonial splendor, when what we need to imagine, as [Achille] Mbembe argues, is an alternative future'.[2]

The dominant tendency on the part of many African scholars is to incorrectly make 'decolonisation' and 'decoloniality' into synonyms. It is beyond the scope of this work to address this here, and it is something for those scholars themselves to justify. But it nonetheless speaks to my contention that the idea of 'decolonising' has lost its way. I hope that my book helps us do a better job of making sense of events, past and present, and generates a greater diversity of opinions, and more and better scholarship, designed to move humanity—not just African humanity—forward.

INTRODUCTION

I would like to begin with an anecdote from when I was at high school in Ìbàdàn, Nigeria, which I think illustrates the core problems that 'decolonising philosophy' was meant to solve. A contingent of students from another high school in Cotonou, Dahomey (now Bénin), had come to our city for a seven-day trip, lodging with us in our dormitories at my boarding school. For the week we were all together, my schoolmates and I spent our time trying to practise our French language skills, while the students from Cotonou did the same with their English. It was not till the eve of their departure that we all discovered, doubtless to our chagrin, that they and we were all, mostly, Yorùbá. That is, we could have had more meaningful, even deeper, conversations in our shared original tongue and primary culture. It was not until 1985 at a conference in Toronto, Canada, held to mark the centenary of the infamous Berlin West Africa Conference of 1884–85, that this experience came back to me, and I was able to expand on it in a presentation entitled 'On the Political Implications of Geography'. It was almost an epiphany when I realised that long before any one of us students in Ìbàdàn or Cotonou had been born, our future mindsets had already been laid out. Our preferences—from victuals (bread/*le pain* and beer/*le vin*) to colonial capitals (London/Paris) to philosophical orientations

1

(empiricism/*phenoménologie*)—had already been rigged in ways that we must, late into advanced adulthood, seek to undo.

So, when Ngũgĩ wa Thiong'o argues for the centrality of language in the task of decolonising the mind, I can't say there is much room for disagreement. And when Kwasi Wiredu insisted that how we think philosophically is influenced by the language in which we learn to do philosophy, one might not object too strongly to that, either. Just as Ngũgĩ reports that during his schooldays in Kenya, the pupils were discouraged (on pain of corporal punishment) from speaking their indigenous languages, and Wiredu's experience during a similar period was not that different in Ghana, I can tell many comparable stories from my own, much later, childhood in Nigeria. The schizophrenia-like condition brought about by going to school in one language and leading our non-school lives in another is one that we'll carry with us forever. Although I do not do so in this book, it's possible to trace a direct causal line from these chaotic linguistic phenomena to some of the contemporary difficulties of much of African knowledge production. It's the reason many African scholars assume that our original languages are good only for 'colloquial' conversations and fall short of the requirements of deep thinking.

Even in religious practice, especially liturgies, the domestication of Christianity has led, in Pentecostal circles, to colonial languages being the primary means of worship, with gaudy translations into our mother tongues provided almost for comic relief. The main assumption here is that anything that requires deep thought is the domain of our borrowed languages; our mother tongues are good only for the everyday, for habits or for ritual purposes, the latter accessible only to the limited few who are appropriately initiated. As a consequence, despite the current anxiety about our languages dying out, it may already be too late to save them from deepening fossilisation, even while they still appear alive. More on this in due course. The drive to rescue future generations from this fate should be welcomed by everyone who understands its terrible implications for a coherent, intellectual identity and for high-quality scholarship.

Given what I just said, why do I then think that it may be time to discard the 'decolonisation' trope in philosophy and elsewhere? When I began this work, I was mainly setting out to rethink 'decolonisation', and I could not have predicted what I end up offering here.[1] As I wrote in the original essay that this longer work is based on, abandoning the trope of 'decolonisation' altogether was only a possibility. But I'm now convinced of the fruitlessness of extending the scope of decolonisation beyond its original meaning—that is, of making a colony into a self-governing entity with its political and economic fortunes under its own direction (though not necessarily control), which I refer to in the book as decolonisation$_1$. 'Decolonisation' today, however, has come to mean something entirely different: forcing an ex-colony to forswear, on pain of being forever under the yoke of colonisation, any and every cultural, political, intellectual, social and linguistic artefact, idea, process, institution and practice that retains even the slightest whiff of the colonial past. I call this decolonisation$_2$.

Decolonisation$_2$ presents itself in a number of ways. Any aspect of an ex-colony that mirrors what was there during the colonial period is treated as evidence of continuing colonisation. Any institution that can be traced to colonial times must be shunned once colonisation has supposedly ended. The ultimate nebulous claim is that decolonisation is complete only after all forms of domination are overturned. In this way, decolonisation is equated with human emancipation, and this is why some people speak of 'the myth of decolonisation' in Africa. It doesn't take too much effort to see how this way of thinking is flawed. In fact, no society, whether former colony or not, is anywhere near human emancipation. Setting this as a goal of decolonisation can only stem from either a lack of understanding or from an ideological commitment. When these terms are conflated, the general objective of seeking human emancipation becomes an unfinished anti-colonial task. This is the conception that I attack in this work. As I argue, it is decolonisation$_2$ that has lost its way and is seriously harming scholarship in and on Africa.

We should rid ourselves of decolonisation$_2$ because no significant good can come from expanding its reach into the broad domain of 'cultural studies', including political, social and religious phenomena. Deploying the idea as an explanatory model, theoretical matrix or descriptive mechanism for our choice of political arrangements, the religious forms that dominate our lives or even the languages we speak in different contexts results, at best, in unsatisfactory or uncompelling outcomes. At worst, it creates confusion and obscurantism, if not outright distortion and falsification. The concept of 'decolonisation', accurately applied, describes the struggle for independence and its outcome, creating a sharp and clear division between one state and another, and aiding in our understanding. But if we extend its parameters beyond this, we are just chasing shadows and incorrectly identifying causality.

My argument follows several key lines. First, the ubiquity of 'decolonisation' in all areas of thought—from literature, linguistics and philosophy, to politics, economics, sociology, psychology and medicine—indicates that either the idea packs an explanatory and/or analytical punch like no other, or it has simply become a catch-all trope, often used to perform contemporary 'morality' or 'authenticity'.[2] I am convinced that the latter is increasingly the case. Second, I contend that many of the tasks 'decolonising' is supposed to help us with are already being, or can be, carried out without invoking this buzzword—and, I might add, without some of the histrionics that go with it. My hope is that my argument is compelling enough to persuade others to take a closer look at the real merits of the idea. Although the original inspiration for the paper which became this book was philosophy, I go beyond this and dive into history and historiography, political theory, the politics of language and the comparative experience of colonialism and its aftermath in Africa and the Caribbean. But the fundamental framework of the book remains philosophy. The reader should bear this in mind as we proceed, as it is the conceptual framing of 'decolonisation' which is chiefly responsible for the unclarity surrounding it.

This book is not so much about what the proponents of 'decolonisation' get wrong; such a focus would smack too much of finger-pointing, and would do little to advance understanding. In that regard, I won't be spending much time highlighting the weaknesses in the arguments of decolonisation's leading lights. Given that the most enthusiastic 'decolonisers' never give any thought to the kind of case I'm making here, I think a more productive approach is simply to offer other ways of looking at the same phenomena, and to allow our respective readers to choose which framework provides the best explanation of today's world. My aim in this book is more to shine a light on the omissions and blind spots of decolonisation$_2$. I believe that addressing these areas will ultimately create a richer discourse with tighter arguments in favour of decolonisation, or with good reasons for limiting its scope, modifying its formulation or even abandoning it outright. My view is that the latter prospects are the ones which will most improve our knowledge and understanding.

To be clear, I would like to see the trope abandoned in most areas, especially when it comes to making sense of phenomena in contemporary Africa. This is not because colonialism plays no role in explaining events, but because we must take care to specify in each case exactly how colonialism features in the explanation, and why a colonialism-driven explanation is better than the alternatives. As I argue, this procedure is rarely followed at present. I make the case for discarding 'decolonisation' in discussions on African philosophy, historiography, political science, the language we should do our scholarship in, and related areas, where it has been inserted without careful thought and in a way that actually hinders understanding. Although the proliferation of the decolonisation trope has reached most, if not all, parts of the world, I argue that its pernicious influence and consequences are more exaggerated in African discourses. Given the central place that many contemporary African thinkers assign to colonialism and its aftermath in the unfolding life of ex-colonies, it is not surprising that the idea of decolonisation has a significant attraction for these intellectuals.

Despite appearances, this is not a fighting book. No doubt, it has a polemical ring to it. But its polemical thrust is not meant to shame or name names. Rather, it simply aims to identify errors or, better still, warn unsuspecting scholars of the dangers of merely deploying the most obvious analytical tools at their disposal, embracing the language of 'decolonising' as if it were unproblematic and, in so doing, writing the kinds of questionable analyses that this book challenges.

'Decolonise This!' is my way of capturing the challenge I present to those who embrace the decolonising trope. I challenge them to show what is wrong with the work of those of us who have engaged critically with and sought to domesticate ideas from the 'West', like modernity, and even with ideas, processes and institutions originating in colonialism, as part of our common (I assume decolonisers share this goal) commitment to creating a better world for ourselves and our progeny. As I have said, I wish to offer new possibilities for those who may not be persuaded by the decolonisation trope, and identify the blind spots which characterise it. Needless to say, if it turns out that those blind spots are non-existent or less significant than I have made out, I will stand corrected and offer my apologies to my opponents. But if I thought that this was the case, it would be foolhardy to issue the challenge at the heart of this book.

Throughout the book, I point to ways in which the ex-colonised, at least in some parts of Africa, have domesticated (and not merely by mimicry) many ideas, processes, institutions and practices that are routinely attributed to colonialism, but are in fact traceable to modernity and other causes. And even if some of those phenomena were rooted in colonialism, that by itself is not enough to condemn them as evidence of the persistence of colonial forms of rule in the post-independence period. This facile attribution to colonial causation of many practices and processes comes from an absolutisation of colonialism and its supposedly almost undefeatable capacity to bend the will of the colonised.

Simultaneously, this approach denies or at least discounts the agency of the colonised. That is, it must and does foreclose the possibility that the colonised could find anything of worth in the life and thought of the coloniser which they could repurpose for their own societies, both during and after colonialism. In fact, one of my motivations in writing this book was a nagging feeling that many of the creative works of the ex-colonised are either not being recognised or not being taken seriously by the zealots of decolonising, insofar as their intellectual products or institutional practices could be considered tainted, even faintly, by the colonial experience. Worse still, due diligence is hardly ever done to establish within reasonable limits to what extent colonialism was a factor in the emergence of such products and practices.

Decolonise this! A running theme among decolonisers is their unremitting opposition to, and their overweening determination to locate, any and every colonial hangover in a process, practice or institution. The problem is that it's not enough to accommodate in our writings the contributions of scholars from the 'Global South', because some of us already do this routinely, without any reference to decolonising. Decolonising scholars cannot escape a Manichaean division in which, (just as during colonial times), the colonised and the colonisers must occupy entirely distinct spaces, and, as the British saying goes, 'ne'er the twain shall meet'. Any colonialism-tinged phenomena must be purged from the postcolonial world. Ato Sekyi-Otu provides a good description of the problems inherent in this absolutisation of colonialism, the accompanying repudiation of universalism and the paradox that a Manichaean worldview generates. He contends that 'to abjure universalism *tout court* because of imperialism, Eurocentric and discriminatory auspices of certain versions—as some Western conscripts to the anti-imperialism cause in common with certain voices from the global South invite us to do—is the last word of the imperial act.' He continues:

> But such is the vicious paradox of some critiques of 'universalism' from Africa and the global South: their obsessive-compulsive Eurocentrism; their willful captivity to the very discourse they are avowedly sworn to divulge and dethrone; their exclusive preoccupation with the things the West does with words in order to enforce its particulars as universals; their trained habit, in contrast, of being utterly incurious regarding what our grandmothers do with words of evaluative judgment that have universals for their predicates. It is as if purveyors of Eurocentrism *and* their critics drink from the same cup and end up inebriated in separate beds but with kindred distractions. That must be the reason why 'universalism' is chief among those ritual anathemas of anti-imperialism or, as they say 'counter-hegemonic' discourse.[3]

My hope is that Sekyi-Otu's caution and my own efforts to bring into the discussion the products of the genius of African agency, in claiming the universal against the false universalism of colonialist ideologies, will enable others to see what 'decolonisation' regularly obscures.

In this book, I wish to present to our 'decolonising' scholars and their audience evidence of how indigenous genius has taken hold of and turned to their own purposes various material and ideational artefacts that were parts of their lives before, during and after colonialism. Some of them, doubtless, either originated in colonialism or were introduced into their lives during the colonial period, without it necessarily following that these ideas or objects were constitutive parts of the colonial infrastructure.

In the following chapters, I challenge our 'decolonisers' to show us why we should decolonise beyond the need to broaden our repertoire or take seriously the works of thinkers outside of the Euro-American canon (which many already do without subscribing to the idea of decolonisation), and to consider what the consequences of decolonising the phenomena I accuse them of ignoring or sidestepping would be. This would be instead of the current preference of our decolonisers for talking in nebulous terms, forever bashing the same Euro-American thinkers for excluding native African scholars' production, even as they themselves have never considered the complexity of the work of African authors, and thereby repeat the same errors as their supposed opponents.

Let's pause for a moment to anticipate the sort of things we'd like our decolonising theorists to try their hands at decolonising. I give two examples, one from music and the other from a combination of music and literature.

The year was either 1984 or 1985. A fellow graduate student at the University of Toronto, not an African, had asked me if I was at 'the concert'. 'What concert?' I asked. 'The performance by King Sunny Ade and His New African Beats', he replied. I was not there, but I am sure now that neither he nor I could have guessed what the consequence of his effusive praise for the maestro's performance would be for me. I was a fan of Sunny Ade from my pre-teen years, when he emerged on the music scene in Nigeria, and I had already seen him perform a few times, both live and on television. And in those days, I was not always keen on going to performances by groups I already knew. Then my friend proceeded to regale me with his account of all the things that impressed him about Sunny Ade and his concert.

It went along the following lines. Sunny Ade's was a roughly 30-piece band, playing instruments, singing and dancing all at the same time, and doing so with such tightness and discipline in the arrangements that nothing was astray. That was when it suddenly struck me that, for people in North America to see that kind of complex, multi-faceted performance, they would, for the most part, have to go to a concert hall, to the opera or to see a choir. Each of these performances would likely have a conductor and sheet music for the players. That was when I realised how little we valued the accomplishments of our Sunny Ades and Ebenezer Obeys, the other maestro, who have jointly dominated Nigeria's music scene for half a century. They—with no formal training and largely self-taught on the instrument they play as leaders of their respective bands, the guitar—have put together complex pieces of music with a creative mixture of indigenous and other instrumentation that is alien to their culture, from electric guitars to accordions, trap drums to Hawaiian guitar, and the organ to wind instruments. I have not looked at Sunny Ade the same way since.

Jùjú, the genre within which Sunny Ade excels, has its roots in Yorùbá civilisation, but it emerged within the modern per-formance subculture that began with the proliferation of Christianity in West Africa from the early 19th century. Unlike other genres in Yorùbá music, which hew more closely to their roots, Jùjú has at its core musical instruments of foreign prove-nance. As we shall see in the coming chapters, the non-African origins of these instruments are, problematically and possibly even wrongly, often identified with colonialism.[4] In this way, Jùjú is unlike genres like Sákárà, Àpàlà, Etíyẹrí, Dùndún and Sẹ̀kẹ̀rẹ̀, and Lúkòrígí, all members of the Yorùbá performance family and almost all—except for electronic recording and amplification—incorporating nothing even remotely related to the former colonial powers.

Before we draw any implications from Jùjú music and its challenge to the decolonisation trope, I want to bring to the discussion another event involving music, which I believe challenges the relevance of decolonisation to creating theories and explanatory models. For some inexplicable reasons, the proponents of decolonising, who enjoy knocking Léopold Sédar Senghor and Chinua Achebe for writing in colonial languages, have never seemed as eager to excoriate Wole Soyinka for prosecuting his craft in English—Chinweizu and his collaborators being the most notorious exception.[5] At the formal presentation of his Nobel Prize in Literature in Stockholm in December 1986, the music Soyinka chose to have played was an orchestra piece by Fela Sowande, a Nigerian composer in the Euro-American classical tradition, titled 'Akinla', from *African Suite* for string orchestra. According to Dominique-René de Lerma,

> Because Dr. Sowande wanted to illustrate to his countrymen some ideas on the unification of African and European music, he selected those melodies and rhythms that would be most readily recognized by African listeners. In its full version, the suite consists of five movements: 'Joyful Day' (based on a melody by Ephrain Amu, a Ghanaian composer and conductor), 'Nostalgia' (a personal statement by the composer about his Nigerian home and family), 'Lullaby' (based on an actual song Dr. Sowande heard just before leaving Nigeria in 1934), 'Onipe' (also after a melody by Amu), and 'Akinla' (a high-life tune, popular in Nigeria and Ghana).[6]

I can think of few candidates who are more ideal for decolonising analyses: an ex-colonised person (Soyinka) handed a prestigious award for writing in the language (English) of the coloniser (Britain) by a section (Swedish) of the colonising world being serenaded by another ex-colonised person (Sowande) with music written in the syntax of the coloniser (European classical) and a song derived from Yorùbá folklore, that would later be covered by high-life—another hybrid modern genre in West Africa—artists Bobby Benson and Fela Anikulapo Kuti. To decolonising theorists, the colonial provenance and even function of Sowande's work is obvious. And to that extent, its African identity must be called into question. The reason that I have cited Sunny Ade and Sowande is that they represent the kind of African intellectual production that 'decolonisers' either fail to recognise or choose to ignore. But, I argue, for 'decolonisation' to be a legitimate lens through which to assess these artists' work, its proponents should be able to show us how the trope can actually help us to place and understand Ade and Sowande in the context of African ideas, borrowed or original.

If we deny that works such as theirs are 'African', which I contend in the following chapters they are, I am perfectly happy to give up the label and keep the music. If, on the other hand, we decide that they are indeed 'African', what on earth does that add to our judgement of their quality as works of art speaking to the human capacity for aesthetic appreciation across boundaries and as worthwhile contributions to that area of cultural life? If decolonising means no more than broadening our horizons of what counts as significant ideas or ways of thinking, many of us are already doing that without the additional fuss of subscribing to a particular ideology. And if it means that we must get rid of anything that smacks of 'colonial' inspiration in our intellectual works, even when some of us have so domesticated these syntaxes as to make them our own, we'd have to acknowledge that African agency does not count for much at all.

I invite decolonisers to apply their critical tools to the omissions in their discourse that we introduce in this book. Where in their intellectual framework is the place for Sunny Ade and Fela Sowande?[7] Sowande is a particularly instructive example of what is wrong with much of the decolonising discourse when it comes to the wilful ignorance of African ideas and thinkers whose works answer questions that our latter-day culture warriors think they are newly posing. As Ato Sekyi-Otu puts it, many of our decolonisers suffer from a 'trained habit of being utterly incurious regarding what our grandmothers do with words of evaluative judgement that have universals for their predicates'.[8] In his short discussion of Fela Sowande in his invaluable 1995 book, *Nigerian Art Music*, Bode Omojola devotes a subsection to what he calls 'Nationalism in Sowande's Music'. What is the nature of nationalism in the work and thought of an artist who, for our decolonisers, is a prime example of one whose work is not African, but European? As Omojola explains, from initially believing that 'study[ing] European music properly ... was a liability ... [Sowande would later] think on looking back it was quite an asset.'[9] According to Omojola, '[n]o other work reveals Sowande's appreciation of Nigerian culture and his strong belief in cultural nationalism more than his *Folk Symphony* (1960). ... The work gives a very strong reflection of African elements and it could be argued that it marked the climax of Sowande's commitment to nationalism'.[10]

Simultaneously, as he was busy idiomatising European musical syntax in Yorùbá, Sowande insistently opposed the metaphysics of difference.[11] As Omojola explains again:

> It is, therefore, not surprising that Sowande's views on nationalism are, despite his commitment to them, marked by a characteristic open-mindedness. He believed in the philosophy of cultural reciprocity and argued against what he called 'apartheid in art'. According to him: 'We are not prepared to submit to the doctrine of apartheid in art by which a musician is expected to work only within the limits of his traditional forms of music'. He therefore warned against: 'uncontrolled nationalism in which case nationals of any one country may forget that they are all members of one human family with other nationals'.[12]

I would like to point out that this refusal to shun anything human and which promotes human progress and well-being, regardless of its origin, is a quality that all great thinkers share wherever in the world they happen to come from. The greatest African minds are no exception to this rule, but, I dare say, many of our decolonisers—who are absolutely fixated with origins and accept the Manichaean division that colonialism caused—can find no place in their intellectual framework for recognising or engaging with African intellectual discourses that come from this inspiration. This is central to the case that I make in this book.

The proponents of decolonisation may wish to connect their 'planetary ambitions', their conclusions about 'the epistemologies of the South' and other such expansive formulations (which homogenise a continent of heterogeneities and heterodoxies) to some specific examples, and show us how our world would be improved by 'decolonising' Jùjú or the Afro-classical music of Fela Sowande, Ephraim Amu, Akin Euba, Joseph Nketia and Sam Akpabot. In other words, I ask that they please stop telling us what is wrong with using knowledge or frameworks derived from the colonial period, and instead try to show us the problem by decolonising specific artefacts, genres, ideas and so on.

This book is not much interested in undermining, refuting or controverting the claims of specific decolonising theorists. The two principal ones that I engage with in the book, Ngũgĩ wa Thiong'o and Kwasi Wiredu, are chosen for their pioneering role in promoting the discourse and being its polestars. This must be made clear from the beginning. There are hardly any contributions to the decolonisation discourse about Africa that do not, at some point or another, cite either or both of these scholars in support of, or as an inspiration for, their arguments. And when it comes to philosophy, my main area, Wiredu looms large, and his many specifications for how to decolonise philosophical phenomena have strongly influenced the discussion, from religion to language to political theory. Hence, my decision to use their work as a foil for my discussion. They made the founding cases, and their successors, up to and including Achille Mbembe and Tsenay Serequeberhan, never fail to reference them in their contributions. Of course, I refer to other thinkers and frameworks, but they do not depart in any significant way from the path laid out by Ngũgĩ and Wiredu.

I am more interested in expanding the record by including areas which are usually left out, in order to cool the enthusiasm for 'decolonising' of an audience which is usually all too eager to embrace such discourses. If this book leads more people to pause and ask questions of the decolonising trope in light of what we offer here, its work will be done. I am convinced that the greatest appeal of this trope and the best explanation for its routine use even by sophisticated scholars is its repeated focus on gross representations of objective processes and events. My goal is to make it harder to adopt this discourse, while also showing how much is obscured by the call to 'decolonise' anything and everything.

The example of music that I gave above is instructive. What would it look like to 'decolonise' African music? The term 'African music' in and of itself is a serious oversimplification which, as I argue, is not a useful analytical tool for any serious theory-making. I've put it in quote marks to draw attention to how quickly we assume that such a phrase describes an objective, concrete phenomenon that can easily be subjected to 'decolonising'. 'Yorùbá music' is problematic enough if some of the things I mentioned above are taken seriously. Does the genesis of Jùjú music under colonialism make it 'colonial music', or music that was framed, or even created, by the coloniser? Does Kimbanguism qualify as 'colonial' because it is a denomination of Christianity which is usually, but wrongly, conflated with colonialism?[13]

Here is my challenge to prospective decolonisers. When you are inclined 'to decolonise X', here are some questions to bear in mind as or before you proceed. First, is X created, caused, determined, conditioned or influenced by colonialism? We can see from my example of music that the relationship between X and colonialism is rarely straightforward or clear-cut. Whether X is 'African music', 'African philosophy', 'African literature' or something else, the place of colonialism in its genealogy must be considered and demonstrated to show why it is a candidate for decolonising. I believe that if this were done, much of the decolonisation discourse would evaporate.

How tight the relationship is between colonialism and X depends on which of the above possibilities is relevant (whether X is created, caused, determined, conditioned or influenced by colonialism). A causal relationship would be the strongest, known in tort law as a 'but for' quality: without colonialism (the cause), X (the effect) would not have come into being. All the other relationships, with the possible exception of 'determined', imply that X emerged for other reasons or from other sources, and colonialism's role in its evolution therefore cannot be critical, much less necessary. In this way, anything that cannot be proven to have colonial origins is a tenuous candidate—if it is a candidate at all—for decolonising. Modernity, for example, was not a product of colonialism—i.e., it was not causally produced by colonialism nor was it introduced into (most parts of) West Africa by colonialism. I will not make the case for this claim here as I have made it elsewhere and, as far as I know, it has not been shown to be incorrect.[14] Efforts to decolonise modernity are both misguided and, worse still, a demonstration of a distinct lack of knowledge and sophistication, which is as bewildering as it is frustrating—especially in an African context. Indeed, part of what makes the colonialism that predominated in Africa, other than in areas of settler colonialism, problematic and inherently contradictory is that it subverted some of the core tenets of modernity as regards the principle of subjectivity (i.e., self-direction, self-ownership) and of governance by consent.

Second, once we've established X's credentials for decolonising, we must identify what sort of colonialism we're seeking to rid it of. Colonialism in Africa was anything but a monolith: settler colonialism predominated in southern, eastern and northern Africa, while exploitation-colonialism was imposed across the rest of the continent.[15] In the beginning, both France and Portugal had an orientation that held out to their subjects the promise of full citizenship if they 'assimilated'.[16] The British never did. Ultimately, all the colonial powers settled for simply pacifying their territories to ensure minimal interference from the 'natives' with the colonial regime of violence and plunder. How this policy was implemented in different colonial territories had implications for the evolution of concepts, practices, processes and institutions there. To attribute the emergence of ideas about liberal democracy to colonial regimes is to conflate two distinct things, and does little to advance our understanding. Here is yet another reason to refrain from referring to the objects of our decolonising missions as undifferentiated wholes.

Third, when X is present in a former colony post-independence, before we rush to decolonise it as a colonial hangover or product, we must consider and, if appropriate, rule out, any alternative explanations. Such explanations might include inertia or a choice by the peoples or intellectuals of this ex-colony to domesticate X in their new situation. That is, we should not be too quick to declare that the presence of X under colonialism and its persistence post-independence represent an unbroken chain of causality. We need to establish in each case whether X has actually endured because the ex-colonised themselves have embraced it. And, if so, we should ask whether this is an embrace which comes from the continuing power of colonialism to bend the will of the colonised, or if it is a case of the ex-colonised choosing, for whatever reason, to preserve X.

As I indicate in subsequent chapters, such investigations are much more illuminating than the easy but misleading attributions to colonialism. For example, it is not frequently, if ever, the case that ex-colonised writers are forced to write in the colonial language. This is one situation where due diligence must be carried out, and unqualified respect be accorded to the agency and autonomy of writers. Daniel O. Fágúnwà chose to write in Yorùbá even during his time working for and with the colonial authorities in Nigeria, while Wole Soyinka chose to write in English at the time of Nigerian independence. It would dishonour the memory of Fágúnwà, and would be a sign of ignorance of his biography, to read his choice of writing in his original tongue as being motivated by some notion of decolonising.[17] To allege, without any evidence beyond the context of Soyinka's or Fágúnwà's decisions, that colonialism played any role in either case cannot be considered serious scholarship. Years after independence, Adébáyọ̀ Fálétí and Akínwùmí Ìṣọ̀lá chose to write in Yorùbá even though they both were polyglots—speaking English, Yorùbá and French—while Ọla Rotimi and Fẹmi Ọṣọfisan chose English as their medium, even though the latter is a scholar of French language and literature. And then there was Ọládèjọ Òkédìjí, an innovator of Yorùbá writing who introduced the detective genre into the literature. Again, it would be an unwarranted stretch to incorporate their preferences into any kind of decolonising discourse. I hope it is becoming clearer why such gross representations are likely to skate over deep issues at the granular levels.

Fourth, given that a positive aim of decolonising is to restore something to X that was taken away from it by its colonial origins, once we've established that there is a causal connection between X and colonialism, we might discover that in the case of an entire discipline, for example, colonial genealogy by itself means very little. Few would deny the colonial origins of anthropology. Even as many hyperventilate about, apologise for and are scrambling to distance the discipline from its colonial roots, few efforts are being made to take seriously the ends to which African anthropologists have put it. Some of the best of them have turned this field of study to making sense of their own reality away from the gaze of disciplinary gatekeepers in cultural anthropology and urban anthropology, without needing to resort to the decolonisation trope. Ironically, our decolonisers hardly ever demonstrate any knowledge of or interest in the works of these scholars.

I offer this book as a spirited counterweight to the decolonising craze, in order to sensitise scholars, and especially students, to the risks they run by agreeing to limit their horizons and engage only negatively with significant elements of the human experience. I hope they open themselves to the ideas and thoughts of African thinkers who have never accepted that their place is just to consider particularities and have always tried to speak to the universal, from within their own historical context—even when they were in thrall to slavery or colonisation.

1

WHAT, AFTER ALL, IS DECOLONISATION?

When it first entered our lexicon as part of the discourse on the struggle for independence, decolonisation as a word, idea or concept had a scope whose boundaries, even if a bit fuzzy, were delimited. It referred to the ending of colonisation and the coming to sovereign status of the polities that had chafed under colonial rule. Its scope covered two clearly defined areas: politics and economics. Perhaps I have put this too simply. As I have argued elsewhere, colonisation has many iterations and is not one entity. But the implicit assumption in the decolonising discourse is that it is one, thereby glossing over this complexity.

In settler colonialism, for example, the aboriginal inhabitants were not candidates for colonisation; it was their land the settlers were interested in controlling, and the people themselves were treated as flora and fauna to be cleared out the way. In colonies divided between settlers and local populations, settlers created their own versions of the metropoles from which they had come, and the only link between the two groups was their exploitation of local labour and natural resources. In colonies designated purely for exploitation—like much of the Caribbean,

Asia and Africa—there were important differences, too. Only in Africa was there absolutely no interest in anything other than the extraction of raw materials, and whatever infrastructure was put in place by the colonial powers was solely intended to enhance this process. These different trajectories have important implications for the type of decolonisation that was obtained and for which challenges had to be met in the wake of independence. For example, in colonies characterised by exploitation alone, the play of culture becomes almost non-existent when it comes to colonial policy. This colonialism is the specific one that is framed by modernity.[1]

I would like to argue that the concept of 'decolonisation' is best understood if we restrict ourselves to conceiving of it as eradicating colonialism, as we have just defined it. I know that this goes against the grain of contemporary discussions. But I'm convinced that limiting it in this way leads to the most consistent and clearest interpretation of the idea. Extending it into events after independence (the putative end of colonisation) can only cause obfuscation, non-explanations and sheer distortions of history. To show how dominant the idea of extending the scope of decolonisation to events after independence has become, it is worth taking a look at Frantz Fanon's analysis in *The Wretched of the Earth* (first published in 1961)—the book that is often hailed as the originator of the decolonisation discourse.

On balance, the central thrust of Fanon's book—framed by the nature, ontological assumptions and core practices of colonisation in Africa—suggests that the most consistent way to read his work is as an indication of what colonisation is and what ending it would look like. Chapter after chapter, Fanon makes it clear that the long, post-decolonisation future will not be framed by colonialism. Contrast that with the current efforts in decolonisation discourse to turn colonialism into the only framework for plotting life and thought in Africa, especially the periodisation of our history. Simultaneously, that future world cannot preclude the presence of elements which may have originated during colonial times, or which are traceable to the practices and culture of the colonising countries, and so on. Ongoing decolonisation₂ discourses about culture, including politics and economics, often claim that Fanon is on their side, but end up papering over the complexity of his thinking where it does not support their contentions. Or they distort, knowingly or otherwise, Fanon's ideas in the service of projects and standpoints he would have had difficulty assenting to.

Here is the key to my interpretation: 'The colonial world is a Manichaean world,' wrote Fanon.[2] What Fanon did not add to this declaration, but which dominates his analysis, is that it was also a unique world. The uniqueness deserves serious attention. Given that the exploitation-colonialism on which Fanon focused was neither the only type of colonialism known to history nor was it typical of colonialism across the world in the modern age, we must take seriously the implications of this uniqueness. It was the only colonialism in which the colonisers convinced themselves that the colonised were not merely inferior; *they were not even human.*

Take a closer look at Fanon's references to the colonised world. For him, it was a make-believe world, one that was neither a natural emanation nor an organic growth from how human beings relate with one another, even where hierarchies predominate. It was a world constructed from whole cloth entirely from the colonisers' imagination. This has implications for how we understand that world and its fate historically. This is the only way to make sense of Fanon's insistence in *The Wretched of the Earth* that 'the colonised' was created wholly by the 'coloniser' and, in *Black Skin, White Masks* (originally published in 1952), that 'the black' was a creation entirely of 'the white'. What this means is that (1) whatever the coloniser reported of the colonised in the colonial world must be treated with a boatload of scepticism; and (2) if we get rid of 'the coloniser', 'the colonised' cannot continue to exist—as Fanon affirmed in *Black Skin, White Masks*, 'the black' cannot survive the disappearance of 'the white'.[3] How we process these characterisations is key to judging the plausibility of using 'decolonisation' as an explanatory model post-independence. That is, whether the idea of decolonising offers any insight into the apparent persistence of pre-independence processes or ideas, or any explanation of why certain political and cultural choices are made by the ex-colonised, depends largely on how much store we set by the story told by the coloniser.

Because it is a contrived world where the humanity of the colonised is denied—although, of course (and this is key), the colonised never thought of themselves as such—we should be wary of building any serious analysis on unreal assumptions about various residents of the colonial world without digging deeper and seeing the reality. The colonised, in the coloniser's image of the world, were 'animals' and their quarters were not human spaces. Yet, each day under colonialism, there were constant and intimate interactions between coloniser and colonised, and the colonised were privy to the innermost recesses of the coloniser's space. What's more, all the things that make us human were shared routinely, without ceremony, by coloniser and colonised in the colonial situation.

When, therefore, Fanon said that decolonisation signalled the birth of a new human from 'the colonised', it is not that 'the colonised' were ever non-human; it is that the world in which they had been considered 'things' no longer existed, and everything pertaining to that world would be superseded. Simultaneously, by insisting in *The Wretched of the Earth* that decolonisation means a reordering in which 'the last shall be first',[4] Fanon is not demanding the subjugation of the coloniser;

instead, he is calling for the restoration of the equality all humans share by virtue of their humanity itself. As far as Fanon was concerned, once this colonial world was overturned, that was the end of decolonisation. 'Becoming human', on this score, was not a process that would be concluded at a later date. In the colonial situation, the colonised were not human; after decolonisation, either the colonised has become human or the colonial world has not ended. But you cannot decolonise in a situation where 'the colonial world' is no more. This is not a semantic issue. Certainly, what kind of human the newly decolonised will become, and how far along the path to creating the best human and to establishing the conditions for the best life for the humans we are, all remain open questions that decolonisation$_1$ was not intended to answer. And the answers the ex-colonies can come up with going forward from the ground zero of becoming the makers of their own history again are no longer limited by the boundaries of colonialism and its negation. That the options of former colonies *are* still limited by colonialism is what decolonisation$_2$ sets up as the main element of its discourse. And it is what I attack because it misunderstands the problem to be solved and generates confusion.

Given this, the use of Fanon's work to legitimise decolonisation$_2$ becomes very problematic. Either 'the colonial world' survived independence and there never was decolonisation; or it did not, and we no longer have a candidate for decolonisation. I should add that I am with Ato Sekyi-Otu here in reminding us that a fundamental humanism animates Fanon's philosophy. Sekyi-Otu puts it well:

> This, it now seems to me, is the profound meaning of the demand that Fanon makes in the introduction to his very first published work: "And truly it is a question of unleashing the human being [*Et véritablement il s'agit de lâcher l'homme*]" .... From the beginning, the central question for Fanon was always that of releasing possibilities

of human existence and history imprisoned by the colonization of experience and the racialization of consciousness.[5]

Unfortunately, a lot of the oppositional discourse, of which decolonising is one example, fully embraces the racialisation of consciousness. We shall see presently how all attempts to frame modernity as an exclusively 'European' or 'Western' inheritance are examples of such racialisation; the same applies to claims about the 'Europeanness' of Reason, rationality, individualism and so on, which represent another concession to the racialisation of consciousness.[6]

If anyone remains convinced that there is no qualitative difference between colonial Africa and independent Africa, I wish them well.[7] If people think that the political and cultural problems that they find in contemporary Africa, post-independence, are still colonial problems, or try to turn colonialism into an eternal category, I wish them well, too. At bottom, this is what much of the discourse of decolonisation rests upon. This persistent ignoring and/or denigration of African agency—whether done with good or bad intentions—reaffirms the racist ideology that Africans are permanent children. The irony is forever lost on the decolonising industry. I want no part of it.

First, given the intimate inter-personal connections that were part of life in the colonial world, it should be no surprise that the colonised, humans that they always were, might have learned or appropriated ideas from the coloniser, and vice versa. To then make it a requirement of decolonisation that no part of the coloniser's life could form part of the colonised's is preposterous. The coloniser never had any qualms about appropriating African ideas or objects for their own use—whether artworks, music, cuisine etc.—confirming that they were lying to themselves in the world they contrived under colonialism.

Again, Fanon was quite forthright about this. Because he never permitted himself to believe the lies that the colonisers told about themselves, he was acutely aware of all the ideological contradictions and distortions they had to embrace in order to make their denial of their victims' humanity plausible even to themselves. Decolonisation means that the colonised also did not embrace such distortions, and from the ashes of colonisation arose humans who could make history, again, *under their own steam*—a capacity that was denied to them under colonialism. The key phrase here is 'under their own steam', and I will be making a lot of this idea throughout the book. For Fanon, as well as for Amílcar Cabral and most of the other leaders of the independence movement in Africa, the key qualitative difference between colonialism and independence was that in the one, their capacity to control their destinies was blocked, while in the other, they could make their own history under their own steam—even if they may have been doing it badly. Kwame Nkrumah had something akin to this in mind when he declared that they 'preferred self-government in danger to servitude in tranquillity'. As Cabral put it, the immediate objective of the anti-colonial struggle, decolonisation, is 'the phenomenon in which a socio-economic whole rejects the denial of its historical process. The national liberation of a people is the regaining of the historical personality of that people, it is their return to history through the destruction of the imperialist domination to which they were subjected'.[8]

For Fanon, either we have colonisation or we do not. I believe that once 'flag independence' was in place and the colonised had become captains of their own ships of state, any talk of colonisation persisting will not pass Fanonian, Cabralian or Nkrumahist muster. The dilemma posed by the continuing appearance of colonialism-like situations in the post-independence polity was accounted for by Kwame Nkrumah with his coining of the term 'neocolonialism'. If it was colonialism, it had to be a kind unlike that which had just ended with the inauguration of independence. But the idea that colonialism has not ended at all is a non-starter. The 'colonised'—considered 'things' in the colonial world—disappeared for good once independence was attained.

Any attempt to affirm an almost unbroken continuity between colonialism and neocolonialism is dubious, if not completely incorrect. But we must not simply dismiss the idea that, contrary to what we argue here, neocolonialism signals the continuation of colonialism beyond independence. Some of Nkrumah's explanations seem to support such a contention but, on closer reading, we must be wary of equating neocolonialism with colonialism. In the book he devoted to the theme, Nkrumah implicitly distinguished between the two: under colonialism, the coloniser controlled the unfolding of history within the colony and the day-to-day running of this territory; after independence, the ex-coloniser—notice the change of terms—would look for ways to subvert the new reality through foreign aid, evangelisation and other ploys, to *undermine*, rather than *remove*, the ex-colonised's control over their own affairs and lives. As Nkrumah explains:

> Faced with the militant peoples of the ex-colonial territories in Asia, Africa, the Caribbean and Latin America, imperialism simply switches tactics. Without a qualm it dispenses with the flags, and even with certain of its more hated expatriate officials. This means, so it claims, that it is 'giving' independence to its former subjects, to be followed by 'aid' for their development. Under cover of such phrases, however, it devises innumerable ways to accomplish objectives formerly achieved by naked colonialism. It is this sum total of these modern attempts to perpetuate colonialism while at the same time talking about 'freedom', which has come to be known as *neo-colonialism*.[9]

This passage is one of several that are key to our insistence that something has drastically changed between colonialism and neocolonialism. What I hope becomes clear in Nkrumah's formulation is that the action or inaction of the ex-colonised is decisive in the success or failure of neocolonialism. That is, it all turns on agency. The same agency that removed the coloniser from the driver's seat of the colonised's history must now work to ensure that this hard-won freedom is not undermined by the ploys of the erstwhile coloniser.

The realisation that neocolonialism's success post-independence was tied to native agency was also articulated by a contemporary of Nkrumah (before Nkrumah's unfortunate dalliance with Marxism-Leninism), Obafemi Awolowo. Both individuals share the distinction of having led the most progressive regimes in Africa. Here is Awolowo in an address in 1973:

> The struggle against involuntary political and economic enslavement under colonial rule was over during the last decade in most parts of Africa.
>
> But the struggle against voluntary subservience and submission to neo-colonialism is yet to begin.
>
> Our frequent and unabating declamation against neo-colonialism appears to me to be pretentious exercise and deliberate diversion.
>
> For the true and real neo-colonialists are no other than we Africans ourselves.
>
> It is we, in spite of our political independence and sovereignty who voluntarily submit to economic, and sometime diplomatic dominance from outside our borders.[10]

Awolowo argued that neocolonialism is not the same as lingering colonialism or the continuing power of ex-colonisers to bend the will of the ex-colonised in the post-independence period. Rather, he pinned the blame squarely on the shoulders of African leaders themselves and their failure to firmly exercise their own agency. In short, as he once declared while excoriating African leaders for being reconciled to their beggar status on the world stage,[11] Africans had the option, with the recovery of their 'political independence and sovereignty', to not 'submit to economic, and sometimes diplomatic dominance from outside our borders'. There is a lesson here for all who engage in the discourse of decolonisation$_2$ and are fixated with the actions of ex-colonisers as the main, if not only, focus of their explanatory models. My point here is not that Awolowo is necessarily right. It is that those who continue to talk as if African agency does not matter, except when it coincides with their preference, would do well to rebut arguments like his.

For me, the insistence on talking as if we are still in 'the colonial world' is the most unhelpful dimension of the decolonising discourse. Constructing new societies and the new humans that are to emerge from the ashes of colonisation, and forming states headed by governments that respect the inviolate dignity of their citizens and are answerable to them—all the things that were not part of 'the colonial world'—are not the domain of decolonisation.[12] Colonialism, while it lasted, was the unique bulwark against such outcomes. But the failure to achieve them post-independence cannot solely or even principally be attributed to colonialism. If it were, we would be right to conclude that independence never happened. But 'flag independence' is still independence! As insignificant as it may seem, it may actually be the main way to represent the qualitative difference between a colonial situation and an independent polity. Awolowo's list of Africa's repeated failures to move its inhabitants towards attaining better humanity includes what he called 'tenacity of office', the proclivity of African leaders for begging, and wrong governance structures, such as, in Nigeria's case, the replacement of federalism with unitarism.

Fanon already predicted the many ways in which the 'new humans' born from independence might fail at their task. But, at the same time, he was clear that nothing was off the table in conducting the all-important task, kick-started by decolonisation, of building this new world. It could not be conceived of as retrieving some illusory pristine past, untouched by time (including time under colonisation). This was the subject of Fanon's chapter 'The Trials and Tribulations of National Consciousness' in *The Wretched of the Earth*. Nor would that new order be totally devoid of aspects of European civilisation. In other words, Europe is as much a quarry for models of future world-making as the various other cultures of the ex-colonised. It is worth quoting Fanon on this final point as a counter to our decolonising zealots' desire to dump what they call 'Euro-modernity':

> All the elements for a solution to the major problems of humanity existed at one time or another in European thought. But the Europeans did not act on the mission that was designated them and which consisted of virulently pondering these elements, modifying their configuration, their being, of changing them and finally taking the problem of man to an infinitely higher plane.[13]

No doubt, even back then, no-one thought that the business of creating a new order with a new human would end with formal independence. The expectation that there would be additional steps to complete what decolonisation set in motion is best captured in Kwame Nkrumah's much-quoted injunction: 'Seek ye first the political kingdom, and all other things shall be added unto it'.[14] 'All the other things' include, principally, control of the economy—failure on which front prompted Nkrumah to coin the term 'neocolonialism'—and, more broadly, other areas of life, especially, culture, comprehensively understood. It is a mistake to capture this unfinished task under the rubric of decolonisation. If colonisation here is meant literally, it is historically inaccurate; if it is meant metaphorically, as we make clear in the rest of this book, it does not much aid understanding. On the contrary, it obstructs analysis.

Many of the practices and ideas that must be expunged from our lives to move closer to Fanon's 'new human' do not have their origins in colonialism. Whether it is child marriage, polygyny, caste systems, oppressive rule under native hierarchies denominated largely by chieftaincy, gender oppression, ethnic chauvinism and so on, it would be difficult to make sense of the struggles against these in terms of decolonising. We can see how the preoccupation with decolonising is likely to block serious analyses of endogenous practices and ideas that need to be severely criticised for our societies to move forward. Worse still, because of the continuing conflation of modernity and colonialism, the appropriation of modern tenets as antidotes to those practices is hindered. Indeed, I hardly see any serious criticisms of our original societies in decolonisation discourse. I take this up more fully in Chapter 3.

Decolonisers hardly, if ever, engage with Kwasi Wiredu's call for a 'critical and constructive analysis' of 'African culture', which is rendered imperative by 'the exigencies of the cultural transition that is taking place in contemporary Africa'. He offers a model of such analysis in his 'philosophical treatment of a particular African culture, the Ghanaian'. He then calls attention 'to three complaints which can afflict a society. They are anachronism, authoritarianism and supernaturalism'.[15] If these afflictions were not created by colonisation, but instead predated it, what sense would there be in thinking that decolonising is the solution? One of the main aims of this book is to focus on similar conflations in the decolonisation$_2$ discourse, rather than engaging in takedowns of specific theories.

I argue that the globalisation of the scope of decolonisation, its generalised deployment across all disciplinary boundaries, and its application as the core of explanatory frameworks for understanding anything and everything has produced a concept that, for the most part, now no longer improves comprehension but obscures it. More and more it is used as a cure-all that cures virtually nothing. The consequences of this are most pernicious in African scholarship, and this is the sphere on which this book focuses.

WHAT, AFTER ALL, IS DECOLONISATION?

The Two Decolonisations

As we have already established, the original concern of decolonisation was the struggle for independence from colonialism. Independence would mean the departure from Africa's shores of colonial rule and all that came with it. The key phrase here is 'all that came with it'. The two dominant aspects of colonialism that decolonisation₁ sought to tackle were politics and economics. While the cultural and ideological dimensions are also important, I think it is fair to say that these were not as central to the discourse and practice of the initial anti-colonial struggle. The reason for this is not difficult to understand. Many of those countries were pluralist societies with diverse cultures, and it is an oversimplification to claim that those who led the struggle for independence were at the same time cobbling together a 'national' culture for their post-independence polity. The demand that the world must be remade entirely, that we must create societies and cultures that would embody the best of our nature and the slowness of our march towards it—especially in light of a seeming failure to make a clean break with our former colonial overlords—was what led some African intellectuals to adapt the discourse of decolonisation₂, and expand its boundaries to cover culture, expansively conceived. It is decolonisation₂ that I wish to swear off and expunge from our discussions.

In the political sphere, colonialism was characterised by the denial to the colonised of the modern philosophical tenet of political legitimacy, which insists that no-one should have to obey the rule of any government to which she has not consented.[16] Decolonisation in politics would therefore mean that the colonised would no longer chafe under the rule of governments (especially by colonialists) imposed without their consent.[17] In economics,[18] control over the levers of economic power—previously under the authority of the coloniser—reverts to Africans after colonialism. Other areas of culture, writ large, are supposed to be marked by the exercising of African agency in determining how life and thought are to be organised. In short, self-determination should inflect life in ways that are exactly contradictory to those of colonisation. What matters here is that people, individually or collectively, write the scripts of their own lives, a prerogative that was denied to them under colonial rule. How this unfolds, post-independence, is only partly understood as being the continuation of decolonisation. It also goes much beyond it.

A key problem suggests itself: it is not always easy to identify how agency might be expressed. But the centrality of agency and the importance of autonomy are everything in the modern system. Self-determination, individual and collective, cannot be forced or be deployed in only one predetermined way. The major difference between being under colonialism and being free from it is that the will of the colonised is bent in one and it is free and self-actuating in the other. So, when we see what appears to be the survival of aspects of the colonial, we should ask if they are still sustained by (1) the previous coercion, (2) inertia or (3) the choices of the ex-colonised. One thing is certain: we cannot simply assume that the colonised will or can never be free if they use their agency in ways that we find unacceptable or difficult to endorse.

What this means is that if we see patterns of life and thought characteristic of the colonial world occurring in the post-liberation period, we must investigate their causal antecedents before insisting that they are instances of the failure of decolonisation$_1$. That is, while there may be post-independence phenomena that mimic similar ones in the colonial period, we cannot automatically assume that they have the same pedigree. If it turns out that some do, we need further evidence to determine if the same causal agents were responsible for them both under and after colonialism. Such would be instances of a failure to decolonise. But we must break down the idea of decolonisation to isolate the causes in different cases. And if such were indeed failures, we would need to determine whether the will of the newly free is still being bent by the same colonial forces. We would also need to rule out inertia, the exercise of the will in the service of choices that negate freedom, and clear preferences for certain ideas and arrangements (even if they had colonial origins). Unfortunately, much of the discourse of decolonisation does not often apply these cautions. Yet, apply them we must if we are to come up with sophisticated accounts of how life and thought have unfolded, or ought to unfold, after the removal of formal colonialism. We must question the ease with which the decolonising trope is used without deep attention to the complexity of the issues involved.

The core of decolonisation$_1$ was the extirpation of colonial rule, symbolised by the replacement of colonial rulers with Africans and the steering of African life under the direction of African agency. I would like to style this the original 'struggle for freedom', and the significance of this characterisation will soon become clear. I put it this way because, all too often, hardly any care is taken to drill down into the many elements of this broad assignment of 'freedom' as the goal of decolonisation. Yet, it is in doing so that some of the fog hanging over the contemporary discussion of decolonisation begins to clear. If we say that Africa has failed to decolonise in this original sense of the term, we must identify the reason behind this failure. Here is why.

Decolonisation$_1$ is simple, straightforward and genuinely universal in its theoretical scope. From Greece in 1821 to Turkmenistan in 1991, from the United States in 1776 to Gambia in 1966, when a polity is decolonised, its members, at a minimum, recover the capacity to become history-makers again—as we saw earlier with Amílcar Cabral. They take back their ability to call the shots in determining the direction of their country's life as an independent entity, which had been taken away from them by colonialism. *All* ex-colonies—and here we are talking of the type of colonisation that involves one set of people (the colonisers) controlling the lives of another (the colonised)—answer to this description. This differs from the type of colonisation present in countries like the United States, Australia and South Africa, where the colonists (settlers) were not interested in administering the aboriginal inhabitants; they wanted the latter cleared from the land for their convenience.

But this is one of the complexities that much of the decolonisation discourse fails to consider. In their capacity as colonists in the United States or *colons* in Algeria, for example, the British and French settlers, respectively, were *not* colonisers; they, too, were the *colonised* and it is only as such that it makes sense to speak of them as candidates for decolonisation and prosecutors of struggles for independence. It is in this sense that Canadians are not different in any significant way from Nigerians or Indians when it comes to their status as ex-colonised. And if decolonisation$_2$ is of service in understanding the situation in any of them, it should be in *all* of them.

It is instructive to consider that once the American settlers attained independence, ridding themselves of the monarchy and the ideological legitimacy that underpinned it, they largely hewed to what they had inherited from old Europe—whether that was in terms of the philosophical grounds for their new political organs, their judicial systems or their economic models. What's more, when it came to the areas of cultural life that come under decolonisation$_2$—from music to philosophy, from language to architecture—the United States was largely content until late into the 20th century to be a pale imitation of the country against which they waged a war of independence. If there is anything wrong with the ex-colonised borrowing from the repertory of ideas, institutions, processes and practices inspired by their erstwhile colonisers, it cannot only be a problem in the former colonies of Africa and South America; it must be a blemish shared by *all* of them.

It may be argued that the examples I've cited here can be easily explained away by the fact that the coloniser and colonised in these countries shared racial identities, and that this was the basis of the continuities I identified. That argument does not tell us much. India, for example, is an ex-colony that also chose continuity in its political and legal institutions, and has domesticated them so successfully that some of the cases decided by its Supreme Court are cited by courts in countries as diverse as the United Kingdom, Nigeria and the United States. Add to this the countries of the English-speaking Caribbean that have also developed their colonial political and judicial inheritances in ways that, as I argue in Chapter 4, Africa would do well to emulate.

Once independence is secured by decolonisation$_1$, the type of philosophical or ideological models that the ex-colonised choose to use cannot be limited to only those options that we, anti-colonial scholars, prefer. If we find that the independent state continues to exhibit features of colonialism—such as denying freedom to its citizens, being obsequious towards the ex-colonial overlords, acting in ways that are inconsistent with their being sovereign states—we must establish, in each case, the causal factors at work. We must not automatically conclude that colonialism has not ended, unless we are prepared to grant that the rulers of such states are permanent children who are forever beholden to their former colonisers. In other words, if we find choices that mirror old colonial forms of rule, we should not rush to conclude that these could only be the result of continuing colonial hold on the ex-colonised's capacity for choice-making. We need to be reminded that the exercise of agency on the part of the colonised cannot be limited to those choices that are 'anti-colonial'. A free people can express their freedom in any manner they choose. One of the defining features of colonial rule was the denial and displacement of local agency but, as we see below, while this agency may have been curbed, it was never dormant, much less non-existent, even as colonial rule lasted.

Speaking of the post-independence period as if native agency matters little, if at all, is a remarkable failing of the decolonisation discourse. We must change course. Doubtless, in most parts of Africa, the project of decolonisation, expansively conceived, was never really consummated. One can concede that many African states have not provided the best examples of being the self-governing, sovereign states that decolonisation$_1$ was supposed to usher in, post-independence. But this does not mean that the only conclusion to draw is that colonialism never ended. Indeed, part of the challenge that I issue to our decolonisers is to lay out clearly and in detail what a decolonised world, on their terms, would look like.

We must sound another note of caution here. When we talk about the failure of decolonisation$_1$, there is a general assumption that this is due to external causes including, but not limited to, the machinations of the former colonial powers. However, often it is better explained by the failure of successor regimes helmed by Africans to domesticate the institutions that our forebears who fought for independence gave their lives to install. It is simplistic to attribute this failure solely or even primarily to the continuing power of colonialism. We must attribute some causality to the exercise of indigenous agency even if we do not thereby substitute another unhelpful monocausal explanation. This is the road to more complex analyses and more effective theories. This is what many who push decolonisation$_2$ do not pay attention to. But Africans did not think that freedom, control over their lives, respect for their individuality or a state whose functionaries serve them and are legitimised by them were

'European' or 'Western' concepts. Julius Nyerere counted himself among those Africans who accepted the promise of change and sought to hold the colonialists to their pledge when it came to the installation of liberal representative democracy in Africa. As he explained in 1961,

> When, later, the idea of government as an institution began to take hold of some African 'agitators' such as myself, who had been reading Abraham Lincoln and John Stuart Mill, and we began demanding institutional government for our own countries, it was the very people who had not come to symbolize 'Government' in their persons who resisted our demands—the District Commissioners, the Provincial Commissioners, and the Governors. Not until the eleventh hour did they give way; and free elections have taken place in most of our countries almost on the eve of independence.[19]

The problem is that many of our decolonisers too easily conflate modernity and Westernisation. It is a big and unwarranted mistake.[20] Needless to say, they never engage with those of us who argue the opposing view,[21] but I hope that this book helps to improve the understanding of those who are somewhat puzzled by this issue. India never abandoned the legacy of modern liberal democracy, although it is currently under severe strain with Narendra Modi's unbridled national and religious fundamentalism; South Korea has embraced it in the aftermath of dictatorial rule; Japan, literally under an American diktat, modified its monarchy after its defeat in WWII to domesticate liberalism's core principles; and young people in Hong Kong are confronting the might of the Chinese government in defence of such principles, even though they have only enjoyed these freedoms since 1997, when colonial rule ended in the city and it was handed back to China. Not to mention the hundreds in Myanmar who, in defence of the modern principle of governance by consent, have been mown down by the country's military; or the people of Sudan, where the military is killing protesters to keep hold of power they seized illegitimately; and, lately, the youths and democratic forces in Eswatini, the only surviving absolute monarchy in Africa, who are defying death and imprisonment to call for the installation of a regime authorised by the governed, rather than by hereditary principles. The same demands are being made by forces in Thailand against a so-called God-king! I am yet to see a positive programme for what a decolonised political system would look like based on the proposals of our decolonisation theorists.

As I have established, there is a conceptual distinction between decolonisation$_1$ and decolonisation$_2$, with confusion coming when decolonisation is used to describe cultural forms, philosophical orientations, language choices and so on. When scholars use the concept of decolonisation, there is an unstated assumption concerning the relationship between its two different iterations. It is almost as if (1) there is no possible difference between the two; and (2) that one can easily jump from neocolonialism and incomplete decolonisation to the decolonisation of philosophy and other cultural forms. But I argue that not only is there a difference, it is significant enough to require us to rethink our very conceptual structures and to come up with clear guidelines for our thinking, going forward.

We should not use the same terms to describe decolonisation$_1$ (the struggle for independence and/or self-determination, the journey from colony to sovereign polity) as we do for decolonisation$_2$ (the continuing dominance in the contemporary world of ideational structures, patterns of thought, etc. ascribed to colonialism). The outlines of colonial rule in politics and economics are easy to delineate. In politics, we distinguish between what we now call 'flag independence' and 'real independence', by which we mean the ex-colonised being in fuller control of the levers of economic power within their respective territories, and being able to order their political lives without even the appearance of control by their former colonisers. I do not think that, beyond metaphor, this distinction is meant to signal the continuation of colonialism.

Deciding on which philosophical orientations are to be embraced, which political systems to be installed and which ideological frameworks ought to dominate in this 'really independent' realm is another issue altogether. Many scholars tend to emphasise the impact of colonialism as the source of almost anything that comes after it, except in whatever we choose to ascribe to the indigenous societies and institutions themselves. This is both analytically unhelpful and historically incorrect. Many of the ideas that predominated in the colonial setting—democracy or lack thereof, modernity, etc.—did not have colonial provenance in, say, West Africa. But the call to 'decolonise' lumps together modernity and colonialism, and, in doing so, insists that the rejection of colonialism means the rejection of modernity. This is a mistake.[22]

Because the ideas and processes involved in decolonisation$_2$ (deciding which philosophical and ideological frameworks to embrace) do not always have the same origins, nor the same solutions, as the challenge posed by decolonisation$_1$ (achieving 'real independence'), we must exercise caution when talking about both in a single breath. Indeed, I believe we must stop conflating these two distinct ideas altogether. For example, in the economic sphere, capitalism is not essentially colonial. In fact, in Africa, colonialism deliberately blocked the development of capitalism, and took active steps not only to restrict the rise of a local bourgeoisie but, also, to destroy local examples and forbid Africans from ever competing with ventures based in the metropole.[23] Some former colonies, whether settler, exploitation or a combination—including South Africa, India, Malaysia, Singapore, Canada and the USA—have managed to build robust and successful capitalist economies post-independence. To suggest that their choice of a capitalist path to development is a sign of lingering colonialism demonstrates serious ignorance or a lack of sophistication concerning the historical evolution of both phenomena.

This intellectual carelessness leads people to think that decolonisation$_2$ should also pursue the sort of total break with colonialism that decolonisation$_1$ mandates. African philosophy grew into a legible and legitimate subdivision of the discipline as a reaction to the racist theory that had consigned Africans to the status of philosophical non-beings. But decolonisation$_2$ which, if I understand it correctly, would also demand the removal of the philosophical model in which Africans were denied the status of humanity and which consigned our ideational exertions to nothing, makes some implausible or even counterproductive assumptions.

Take, for example, the most extreme case of the denial of another's humanity: chattel slavery. In the United States, slave-owners convinced themselves that their enslaved workers were objects, consistently listing them on the same side of the ledger as farming equipment. As Aimé Césaire pointed out, in the type of colonisation that took root in Africa and in the French Caribbean, populated by African-descended peoples, colonisation was synonymous with 'thingification'. Of course, we owe our understanding that the colonised were considered non-beings to Frantz Fanon's characterisation of colonialism. No doubt, colonisers proceeded to organise life, work, space and thought along these lines.[24]

Did slave-owners and colonisers succeed? Not quite.[25] For one thing, it is questionable whether, beyond bluster and self-deception, the slave owners really believed their own lie about the non-humanity of the enslaved, given their repeated rapes of enslaved women and their widespread interest in producing off-spring with them. Either slave-owners did not really believe their own tales, or theirs must rank as the only civilisation in history built on mass 'bestiality'. If you are participating in a 'breeding' scheme—the preferred term of the slave-holding establishment—you can rise no higher than those you 'breed' with. It is part of the hubris of slave-owners that they did not acknowledge their bestiality if, indeed, as they held, their enslaved victims were 'animals'. What is more, other farm implements never invented anything or created music, never improved productivity or constructed religions. If we cannot be sure that the enslavers really believed that the enslaved were non-human, we have reason to question the efficacy of those ideas even while slavery and colonialism lasted. It was why violence was so widespread and mindless while these practices lasted.

Moreover, it was one thing for slave-owners and colonisers to deny the humanity of their victims; it was another thing entirely to consider what those victims thought of themselves, their situations and even of their oppressors. Otherwise, we would be taking the oppressors' narratives as the only ones that matter. I argue in this work that much of the discourse on decolonising treats the colonised as if they are mute presences in the drama that other people are writing, and acts as if only two viewpoints matter: that of the oppressors and that of the analysts who think they know best what works. What is often ignored or dismissed is the work of the ex-colonised themselves, unless it squares with the expectations of decolonisers that anything with even the appearance of being related to colonialism must be discounted. This is why I have invited our decolonisers to take seriously such work.

Again, the situation of the enslaved is a good guide for how to handle what ought and ought not to be required for decolonisation$_2$. Enslaved persons in the United States were quickly deracinated and enormous efforts were made to denude them of their original cultures and expertise (whether in religion or medicine, agronomy or statecraft), as well as to rid them of any language they could use to conspire against their enslavers. But their enslavers could not deprive them of the human prerogative to appropriate what is to hand to tell their stories, to make sense of the world—especially one so cruel and inhumane—and generally to name themselves and fashion the world in their own image. The 'owners' of 'chattels' were free to believe their own lies. But the so-called 'chattel' always shocked their 'owners' by talking back and doing so in the same syntax as their supposed owners.

While enslaved persons had lost or had been taken away from their original world-making tools, must we object that English— or some variant of it mixed with elements of their previous cultural inheritances—became their vehicle for articulating their respective worldviews and experiences? If the answer is no, how much sense would it make to demand that they jettison this language and the conceptual framework it provides them with as evidence of their separating themselves from their enslaved past? By its very nature, no language can be owned by any person or any people.[26] Anyone who is willing and able to acquire a language becomes a part-owner of that language. Even when enslaved persons were forbidden from learning to read or write, their common capacity to acquire language by ear—which the slave-owner could not take away from them—allowed them to become proficient in the shared language and turn it to devastating use in calling their owners out on their hypocrisy, inconsistency, illogicality and their unspeakable cruelty, especially when they claimed to be pious Christians.

This is where the disanalogy between decolonisation$_1$ and decolonisation$_2$ comes into sharper focus. We know clearly what was wrong with colonialism when it came to political and economic operations in Africa. African lands were considered only good for extraction, and whatever infrastructure was put in place was not designed to improve the welfare of the colonised or the future development of their lands. They were colonies earmarked for supplying raw materials for the industrial enterprises of the metropole and, simultaneously, held as captive markets for the finished goods manufactured there. That is, the colonies were not permitted any choice in trading partners or the source of the manufactured goods they needed. We confront, yet again, how the issue of autonomy, of self-governance—the central credo of the modern age—was the *differentia specifica* when it came to defining the economic organisation of the colonies, with the interests of the colonised subordinated to and determined by the colonial powers.

In the political sphere, the signs are even clearer. As I argue in Chapter 4, the self-ownership of the subject underpins the demand that no government can have legitimacy unless it has been consented to by the governed—the principle of governance by consent—and this is the defining characteristic of the modern age. Modern colonialism in Africa failed this simple test where it concerned the fortunes of indigenous Africans. Colonial settlers, colonists and *colons* all travelled with their citizenship intact, and their revolts or resistance against the mother country, when they occurred, were conducted in the name of the principles guaranteed by their citizenship. The colonised never enjoyed that privilege even when the policies of 'indirect rule' (in British territories) or 'association' (in French ones) were imposed on the continent, lasting right up until the eve of independence in colonised African countries.

The parameters of decolonisation$_1$ are thus very clear. In politics, Africans should be in control of who governs them, and that governance must be based on the consent of the governed. The country in which this governance is exercised must be sovereign over its space and its social ordering, and may not be beholden to any other outside its own boundaries unless by acts voluntarily entered into and able to be reversed when the country so determines. This simple requirement is one of the strongest signs of the errancy of the decolonisation discourse even in this area. For example, when it became public knowledge that the then government of Nigeria had negotiated the Anglo-Nigerian Defence Pact with Britain in 1960—which would allow the former colonial power to have a military base in the newly independent country—all hell broke loose. Public opinion, led by opposition parties and the new country's intellectuals and students, forced the abrogation of the pact. Think of it, we are talking of a time closest to independence, a time when the new state's vulnerability to sanctions was most acute. Yet, the new sovereigns, the newly minted citizens of Nigeria, decided to take the risk and dare their former colonisers. Incidentally, Obafemi Awolowo was the leader of the opposition in Nigeria's federal parliament when this pushback occurred.

But years later, various African countries started making pacts with ex-colonisers and even with those, like the former Soviet Union, who never had a colonial presence on the continent, that allowed the latter to have bases inside their territory. If this is the sort of thing that is meant by those who argue that colonialism never ended in Africa—and this is the crux of the continuing appeal of decolonisation discourse—it is either that they have made the definition of colonialism so elastic that it no longer has any meaningful boundaries, or they have chosen to ignore African agency after independence. I refuse to accept this dangerous move.

In economics, the direction of the country's economy must be steered by its citizens, with a government that they have freely chosen at its helm. It must be driven with the interests of its citizens in mind and with the goal of creating a self-sustaining, independent, internally robust mode of production. How this outcome is achieved—capitalism, socialism, mixed economy—becomes less important than whether it is driven by the will of the free country and its government. Again, if anybody holds

WHAT, AFTER ALL, IS DECOLONISATION?

France responsible for her ex-colonies' decision to tie their currency to the French Central Bank and regards that as evidence that colonisation never ended in those countries, I beg to differ. What were Africans leaders who signed on to such deals thinking when they did? Yes, they were subjected to threats. But we must either hold them liable for their lousy choice or we must assume that they are, one and all, minors who could not say no to their 'guardians', the French. And we have evidence of various African countries exercising their autonomy in choosing which economic systems they were going to embrace after independence: Kenya was unashamedly capitalist, Tanzania went down the socialist path, Nigeria chose a mixed-economy model, and so on. Meanwhile, as I write this, various African countries are allowing military bases to be set up within their borders; are selling land to foreign countries so that its purchasers can grow food for export; and borrowing money under terms which make their major infrastructure, like seaports, vulnerable to seizures by their foreign creditors.

I am arguing that decolonisation has no place where there is no colonial presence. Whatever problems there may currently be in Africa's political and economic spheres, since the day after independence, they are no longer colonial problems. If, indeed, my distinction between the two senses of decolonisation holds, it turns out there is a paradox in the discourse that has been hidden from analysts until now. If colonialism, as I argue, represents a subversion of modernity and its core tenets, processes and practices (the principle of subjectivity, the centrality of Reason, the importance of governance by consent), and the anti-colonial struggle was carried out, at least in part, to force the colonisers to live up to the ideology used to justify the colonial adventure, it stands to reason that post-independence, decolonisation would not be identified with the abandonment of those principles. Decolonisation would raise the demand not only for their realisation but for their deepening in the lives of the ex-colonised. It may be that some of our 'decolonisers' have understood this paradox but are afraid to confront it.

This may be one explanation for their deafening silence on the ongoing second struggle for freedom in different parts of Africa, best illustrated by the 2010 Jasmine revolution in Tunisia and the ensuing Arab-African Spring, as well as by other movements in Africa which began with the overthrow of the military by the Béninois people in 1991. Those movements have not been driven by flag or food, religion or creed, ethnicity or nationality. And they surely were not a struggle for independence from or against colonial rule. It was not Britain, France, Portugal or Spain who were the objects of the protesters. Nor did the protesters speak or act as if they believed that the local objects of their animus—their ruling classes—were minions of a colonial master. Rather, from Bénin in 1991 to Eswatini, Tunisia and Sudan in 2021, their demand has been for human dignity; for the state, run by people from within their own ranks, to serve and respect them; and for individuals, in their capacity as humans and citizens, to be the authors of their own scripts, and for the integrity of their person to be held sacrosanct by the state, its agents and their fellow citizens. I argue that these are the core elements that set modernity apart from previous modes of social living and principles of social ordering. Ordinary Africans had thought that flag independence would lead to this outcome, and when one-party and military rule distorted and diverted this political progression, they never gave up on the goal. While the first struggle gave freedom to their polities as states, this second struggle is designed to wrest freedom for them as individuals deserving of dignity by reason of their humanity alone. When we speak as if this struggle is about decolonising, we misdescribe what is happening, and we fail to hold accountable the native successors to the colonial regimes for their failure to treat their people with respect. And it does not help the argument to accuse them of being lackeys of the former colonial powers. In so doing, we lend support to the racists who contend that Africans are permanent children.

The Philosophical Case Against Decolonisation

This brings us back to the centrality of philosophical and cultural ideas to decolonisation$_2$, and how much of a problem it poses to the decolonisation trope. African thinkers in the period immediately after independence had begun to grapple with the issues of freeing African philosophy from the grip of colonialism and its ideological manifestations. That is, they had started to question the provenance of ideas and ideational structures that dominate life and thought, tracing them to the colonial period. This is the root of the discourse of decolonising philosophy as it manifests itself in Africa. Philosophers and other cultural thinkers are no less susceptible to the problems that we have highlighted so far in this discussion.

I need to be very specific in this context because much confusion is caused by what I see as unfounded generalisations about the nature of colonialism and the erasure of its specific features in different parts of Africa. In a country like Senegal, for example, where French colonialism unfolded in two distinct phases—assimilation and association—one can see the different fruits born of those phases. The differences were deeper still in areas of settler colonialism. I have searched for, but have been unable to find, examples of decolonising discourse applied to the Afrikaner experience in South Africa of being colonised by the British, and how this was incorporated in Afrikaner philosophy. Of course, it is entirely possible that Afrikaans-inflected philosophy is full of such discussions. Similar considerations can be raised for Zanzibari philosophy or Hausa philosophy, and their iterations in Islam-dominated countries in Africa. What am I hinting at? It is all too easy for us to talk about decolonising philosophy when we take Africa to be our primary referent. But, once we begin to dispel certain assumptions that inform our current discourses, things become rather more complicated. Given that much of the focus has turned on language and political philosophy, we similarly limit ourselves in this book.

I argue that the impact of what Kwasi Wiredu called the need for 'conceptual decolonisation in African philosophy' may be having some very problematic, even if unintended, consequences. These consequences can be traced to the very conception of the problem which I have just hinted at. The very concept of decolonisation, as applied to culture, is beset with significant confusion. Even among its sophisticated proponents, there is little clarity as to what a fully decolonised philosophy (assuming that were even possible) would look like. Here, one finds as many variations of decolonisation as there are thinkers promoting it.[27] If this is the case, it is only fair that I show how and why it has happened. But this can be a tricky move to pull off. I am not interested in highlighting arguments with which I am unable, given the scope of this book, to engage. What I will do over the following pages is draw attention to some of the representative samples of the confusion that I see, encourage us to identify it and avoid it in our and others' thinking. In subsequent chapters, I give more details about how inattention to the confusion that arises from the indiscriminate deployment of the decolonising trope actually subverts efforts to solve the problems that its proponents are interested in solving, either by misdiagnosing their causes or simply by inappropriately applying the decolonisation trope. This confusion includes:

(1) If we find the term 'decolonisation' used in a paper to lump together different phenomena without any attempt by the author concerned to acknowledge the shifting usages, it is fair

to say this does not aid reflection. These shifting usages are not rare in many otherwise self-contained discussions. Here is an example of inconsistent usages. In a 2016 piece by Achille Mbembe, promising 'new directions' for 'decolonizing the University' and dealing primarily with South Africa (but with the usual nod to the rest of the continent), we have the following characterisations of decolonisation: first, 'decolonization on campus' refers to removing iconography that depicts racist figures. This is a specific recommendation for South African universities. Second, 'decolonization' is defined as rolling back 'neoliberal' influences on the university, instituted in what the author calls 'this tide of bureaucratization'. Third, we are told that 'to decolonize implies breaking the cycle that tends to turn students into customers and consumers'.[28]

We should not assume that decolonising means the same thing in each of these three characterisations. For one thing, the line that goes from colonisation to removing iconography that depicts racist figures, to removing neoliberal influences, to breaking the cycle that tends to turn students into customers and consumers is neither obvious nor straight. For all three things to refer to the same cause it must be the case that colonialism plays a causal or, at least, a quasi-causal role in their emergence and their current manifestations. In other words, we must be able to trace these phenomena to colonialism, and attributing them to such a cause must provide a more convincing explanation than competing ones.

Many who subscribe to decolonising models already take for granted that these phenomena are directly caused by colonialism, and this assumption is rarely questioned. What's more, it is difficult to persuade the proponents of decolonisation to locate themselves outside of this theory and consider that there may be alternative genealogies for processes or practices that they are all too content to trace back to colonialism. It is for this reason that

I am more interested in addressing myself to those who may be considering embracing the trope, in order to prompt them to take a second look before signing up.

For now, let's stay in South Africa. To begin with, there was more than one colonialism in South Africa. Even if we were to incorrectly assume that colonialism in South Africa was a monolith, we must still admit that its victims did not all have the same experiences with it nor were they impacted upon in the same way by it. Boer settlers colonised the land, not indigenous South Africans. Some native groups imperialised, even if they did not colonise, other native groups. The British subdued the Afrikaners as well as various indigenous groups. It is British colonialism that is the focus of Mbembe's essay. Properly speaking, if the original peoples of South Africa are interested in removing iconography that depicts racist figures, it is not far-fetched that Afrikaners would be interested in removing iconography of the British figures who placed them under colonial rule (and from which they were freed in 1910, to the detriment of indigenous South Africans). I don't subscribe to the notion that the psychological harm caused by colonialism is essentially racially defined. The Irish and the English are of the same racial stock, for example, but, if the continuing struggle of Irish Republicans in Northern Ireland is any indication, they would be as invested in decolonising as descendants of South Africa's original peoples.

Even if we grant the colonial provenance of iconography—Mbembe's first object that must be 'decolonised'—it is more difficult to link 'neoliberal influences' and colonialism. Neoliberalism is a global phenomenon, which has rampaged across the world affecting coloniser and colonised alike—whether this is in the United Kingdom in the transition from Edward Heath to Margaret Thatcher in the 1970s; in South Korea and Indonesia during the financial collapse in the 1990s; in Argentina in the opening decade of our present century; or more recently in Italy,

Spain, Ireland or Greece in the aftermath of the economic crash of 2008. And if one wants to focus on its specific colonial manifestations as a basis for pulling it into decolonising discourse, we must say much more than our decolonisers usually do.

The connection to colonialism is established by linking the business of knowledge production to the continuing dominance of so-called 'Western epistemic traditions', which exclude or even kill local forms of scholarship. Decolonisers have even come up with a name for this: 'epistemicide'.[29] It is this dominance with which decolonising the university and its curriculum is concerned. It is an irony that those who criticise Léopold Sédar Senghor for committing the crime of writing in French are also the ones who, simultaneously, call for precisely the kind of epistemological standpoint that he had advocated: community-oriented, emotion-inflected, spirit-infused. Dethroning so-called Western epistemic traditions from their hegemonic pedestal in the ex-colonies is one of the declared aims of decolonisation.

This is a type of decolonisation that I am convinced is totally unwarranted.[30] When decolonisers accuse colonisers of killing local epistemes, I am often at a loss to make sense of this accusation. If you wish your papers to be published in so-called prestigious journals dominated and curated by those you accuse of being colonisers, then they will insist that you meet *their* criteria for what merits inclusion. But why do we not create alternative outlets for ourselves and our audiences?[31] When the *Journal of the Historical Society of Nigeria* was considered the place to publish when it came to African history, did anyone from Britain or the United States complain? On the contrary, it used to be the case that the most celebrated Africanist scholars touted their work's inclusion in the journal as a mark of excellence and legitimacy. Why are we now asking Cambridge University Press's *Journal of African History*, dominated by British and American Africanists, to decolonise? Why are we holding outsiders responsible for our own failure to commit adequate resources to studying Africa?

The complaint about colonial domination of knowledge production is, for the most part, an implicit acknowledgment that we dropped the ball on owning our reality. What's more, because Africans keep hankering after the approval of those whom we routinely accuse of not recognising our scholarship, we never fail to cite them as authorities—a move that prolongs their domination over our story-telling. We keep reinfusing their outlets with our fresh ideas, rather than moderating and curating them under our own agency. Never mind that many of those outlets would not have the depth of knowledge required for them to be competent judges of African work, if that work were really directed at creating and furthering our own intellectual traditions. Hence my argument later in this book that much of the output of the decolonising trope is dominated by extraversion. We need to turn inwards, take our agency seriously and act as if we value it.

No account of decolonisation would be complete without the usual, often unthinking, nod to Ngũgĩ wa Thiong'o's demand, as paraphrased by Mbembe, that 'a decolonized university in Africa should put African languages at the centre of its teaching and learning project'.[32] Unlike Ngũgĩ, however, Mbembe believes that French, Portuguese and Arabic have already become African languages. Since I devote a whole chapter later to the topic of language in decolonising, I do not need to dwell on it here. But a comment is relevant. This is one of those situations where a little more digging shows what decolonisers may be missing. If these foreign languages all came via colonialism and part of what decolonisation entails is the expunging of colonial modes scholarship, we must show how the French, Portuguese and Arabic colonial modes of scholarship that have become African have been decolonised and made suitable for African use. But, if this is possible with an artefact that is still so bound up with its external origins, why is the same not true for other areas or processes that are the targets of decolonisers?

(2) We next consider a second set of defects. There are those calls for decolonising which, when we reflect more deeply, place items within their domain which can either be differently explained, do not address a real problem or which address a problem that can be resolved without resorting to the drama of 'decolonisation'. When we are asked to decolonise a discipline, a discourse or a movement, there is always the assumption that our subject matter is a creation of colonialism, or that it is so steeped in colonialism that it needs a complete makeover. Here, again, we run into difficulties that are often obscured by this assumption that the process in question is inseverable from colonialism.

To illustrate the point, consider the 2015 essay, 'Decolonizing Western Political Philosophy', by the late Charles W. Mills. What does it mean to decolonise 'Western political philosophy'? According to Mills, '[w]hat we have to do, then, is to expand the current vocabulary of Western political philosophy to admit colonial and imperial dominations as political systems themselves, not merely national but global, and centrally constituted by race'.[33] If we are not co-owners of 'Western philosophy', why are we asking its chroniclers to include us in their annals? I do not see us asking to be included in Chinese or Indian philosophy. If we are asking that Western philosophy account for the historic violence, subjugation and even genocide that it abetted or caused, that is only fair. But I do not think a whole new discourse is needed to ask a discipline to tell the truth about itself.

Moreover, Western philosophy is never monolithic. As 18th-century philosophers David Hume and Immanuel Kant were libelling African-descended peoples, their contemporaries James Beattie and Olaudah Equiano, and James Africanus Beale Horton a few decades later, were rebutting their arguments within the same epistemic, metaphysical and ethical frameworks—a development that made the latter two African-descended thinkers co-owners of Western philosophy! And if Africans can be co-owners, what is called for is not decolonisation, but a more honest telling of the story of this branch of thought. If, as Charles W. Mills's piece argues, some ex-colonised thinkers can be considered Western philosophers, does that make their writings, too, candidates for decolonisation? After all, in the view of many in the decolonising community, there is no distance between colonial and imperial domination and the philosophical heritage of the colonising and imperialising countries.

Does that mean that the philosophies of the ex-colonised which are considered part of the Western inheritance are equally guilty? If the answer to this question is yes, efforts at decolonising must include philosophers like Ottobah Cugoano, Olaudah Equiano, Anton Wilhem Amo, Edward Wilmot Blyden, James Africanus Beale Horton, Alexander Crummell, Aimé Césaire, Frantz Fanon, Albert Memmi, Kwame Nkrumah, Léopold Sédar Senghor, Amílcar Cabral, Mourad Wahba, Fatima Mernissi, Obafemi Awolowo and Paulin J. Hountondji, because all of them worked within the framework of 'Western' philosophy and wrote their own 'J'accuse' from within it. If not, why are some Western thinkers candidates for decolonisation and others are not? Are we giving Frantz Fanon a free pass because he comes from 'our' community or are we implicitly conceding that there are liberatory political philosophies in the Western tradition sitting, however uneasily, alongside the philosophies of domination? What's more, whatever can be decolonised cannot at the same time have colonialism as part of its very constitution. To that extent, the colonial moment must then be incidental to Western political philosophy. Mills's essay actually seems to corroborate this point, because, as we saw above, it holds that to decolonise Western political philosophy is to recognise its underbelly of political domination denominated by race, and make the discipline more self-aware of the imperial genealogies of some of its key categories.

A similar point can be made about Adam Branch's position that 'decolonising would mean starting with attention to and learning from the specific, concrete debates that have taken place in specific locations in Africa and global Africa'. For example, it would mean going against the compartmentalisation of African thought and 'insisting on the fact that African political thought is political thought'.[34] If there is any situation for the application of Ockham's razor,[35] which cautions against the multiplication of entities beyond necessity, this is it. Many of us do what Mills and Branch are asking without any need to turn to the trope of 'decolonisation'. These are demands that a keen attention to good scholarship, especially one that answers to the call of a liberal education, should take care of quite easily. How good can scholarship be if it is blind to the experiences of a significant portion of humanity on account of their 'difference'? Can the 'best' scholarship really be produced if it conveniently ignores the ideas of a particular people and the products of their intellectual engagements with questions that have inspired other peoples to create philosophical models?

These characterisations indicate that colonialism is not integral to the constitution of Western political philosophy. Instead of calling for the decolonisation of philosophy, given that the colonial period is time-specific, why can we not answer this call by recasting the narratives of the discipline to reflect the breadth and complexity of the human experience? Why create another genre? Why not just insist that people write better histories of philosophy without reducing the problem to one of the machinations of colonialism? If we may take a leaf out of the book of feminist engagements with Euro-American philosophy, they did not create a whole new genre of 'demasculinisation'. Instead, they began to retell the story of philosophy by reemphasising the role of women in its evolution and insisting that more inclusive language be adopted to show that philosophy does not come in only one gender. They realised that androcentrism was not a constituent part of philosophy, and was merely an accident of its development.

To anticipate an argument that is developed in Chapter 2: if all that decolonising requires is that we critically consider artefacts inspired by colonialism, and can give good reasons for embracing them, then it cannot be the case that the colonial element in them is dire. Some of us have done exactly what is being asked in our own accounting of the philosophical discourse of modernity without deploying the decolonisation trope.[36]

(3) The final part of the confusion that I identify with the decolonisation discourse is the almost indiscriminate deployment of it to address anything and everything. This promiscuous application is part of what led me to think that the idea has lost its focus, and that its explanatory power has become so attenuated as to be non-existent. Under this heading, a lot of the discourse is either faddish or lends itself to bad ideological purposes. Works on this subject range from 'Decolonizing Globalization Studies', 'Decolonizing Sociology' and 'Decolonizing African Educational System as a Panacea for Africa's Educational Advancement in the 21st Century' to *Decolonising Knowledge for Africa's Renewal: Examining African Perspectives and Philosophies, Decolonizing Enlightenment, Decolonisation and Afro-Feminism* and *Decolonizing Universalism*.[37] My hope is that drawing attention to the catch-all use of this might cool our ardour for throwing 'decolonisation' at whatever ails our discussion in philosophy and culture more broadly.

In this section I've shown how a little attention to our conceptual framings might help improve awareness of the fact that many of the theories we take for granted may not have the solidity and coherence that we had previously thought. In addition to the above conceptual confusions, there are four other defects in the decolonisation discourse, which together make up the fundamental reasons why I argue we should dispense with the idea of decolonisation$_2$ entirely. Even if we pay more careful attention to and clear up the confusions outlined in the preceding section, I think that the trope and the discourse built on it cannot escape these defects:

a) When it comes to language, both Ngũgĩ wa Thiong'o and Kwasi Wiredu may be raising or have raised unrealistic expectations regarding what can and/or ought to be done.

b) A trope that emerged to break down the walls erected by Eurocentrism around philosophy may have become a new barrier that obscures much more than it reveals.

c) The dominant conception of colonialism in the decolonisation discourse is somewhat stilted and does not take seriously the complexity and historicity of the concept or, importantly, the different paths of modernity and colonialism in Africa.

d) The discourse ignores or plays fast and loose with the intellectual contributions of thinkers in the ex-colonies, and their reaction, relation to and engagement with the legacy of colonialism and modernity.

These last four problems will be critically discussed in the remaining chapters of this book.

I will frame my discussion by using as foils the case for 'decolonizing the mind' made by Ngũgĩ wa Thiong'o and Kwasi Wiredu's case for 'the need for conceptual decolonization in African philosophy'. I use them in this way because these two thinkers have loomed large in the debate on decolonising the humanities since they elaborated their theories in the early eighties. Both, especially Ngũgĩ, have had a far-reaching influence on university organisations in Africa. Soon after Ngũgĩ and his brave comrades in Nairobi forced the Department of English to be renamed the Department of Literature in English, my own alma mater, the University of Ife (now Obafemi Awolowo University) in Ile-Ife, Nigeria, was where the train next stopped. It led to the dominance of a Marxist-inflected sociology of literature and literary criticism, which generated such fierce debate that Wole

Soyinka had to address its impact in his Inaugural Lecture deliv-
ered there in the 1980s.[38]

Wiredu's voice in the emergence of African philosophy as a
subdiscipline is a pivotal one. His *Philosophy and an African
Culture* (1980) was one of the earliest articulations of academic
African philosophy that did not allow itself to be deflected by the
racism-tinged, sterile 'question' of African philosophy and the
conditions of its possibility. So, in challenging his and Ngũgĩ's
submissions, I am paying tribute to the enduring significance of
their contributions. But challenge I must, to push back the frontiers of a debate that, I believe, is fast ossifying. As with other
pioneers and trailblazers, the problem is less with the originals
and more with their imitators, who remain stuck on the same
note either through simple inertia or because they are too petri-
fied to strike out on their own.

In the subsequent chapters, I address certain framing questions (outlined below) which, unfortunately, are regularly
neglected by much of the discourse on decolonisation. It is
likely that the enthusiasm for decolonisation stems from the
fact that everyone seems to believe that they know what everyone else in the discourse is talking about. But if we put these
questions at the forefront of our minds, it forces us to deal with
otherwise hidden conundrums. We have seen that, for decolon-
isation$_1$, there are clear criteria to establish when it has been
attained. So, to a great extent, these questions are more pertinent to decolonisation$_2$.

When we have decolonised our literature, philosophy and other
areas of thought, what would things look like? To put it differently, what goal do we have in mind and how would the world
look were we to attain a decolonised discourse in philosophy?
Another way of phrasing the question is to ask what we are to
understand by decolonising anything. This is not the place to get
into it. Maybe someone will one day put together a taxonomy of

conceptions of decolonisation in the literature. As we saw above, even in the work of a single author, decolonisation can often come in three or more variations, and the confusion is compounded when the idea is promiscuously deployed in all spheres.[39]

Some of the thinkers usually cited as authorities by the decolonising discourse do not always answer to what decolonisers believe them to be saying when it comes to the relationship between the two versions of decolonisation. They cannot be used to legitimise much of what currently passes for decolonisation. Consider Frantz Fanon and Amílcar Cabral. As we saw above, Fanon was very clear about what decolonisation would look like. So was Cabral. Cabral, indeed, is more helpful here given that he was clear that national liberation and culture are not judged by identitarian criteria—no spurious authenticity for him—but by whether the process of creating them unfolds under the power of the people. That is, whether it is self-directed. When it comes to decolonisation$_2$, Fanon, too, was very clear that the pieces that would be used to create a new culture, post-colonisation, would not be limited to some 'authentic', pristine past of the colonised.[40] Neither Fanon nor Cabral were worried about the colonised appropriating elements of their experience under colonialism that they deem helpful to creating their new metaphysics and social philosophy, which would reflect the humanism to be incorporated in their recently independent social formations. So, their argument is less about pedigree than it is about who chooses, what is chosen and with which goal in mind.

Neither Fanon nor Cabral set much store by decolonisation. Yes, it was important, but they did not permit themselves to think of it in absolute terms or to extend its reach beyond very narrow boundaries of economic control and political sovereignty. They therefore knew that what we have identified as decolonisation$_2$—a nod to the decolonisers but designed to show the irrelevance and problematic nature of using the term to describe something that is not continuous with its original iteration, decolonisation₁—would require a lot more, and its boundaries could not cover objects, processes or practices that may have been there under colonialism but were not caused by it. And even if these ideas or institutions did have some connection with the colonial period, Cabral and Fanon were not willing to make such things inseverable from colonialism.

Once we grant this, neither Fanon nor Cabral were interested in pedigree because they both knew that transforming the struggle against colonialism into a call for renouncing any aspect of the cultural, social, political or scientific life of the coloniser would be to give up on the oneness of humanity—the ultimate racist trope—and the fact that hybridity is the very core of human civilisation. They worried that such a move would mean a reversion to atavisms, identitarian politics—including ethnocentrism—and other forms of unacceptable cultural nationalism in post-independence polities, and a forswearing of what they both embraced: the politico-philosophical discourse of modernity which accused colonialism both of baiting the colonised with its promise and of switching when the time came to deliver on it. It was part of their theoretical sophistication that they did not make the error that is now rife among decolonisers—conflating colonialism, modernity and Westernisation.

For example, Cabral does not rule out borrowings from colonisers:

> Whether our new culture is in or outside of school, we have to place it in the service of our resistance, in the service of compliance with our Party program. It has to be that way, comrades. Our culture should be developed at the national level of our land, but without disparaging (or considering as lesser) the culture of others, and, with intelligence, availing ourselves of the culture of others—everything insofar as it can be adapted to our living conditions. Our culture should be developed on the basis of science, it should be scientific— which is to say, not involve believing in imaginary things.[41]

Beyond decolonisation, his commitment to humanism is very clear:

> From the beginning of our struggle, even with documents that the comrades may recognize, we addressed ourselves to the colonialists of our land, telling them clearly: 'You are the wheel of the old colonialist car that wants to continue exploiting our people.' Even they have a place in our land if they want. We want to make a land where anyone, from whatever part of the world, can live, work, and live properly, provided that they respect the right of our people to direct itself.[42]

This passage neatly, almost imperceptibly, shows that decolonisation$_1$ is what matters when it comes to demarcating a boundary between colonialism and post-independence. How we structure life after independence, and where we draw inspiration from for that purpose, is a separate issue from whether we do so under our own power or the power of another. We could have the same mode of social living forced upon us in the one case, pre-independence, or freely adopted by us, post-independence. 'Respect[ing] the right of our people to direct itself' means that we are independent, and if we remain under the direction of another, we do not have independence. But analysts may not dictate the limits of from where a free people may draw their models for organising life and thought, nor may they easily conclude that only the power of the coloniser can explain any continuities between the pre- and post-independence periods in the life of any people.

According to Fanon, colonisation and decolonisation do not form a continuum such that we can affirm of them the kind of dialectical relations that exist between moments of a whole. They are mutually exclusive, and when we move from one to the other, there is annihilation of the previous state, not a sublation of it. In the specific colonial situation in much of Africa, the colonised were non-persons; they were consigned to a 'zone of non-being'. Becoming decolonised means vacating this zone, not amending or ameliorating it. It must be ended, period.[43] For this to happen, the coloniser qua coloniser must also become a non-being. If any piece of colonisation were to remain in the aftermath of decolonisation, that would be an indication that the latter had not occurred.

Put differently, were philosophy to be an integral part of colonisation, we cannot claim to decolonise while retaining philosophy. If we use this as our metric, then any areas of life that have anything to do with the coloniser must be eradicated. This is why it is crucial that we must not carelessly attribute more to colonialism than can be supported by the historical record. If modernity were part and parcel of colonialism, a decolonised society would clearly have no truck with it. We can easily see the many contortions analysts are forced into once they decide that modernity and colonialism or modernity and Westernisation are one and the same. It is why the theoretical landscape is now littered with such strange neologisms as 'pluriversals', 'coloniality', 'transmodernity', 'multiple modernities' and so on. Either we must establish a sharp distinction between modernity and colonialism, as I argue, or they both go down together and the ex-colonised's relationship with modernity would be forever conflicted, if not impossible. But we know that this is problematic or even implausible. It would require us to take an extremely narrow and monistic view of life under colonialism and attribute every artefact from the colonial situation to colonialism. That is, anything that is present while colonialism lasted is irremediably sullied by the colonial imprint and, therefore, can have no place in the world beyond colonialism. Given this implausible scenario, we need to be more modest and more specific in identifying the inventory of colonisation and to take a more expansive view of the plural forms of life under this system of rule.

As I argue throughout the book, we must separate changes under colonialism that were essential constituent parts of it from those that were incidental to it; those that unfolded under the direction of colonisers and were designed to reinforce the non-being of the colonised from those that were driven by the autonomous will of the colonised, however much the coloniser pretended that the colonised were incapable of choice-making. We must strive to draw out the provenance of ideas that may have been inducted into the colonial situation but were not necessarily inherent to it. This is why I insist that we do not conflate modernity and colonialism.

We must be clear which decolonisation dominates the historical and political discussions that we are interested in. What decolonisation signifies is inseparable from which iteration of colonialism, historical or conceptual, we are speaking about. When historians talk about the period of decolonisation in Africa, what should we take them to be referring to? Similarly, what was the focus of the anti-colonial struggle? This is one iteration of decolonisation, and its outcome was independence. But what was independence supposed to herald? What new state of being was to be ushered in at the dawn of independence? Certainly, there are material structures, political processes, social relations and ideological commitments involved, and we must take care to delve into some of these in this discussion. When it comes to these latter ideas, structures and processes, it is less complicated to come up with metrics for determining the relative success or failure of any decolonisation regime. It was what made it possible, maybe even easy, for Kwame Nkrumah, Amílcar Cabral, Julius Nyerere and others to (1) set a goal for what independence would mean and test for how close to those goals their polities came post-independence. And it is why Cabral could (2) make a distinction between independence and human liberation and argue that decolonisation is a mere condition for the building of a culture that has human emancipation as its ultimate goal. As he explained:

> We are struggling to build in our countries ... a life of happiness, a
> life where every man will have the respect of all men, where discipline

will not be imposed, where no one will be without work, where salaries will be just, where everyone will have the right to everything man has built, has created for the happiness of men. It is for this that we are struggling. If we do not reach that point, we shall have failed in our duties, in the purpose of our struggle.[44]

But the movement towards this outcome is no longer part of the anti-colonial struggle. As I continue to insist, colonialism has not survived independence.

Might this be what the current preoccupation with decolonisation is gesturing towards? That is, that today's decolonisation$_2$ completes the anti-colonial struggle of decolonisation$_1$? The link between the historical iteration and the current confused attempt to turn this into an explanatory model for the contemporary political, social and ideological reality of Africans and their societies may be the work of Frantz Fanon. The continuities are remarkable. But when we let (1) having our polities' evolution under our direction become synonymous with (2) using this control over our destinies to build a superior human society, we set the stage for the current situation where we no longer have clear, helpful metrics to test our progress. Concrete measurements like whether we have implemented governance by consent, determined what economic models to adopt and changed our education system to reflect our own preferences are replaced with vague calls to decolonise anything and everything, making it seem as if we are still on the path to decolonisation. The term has become so slippery that it no longer offers a sure handle on what success would look like in a decolonised world.

2

DECOLONISATION AND THE POLITICS OF LANGUAGE

AN OVERSOLD PROMISE?

*Let us turn to the question of African languages. They were long consid-
ered dialects and it was said that Africa had no culture. Now we have
gone beyond that, even though the notion still remains in the heads of
certain academics. But that is not a serious problem. What is alarming
is that those who govern us, the African governments, do not have the
courage to consider that language sustains culture and the economy.
What matters is not to think of Gikuyu as a rich language. It is a language like Masai, Wolof and other languages. This is the struggle we have
to fight back home before we even start carrying it into Europe or the
United States.*

Ousmane Sembène[1]

I do not think that it is an exaggeration to say that people probably know Ngũgĩ wa Thiong'o more as a theorist of the adoption
of African languages as the principal criterion for defining
African literature than as the important writer that he is. From
the time that he forcefully asserted that the very identity of
African literature is inseverable from the language in which it is

written, he has become the most insistent voice in the decolon-
isation$_2$ discourse. It has since become a basic tenet of decoloni-
sation$_2$ that one of the identifiers of a genuinely decolonised
intellectual contribution is that it must be articulated and presented in an African language. There is a sense in which this is
so widely accepted that it is hardly ever problematised, much less
interrogated. Even for Ngũgĩ's critics, their main concern is to
dispute the claim that English and other colonially derived languages are forever marked by their alienness, neglecting other
key issues with his theory.[2]

The other thinker whose work serves as a foil for the argument of this book, Kwasi Wiredu, also takes as an important
principle of his idea of the decolonisation of philosophy that we
must think our concepts in our original, indigenous languages.
As we shall see, there are some significant differences in their
respective standpoints as regards what the desired outcome of
linguistic decolonisation is and what is the best path to it.

This chapter submits to careful scrutiny the promise and challenge of decolonising language and of reducing the influence of
colonially derived languages in our discourses. I will present and
explore the respective cases made by Ngũgĩ and Wiredu and
show the limitations of their arguments and their severe consequences for current and future thinking and writing. First, I
argue that the promised results of conducting formal intellectual
work in our original languages may have been oversold by its
canvassers. I am surprised by how little, if at all, this is flagged in
the literature. Second, I contend that using one's choice of language as the only or primary measure of 'African' identity has an
unintended consequence. African thinkers who do their intellectual work in colonially derived languages are often excluded by
scholars who are looking for 'African' contributions to ideas and
discourses. They are rendered almost peremptorily illegible, and
their output is automatically discarded regardless of its themes,

quality and relevance. These thinkers are considered not properly 'African'. I do not know how many people, on realising this, would persist in thinking that there is any good to be had in this manner of proceeding. Third, and related to the second problem, the insistence that 'African' work must be done in local languages makes light of or even summarily denigrates and delegitimises African agency. If people lose their status as African thinkers because, for whatever reason, they do their intellectual work in ways that are not deemed 'African', it means that African agency is only to be embraced when its choices are to our liking! Fourth and finally, the assumption that it is easy to ascertain what is or is not an 'African language' is implausible, and I will make a case for this presently.

For Ngũgĩ, the need to decolonise the mind was a continuation of the battle that Africans were waging against imperialism, notwithstanding the fact that most African countries had been nominally independent since the early sixties. In other words, decolonisation$_1$ had not been completed. This is where the distinction between the two iterations of decolonisation becomes important. These two concepts are neither continuous nor is there any necessary connection between them. The specificity of the first stands in marked contrast to the fuzzy nature of the second. What's more, while there is no room for any continuity between the colonised state and decolonisation$_1$, an ex-colony may choose to retain certain cultural forms, from language to religion, from architecture to literature, derived from the previous colonial situation. South Korea, Japan, Russia and Ethiopia all, at different times, reached out to various European countries for models of social living to improve their societies. In the 16th century, kingdoms in Central Africa and in the Niger delta sent their children to learn the ways of the Europeans, and so on.

Ngũgĩ identifies two 'mutually opposed forces in Africa': 'The imperialist tradition' exemplified culturally by the 'African neocolonial bourgeoisie', is the first, with 'its culture of apemanship and parrotry enforced on a restive population through police boots, barbed wire, a gowned clergy and judiciary; their ideas are spread by a corpus of state intellectuals, the academic and journalistic laureates of the neo-colonial establishment'.[3] To this he opposed '[t]he resistance tradition [which] is being carried out by the working people (the peasantry and the proletariat) aided by patriotic students, intellectuals (academic and non-academic), soldiers [?] and other progressive elements of the petty middle class'.[4] In this case, 'resisters' are able to push back against the 'imperialists', and it is fair to assume that the resistance is not influenced by ideas and structures mimicking those immersed in colonialism. But as we shall see, this opposition may not be a helpful way of understanding the trajectory of ideas and structures in Africa.

For Ngũgĩ, there is a continuity between the dominant concepts and practices under colonialism and those that marked the post-independence period and were purveyed by the local intelligentsia in various African countries. He seems to think, and many who argue for decolonisation agree with him, that the cause of this continuity must be traced to the power of imperialists to bend the will of ex-colonised intellectuals even after independence. The argument is along these lines: under colonialism, the will of the coloniser prevailed. The coloniser's language and other artefacts were the chosen ones. After colonialism, the coloniser's language and other artefacts are still dominant. Therefore, colonisation has not ended. We need to decolonise. As students of logic can see, this is a non sequitur: the conclusion does not follow from the premises. For it to be the case that colonisation has not ended, there must not be any alternative explanations for the post-independence situation, such as the colonised making poor choices, admiration for those practices and institutions, or just inertia.

We need to be careful how we present this problem. Beyond the logical fallacy just flagged, there is also a historical problem. We must drill down into some of the core elements of the discussion. Let us focus momentarily on the following terms from Ngũgĩ: 'a gowned clergy', 'judiciary', 'state intellectuals', 'academic and journalistic laureates' and, in the next breath, 'working people (the peasantry and the proletariat)', 'intellectuals', 'soldiers', 'petty middle class'. These are all concepts that are alien to indigenous African societies, regardless of Ngũgĩ's bifurcation of them into two different functional categories. No doubt, they had their empirical matches in some of Africa's original societies, which had developed sophisticated divisions of labour and class systems. I would like to believe that the difference between the two categories Ngũgĩ identifies here does not turn on identity. But for the most part, they are all products of or have had their configurations shaped by colonialism, modernity and Christianity in many African countries, especially Ngũgĩ's homeland Kenya.

There are two reasons to pause here. First, it is not true for all or even most of the continent that all these forms *originated* in colonialism. In Nigeria and Ghana, for example, many of these 'laureates'—especially intellectuals, clergy and journalists—predated colonialism and fought against it throughout its tenure in their territories. In their fight against colonialism, they were, for the most part, not socialists. Rather, they accepted the modernity which was the supposed ideological template at the heart of colonialism, but which had been subverted by it. They, however, had acquired modernity from a different source: missionary education. Second, some of the institutions that are lumped together in Ngũgĩ's formulation do not unequivocally have the character he invests them with. The judiciary, for example, was supposed to play its core role under modernity of being the impartial arbiter constituted to protect the puny individual from the all-powerful state. But this, too, was subverted by colonialism, and part of the promise of independence was that this function would be restored to its rightful place, and the inviolate dignity of the individual would be respected by the state.[5] It is a mistake to speak as if these institutions—which, properly conceived, could preserve the dignity of the individual—can never be more than what they were under colonialism. Of course, if you think nothing of the tenets of modernity as regards the sovereignty of the subject and the impermissibility of state intrusion upon it without serious justification, it is easy to dismiss this as bourgeois hocus pocus. But Africa's second struggle for freedom that is ongoing across the continent is all the proof we need that ordinary Africans do not buy into this corrosive scepticism. If this is accepted, then what sets one group, in Ngũgĩ's description, apart from the other must be what they do, how they do it and to what end—not their presumed pedigree.

Additionally, none of the classifications used by Ngũgĩ has a univocal meaning and, no doubt, their functions and how they are executed cannot all be construed in only one way. Here is an analogy to illustrate this point. The Catholic Church in Latin America, which for centuries had blessed dictators and counselled congregants to obey their rulers, also managed to birth a radical branch that called on the same congregants to not accept their positions docilely but to resist oppression in the name of God. That is the entire raison d'être of liberation theology. If there was more to the Church than simply kowtowing to the powers that be—even when the original understanding was that scripture did not authorise any specific political philosophy— how much more can we expect of modern institutions like the judiciary? The judiciary has very definite metaphysical groundings and principles of social ordering which, during the colonial period, were in and of themselves an indictment of the type of colonialism dominant in Africa for stunting and violating those principles when it came to the administration of the lives of the colonised. We should therefore be wary of identifying the modern judiciary with its truncated form under colonial rule and—especially given the current military and one-party misrule in parts of Africa, and the ongoing second struggle for freedom across the continent—we should be less sanguine about dismissing the significant leap forward that bourgeois legalism has been for humanity the world over.

So, to put the 'judiciary', 'police boots' and 'barbed wire' in the same box is either to misunderstand the modern legal system or mistake the false form for the true. As we will discuss later, would decolonising the judiciary mean the wholesale expurgation of the system bequeathed by colonialism, or would it mean a commitment to reducing the gap between what the system promises and how it is realised in our society? In other words, once we have decolonised the modern judiciary, what shall we be left with? How would our world be different and better?

Similar points can be made as regards the other terms we have highlighted. The moral economy of the peasantry or of capitalism, within which the relationship between the bourgeoisie and the proletariat is processed and understood, are not organic to Kenya or Nigeria. Rather than uprooting these concepts from their material contexts, we must study their origins, their evolution and their operation in the places from which we obtained them, and do our best to make them work in our domestic situation. Again, does decolonisation involve ridding ourselves of these economic forms? Or should we modify that economy to meet our needs in ways that colonialism never did? And if we opt for the latter, will it amount to decolonisation?

The preceding examples illustrate why we must work with nuances and distinctions, which can only help us to lay out clearly delimited boundaries for our discourse, to identify the problems on which we wish to shed light and, ultimately, to solve them. We should stop wasting precious energy chasing shadows and misdirecting young minds, especially, into intellectual and practical blind alleys.

Ngũgĩ on Linguistic Decolonisation

According to Ngũgĩ, 'the biggest weapon' in imperialism's armoury, and with which it continues to dominate life and thought after formal colonialism, is 'the cultural bomb'. What does the cultural bomb do when detonated? It messes with a people's frameworks for understanding the world; with their cosmologies; with their sense of their place in and relation to the world; their narratives (literary and historical); and, most importantly, 'their belief in their names [and] their languages'.[6] The cultural bomb makes people doubt their sense of who they are and their confidence in their being-in-the-world. As Ngũgĩ explains,

> It makes them see their past as one wasteland of non-achievement and it makes them want to distance themselves from that wasteland. It makes them want to identify with that which is furthest removed from themselves; for instance, with other people's languages rather than their own.[7]

Ngũgĩ assumes that there is some solidity, if not unanimity, in this supposed reaction on the part of the colonised to 'the cultural bomb'. Given what we know of the historical evidence, there is no basis for this assumption. It is this Manichaean view of the relationship between the coloniser and the colonised—which the coloniser believed, according to Fanon, but which the colonised never accepted—that limits the explanatory value of 'the cultural bomb' for understanding how the colonised processed the experience of colonial subjugation. Exploring these assumptions is beyond the scope of the present discussion. But given that imperialism is a global phenomenon with many different specific manifestations, it cannot be the case that the outcome described by Ngũgĩ is the only or even the dominant one. For example, I think it would be a stretch to say that what Ngũgĩ describes captures the experience of Indians with British colonialism, or that of the Vietnamese with French colonialism. And British colonialism did not extirpate Afrikaans or alienate its speakers from it in South Africa, nor did it make Afrikaners unenthusiastic about their culture. Additional reasons, beyond the power of imperialism to assert its will, are needed to explain if and why Africans want to 'distance themselves' from their past, as Ngũgĩ asserts. We must also make clear that the type of colonialism that Ngũgĩ refers to is only one iteration of it: the modern. And we need to specify in each case which variant of modern colonialism is under review, as emphasised in the last chapter. The discourse of decolonisation$_2$ leaves little room for this sort of interrogation.

Given how tightly Ngũgĩ weaves language with our very identity as humans and the culture that we have birthed, it should be no surprise that he insists that decolonisation be demonstrated by creating literature in African languages or thinking philosophical concepts in 'our own' languages.[8] I argue that this demand may be raising or may have raised unrealistic expectations regarding what can and/or ought to be done. The imperialist cultural bomb compelled Ngũgĩ to adopt language as the best terrain to fight for genuine independence and for the restoration of the dignity of African peoples. This is at the heart of his original case for decolonising the mind. As Ngũgĩ puts it,

> The choice of language and the use to which language is put is central to a people's definition of themselves in relation to their natural and social environment, indeed in relation to the entire universe. Hence language has always been at the heart of the two contending social forces in the Africa of the twentieth century.[9]

That is, language is both 'a means of communication and a carrier of culture'.[10]

Recall the story narrated in the Introduction as regards how decisions taken at the Berlin West Africa Conference of 1884–85, even if unintended and clearly unforeseeable, ended up mapping the future contours of African minds by the powers that dominated specific geographical regions in the aftermath. Ngũgĩ's insistence on the centrality of language to the very idea of being human arises from what he sees as the unsavoury consequences of colonialism for African models of being human. He recounted his experience growing up, a peasant child, living at home and in the rest of his daily life in Gĩkũyũ while, once he was enrolled in 'school, a colonial school', the 'harmony' that marked his life and the centrality of one language to all aspects of it was 'broken'. 'The language of my education was no longer the language of my culture', he explains.[11] Again, there are assumptions here that are, to say the least, problematic. Not all of us who share similar experiences to those of Ngũgĩ have processed it the same way as him. Neither Senghor nor Soyinka nor even his fellow decoloniser, Wiredu, affirmed the same near-pathological processing of education in a colonial language which Ngũgĩ presents as an almost inevitable outcome of the experience. This suggests that tying language to identity is not automatically correct, even if it appears plausible. Those who follow his lead tend to write as if those of us who do not embrace this pathologisation are, to put it bluntly, not okay and are victims of a colonial mentality that prevents us from seeing that there is something wrong with our choice. The history of language development and what role to give to colonial or indigenous languages in education is a lot more complex than Ngũgĩ's straight rendering might suggest.

Here is yet another wrinkle in the decolonising discourse that is hardly ever flagged, much less discussed in any detail. Ngũgĩ's experience unfolded under colonial conditions marked by a racially dominated hierarchy. Could we say the same—and if the theoretical assumption is plausible and the model has any explanatory power, we must—of Amazigh children in Algeria and Morocco, who for a long time had to go to school in Arabic and French? If yes, would we still call it 'decolonising'? Do the same consequences follow for component units of the defunct Soviet Union under the sway of the Russian language, or for generations of Welsh, Scottish and Irish nationals under the domination of England? Is the model of 'the cultural bomb' relevant to their experiences? And must we now apply decolonising to South Africa? After all, its 11 official languages do not include all that are spoken there. As I show next, discussing these issues does not necessarily require decolonising language, and only if we absolutise the contingencies of modern British colonialism does the theory gain any serious purchase.

It was Ngũgĩ's introduction to the debate among African writers during the 1962 'Conference of African Writers of English Expression' at Makerere University College, Kampala, Uganda that initiated the protest and dissatisfaction which would culminate first in the University of Nairobi's decision to change the name of its Department of English and, later, in the campaign which had its birth certificate in the book that has become a classic of the decolonisation literature: *Decolonising the Mind*.

Why is all this important? The core of Ngũgĩ's argument about the illegitimacy of European languages as vehicles for the expression of any genre of African literature has to do with the looming, almost inescapable, presence and machinations of colonialism and its consequences for how life is shaped in Africa. 'The language of African literature', he explains, 'cannot be discussed meaningfully outside of the context of those social forces which have made it both an issue demanding our attention and a problem calling for a resolution'.[12] The 'social forces' in question are 'imperialism in its colonial and neocolonial phases' which, in Ngũgĩ's estimation, has continued to control African hands and minds up until this day. The question of which language to use to convey and express Africa's cultures is but one element of the generalised African struggle against imperialism and colonial and neocolonial manifestations.

This problematic, originally formulated by Ngũgĩ and spiritedly canvassed by him since then, has continued to be the go-to formulation for contributors to the debate concerning language. This is why I have used his conception to frame my argument against the deployment of the decolonising trope to the question of language in African discourse.[13] Unfortunately, there is hardly any critical exploration of Ngũgĩ's case among his supporters. They merely cite him and buttress his submissions with their own musings on the subject. My hope is that the case made here will encourage more critical responses both to him and to me, all along the path to expanding the boundaries of discourse on language and its consequences for African scholarship. We shall presently consider one critical reaction to Ngũgĩ's arguments by Biodun Jeyifo.

Decolonisation$_1$ threw off the yoke of imperialism and colonialism, but our minds were never decolonised, as in decolonisation$_2$, because Africans continue, post-independence, to use colonially derived languages as our preferred vehicles of expression in the most significant areas of our individual and collective lives. If, as Ngũgĩ contends, language is 'central' to our very understanding of who we are and our 'relation to the entire universe', and it continues to be dominated by the machinations of imperialist and neocolonialist forces, it is easy to grasp what the problem he wants to solve is and why it concerns him so much.

When we say we are, for example, Yorùbá, but we choose to express ourselves in literature in English or French, we must acknowledge that we are not *really* or *fully* Yorùbá. We are, at best, Yorùbá-English or Yorùbá-French, and the literature, to remain in Ngũgĩ's principal domain, that we produce is *not* Yorùbá—it is English or French.[14] Beyond literature, Ngũgĩ's larger point is that given the centrality of language to our humanity itself and even to our relation to and engagement with the world, anything that interferes with that conception of our being in the world also diminishes our claim to being the authors of our own scripts—the very core of what makes us lawgivers to the world. So far, there is no reason to object to Ngũgĩ's thesis.

Questions arise, however, when we consider the extrapolations that Ngũgĩ derives from the thesis. One question is whether as both 'a means of communication and a carrier of culture' language answers to the strictures that Ngũgĩ wishes to place on it when it comes to the influence and reach of colonialism in our lives. If, as Ngũgĩ argues, 'Language is thus inseparable from ourselves as a community of human beings with a specific form and character, a specific history, a specific relationship to the world',[15] then interference by colonialism, via the imposition 'of a foreign language, and [the suppression of] the native languages as spoken and written' is to break the 'harmony' between a people and their world and the languages with which they engage with the world. It is a diminution of their very being as humans, on this interpretation.

Let me now make explicit a hint I gave above concerning the problem of pathologising African responses to colonial languages and other artefacts. This is where it becomes important to take seriously the complexity and heterogeneity in African thinking. While people are happy to line up behind Ngũgĩ's declamations, hardly anyone bothers to consider alternative takes on the question of language from other African thinkers. I offer one such alternative from what would strike many as an unlikely source. According to Amílcar Cabral, all talk of colonialism killing the culture of the colonised is an exaggeration. Despite the endeavour by imperialism 'to liquidate directly or indirectly the cultural fabric of the dominated people', the colonised

> are able to create and develop the liberation movement only because they have kept their culture alive and vigorous despite the relentless

and organised repression of their cultural life. Even with their resistance at political and military levels destroyed, they continue to resist culturally. Except for cases of genocide or the violent reduction of native populations to cultural and social insignificance, *the epoch of colonisation* was not sufficient, at least in Africa, to bring about any significant destruction or degradation of the essential elements of the culture and conditions of the colonised peoples.[16]

If we grant this thesis of the durability of the culture of the colonised in the face of the ravages of the coloniser—and Ngũgĩ also seems to partly acknowledge this in picking the peasants and the proletariat as 'the resistance tradition' (a testament to the tenacity of their agency)—what are the implications for the question of language? Cabral espouses a very pragmatic view of language, away from the ideological and identitarian one offered by linguistic decolonisers. He argues:

Language is an instrument that man created through labor, through struggle, in order to communicate with others. And this gave him great new strength because no one was closed in on himself anymore; they began to speak with one another—men with men, societies with societies, people with people, country with country, continent with continent. How wonderful! Language was the first natural means of communication that existed. But the world advanced a lot; we didn't advance as much as the world. Our language remained at the level of that world to which we arrived, in which we live, whereas the *tuga* [the Portuguese]—although he was a colonialist living in Europe—had a language that advanced a good bit more than ours, being able to express concrete and relative truths, for example, with science.[17]

This instrumentalist conception of language does not preclude the development of literary and philosophical traditions based on it, but it surely does undermine the idea that language defines the identity or even the very humanity of a people. On this basis, Cabral made a startling claim: 'We have to have a real sense of our culture. Portuguese (the language) is one of the best things that the *tugas* left us, because language isn't evidence of anything, but an instrument for men to relate with one another, a means for speaking, to express realities of life and of the world'.[18] For Cabral, language is dynamic, and its primary purpose as a tool for communication means that, in a situation of backwardness,[19] what is crucial is what will most quickly help us get to that good life that defines human emancipation. As he explains,

> But for our land to advance, every child of our land in the next few years has to know what the acceleration of gravity is. ... There are many things that we can't say in our language, but there are people who want us to put the Portuguese language to the side because we're Africans and we don't want a foreigner's language. Those people want their mind to advance; they don't want to make their people to [sic] advance. We of the Party, if we want to lead our people forward for a long time to come—to write, to advance in science—our language has to be Portuguese. And this is an honor. It's the only thing we can appreciate from the *tuga*, because he left his language after having stolen so much from our land. Until an actual day in which, having deeply studied Creole, finding all of the good phonetic rules for Creole, we could begin to write Creole. ... But for science, Creole doesn't yet suffice.[20]

I present Cabral's very pragmatic reflections as an alternative with which we can argue. Cabral would clearly not enlist in the army of those who believe that decolonising requires a search for an 'African' science or for other modes of explaining reality that are to be recommended because they have no truck with 'colonial modernity', 'Euro-modernity' or 'Western rationality'. If you can convey an idea to the world and make sense of how things work, it matters less to Cabral what language you use to do so and more how successful you are at communicating your point. He did not argue that we should be content with using Portuguese, in his case, for ever. Rather, he contended that Africans should continue to develop our local tongues to a level that will enable us to articulate even the most recondite thoughts. This capacity is not automatic; it is a product of the language's evolution towards ever more sophisticated comprehension of our world and our place in and relation to it.

But this is not so for those for whom completing the process of decolonisation—i.e. decolonisation$_2$—means purging from our collective and individual imagination all of the artefacts that have proven colonial provenance, including language. Ngũgĩ assumes that if a language was imposed by force, the subsequent history of that language can never escape that.[21] This is where the significance of the distinction we make between the two forms of decolonisation asserts itself, again. Unless we assume that Africans, especially their elites, are singularly incapable of autonomy, it is implausible to write as if those who, post-independence, kept English as their vehicle for expressing ideas, have necessarily had their wills bent by neocolonial forces. Many decolonisers, following Ngũgĩ, work with this dubious assumption. But as I will argue, many things unfolded under colonialism whose causes cannot plausibly be ascribed to it. What's more, many other things occurred under colonialism which were legitimately ascribed to it and which the coloniser is all too eager to claim—e.g., the idea of liberal representative democracy. Simultaneously, thanks to the deployment of the subjectivity of the colonised—which was never absent, even if it was not dominant—the colonisers' will and designs were actively subverted and domesticated by the colonised, who put their own stamp on many such phenomena. This is like what we saw earlier with enslaved persons becoming better singers of freedom's song.

The appeal of decolonisation$_2$ fades once we write this alternative into the explanatory matrix. The idea that colonialism's cultural bomb is so powerful that it 'annihilate[s] a people's belief in their names, in their languages, in their environment, in their heritage of struggle, in their unity, in their capacities and ulti-mately in themselves'[22] is hyperbole, and is not very convincing as an explanatory model. The historical record points in a different direction. The contention that the peasants are the sole or prin-cipal vectors of indigenous languages, and that the elites wielding their colonially derived languages are, by definition, imperialist stooges, cannot be supported, even on Ngũgĩ's own terms. Intellectuals of the proletariat are still intellectuals and, for the most part, do not enact their 'resistance' in native tongues!

The situation while colonialism lasted was a lot more fluid. To suggest that language offers us a useful tool for classifying Africans as either resisters or collaborators is simply false. What of those who saw through the false universalism of colonialism, its incompatibility with the core tenets of the modernity that it deployed to justify its plunder, and decided to use these very prin-ciples to indict colonialism in the name of a genuine universalism, borne of the equality and dignity of all humanity? There is no place at the table for this class of thinkers. In the 'imperialist' versus 'resister' schema, where do our decolonisers place the likes of Wole Soyinka, Nelson Mandela, Obafemi Awolowo, Alexander Crummell, James Africanus Beale Horton, the denizens of the Fanti Confederacy (see Chapter 3), and others? None of these thinkers can be seen as victims or collateral damage of the cul-tural bomb. On the contrary, some of them were the first in the 19th century to challenge the idea that Egypt was not an African civilisation, while others in their ranks led the movement to cre-ate scripts for our autochthonous languages. More on that soon.

If the evidence cited by the late Lalage Bown in her landmark study *Two Centuries of African English* is accepted, 'African English' has been in existence since 1769, a 250-year period that is not even remotely convergent with the rather short career of colonialism on the continent.[23] What this means is that colonial imposition could not have been the sole way that English was disseminated across the continent. In many parts of West Africa, Christianity, not colonialism, was the vector of modernity, and many who welcomed English did so not out of compulsion but as part of their embrace of the new life brought by their faith.[24] Many of those missionaries who staffed the mission stations and did the crucial leg work were returnees from enslavement in the Americas and Europe, or 'recaptives'—captured Africans destined for enslavement in the Americas but rescued at sea by the British—after the abolition of the slave trade (but not slave-holding) in 1807. Their adoption of English did not prevent them from becoming the first scholars of our local languages and the most celebrated of them, Samuel Ajayi Crowther, authored the first primers in at least four languages: Yorùbá, Igbo, Nupe and Igala. And before the second evangelisation spree, while the ignoble trade in humans lasted, many of the trading posts on the coast were cosmopolitan centres, and a large number of Africans who took part in the trade learned the languages of their trading partners, from English to Portuguese, Danish, Spanish and French.[25] We need to take our history more seriously.

This leads us to the second major issue that I have with the idea of linguistic decolonisation. Whether people chose to use the colonially derived languages or had them imposed by others, it stands to reason that—and let's use the time frame of Bown's collection here—there is a vast community of people who use English as the medium of expression for their thoughts. In the world constructed by our decolonisers, those within this community who cannot be accommodated as 'resisters', à la Ngũgĩ, can only attract opprobrium but never be recognised as serious thinkers whose works deserve critical but respectful engagement, even if in disagreement. The sad consequence is that such thinkers are rendered illegible to many latter-day congregants in the church of decolonisation, and the insights contained in their works, as diverse and informative as they often are, are lost in the frenzy of excoriation and name-calling to which they are routinely subjected.

Once we acknowledge the presence of this category of thinkers, we must necessarily reckon with their intellectual production, being less concerned with their pedigree and more with the integrity and cogency of their ideas. When I spoke earlier about African thinkers of this type being walled away from the purview and interest of decoloniser-scholars preoccupied with 'African' contributions, this is how it goes. I can only hope that no decoloniser is desperate enough to retort that the only issue at stake is that of genealogy.

When Ngũgĩ reported on the Writers' Conference where the debate took place over what language to use to present African literature, one would get the impression that what mattered to him was the question of the origins of the language and of what writing as Africans in colonial languages meant for the very subjectivity of the ex-colonised. The problem we are talking about here—what to do with the large body of literature from Africans in 'colonial' languages over almost two centuries—had been posed in as forceful a manner as possible by Ezekiel (Es'kia) Mphahlele. Let's examine it in some detail to situate the problem of amnesia and selective vision that the decolonising trope encourages.

Interlude: Mphahlele's Question

In the early 1960s, Mphahlele complained about the direction that the celebrated journal *Présence Africaine* had taken not long after its founding. He noted that the journal had been established by the same people who had birthed the Society of African Culture in Paris in 1955. Their founding philosophy was Négritude, 'a word coined to embrace all Negro art, or the negroness of artistic activity'.[26] Mphahlele also noted the irony that it was the 'assimilated' African intellectuals, 'not the African in British-settled territories—a product of "indirect rule" and one that has been left in his cultural habitat—who readily reaches out for his traditional past', 'who have absorbed French culture, who is now passionately wanting to recapture his past'.[27] For Mphahlele, it is significant that, apart from writing in the colonial language, Léopold Sédar Senghor,

> in his poetry extols his ancestors' ancestral masks, African wood carvings and bronze art and tries to recover the moorings of his oral literature; he clearly feels he has come to a dead-end in European culture, and is still not really accepted as an organic part of French society, for all the assimilation he has been through.[28]

As enlightening as Mphahlele's analysis is so far, what is more remarkable and of greater relevance to this section is that he was concerned by what he saw as a worrisome turn by the journal, which made it less interested in the problems of the artist. 'Lately, *Présence Africaine* has, unfortunately, been too preoccupied with anthropological creepy-crawlies to devote enough attention to the problems of the artist in his present predicament', Mphahlele explained. Anticipating some of our present criticisms, the journal, he argued,

> did not seem to be aware of cultural cross-currents that characterize artistic expression in multi-racial societies. They seemed to think that the only culture worth exhibiting was traditional or indigenous. And so they concentrated on countries where interaction of streams of consciousness between black and white has not taken place to any significant or obvious degree, or doesn't so much as touch the cultural subsoil. A number of these enthusiasts even became apologetic about the Western elements in their own art.[29]

Mphahlele never begrudged the men of the journal their choice when he stopped in Paris in 1959 'to exchange ideas with' them. It is the question he posed which has resonance for our current discussion and the contemporary discourse of decolonisation: '*Where do we come in—we, who are detribalized and are producing a proletarian art? Has the Society of African Culture no room for us? This is what I wanted to know*'.[30]

This simple question has significant implications for our time. First, given that Ngũgĩ's category of 'resisters' includes the kind of 'proletarian artists' that Mphahlele took himself and his friend, Gerard Sekoto, to be, it is curious that this did not command Ngũgĩ's attention. And nor has anyone else in the discourse of linguistic decolonisation paid it much heed. Once we see that 'resisters' are not, in the main, defined by their working in African languages but only, in Ngũgĩ's own formulation, by their drawing of inspiration from the peasants to whom Ngũgĩ consigns the task of keeping African languages alive, the force of the insistence on linguistic identity is attenuated. Second, the charge that the journal had succumbed to the seduction of 'anthropological creepy-crawlies' mirrors one I level in the next chapter. That is, I contend that much of the decolonisation discourse lends itself to the proliferation of atavistic retrievals and essentialist characterisations of cultures and their manifestations, which have little connection with history or truth.

Recall who is excluded: those whose art is not strictly 'negro', 'African', or suchlike, whatever that means. Mphahlele used the example of his fellow countryman in whose company he made the journey to Paris, and an artist to boot: 'Gerard Sekoto, the Pretoria painter' who, despite having lived for ten years in Paris, 'still uses African themes .... [His paintings] exude ... a wonderful spirit of freedom and display a universality which could only result from an impact of cultures in the artist'.[31] He and Sekoto

[t]ried to bring home to our friends the problems facing culture in multi-racial communities like those in South Africa ... Our choral and jazz music, literature, dancing in South Africa have taken on a distinctive content and form which clearly indicate a merging of cultures. And we are not ashamed of it .... [Jacques] Rabemananjara

argued that there could be no conscious merging of cultures until we had attained political independence. But then the artist never waits for that kingdom to come: our vernacular and English writers had been producing work since 1870—long before organized political resistance took shape in 1912. And we in South Africa are poised between the two main cultural currents. We have got to do something about it, as we indeed are doing, more than the whites with blinkers on are prepared to admit. That is why our music will always be more vital, vibrant and meaningful than *boere-musiek* (Afrikaans music) which is a monument to a dead past, full of false posturing, hemmed in as it is by a frontier laager ...

When I am engaged in creative writing, for instance, my characters interest me in so far as they are in a so-called mixed society. What they were and what they did before the white man came interests me only as far as it throws light on their present behavior and human relationships. And then I don't want to depict African characters only. I first came to know the white man at the point of a boot and then at the point of an index finger—as a servant to him. I know there is much more to him than his fear of me, and I want to explore this other side. But then he won't let me.[32]

I hope that the rejoinder to Mphahlele's argument in the above passage is not 'is it African?' And we should also not read him as saying that only mixing produces great art. There is a way in which some of my strictures against the decolonisation of language mirror those of Mphahlele. There is a real sense that, beyond Ngũgĩ himself, a lot of the decolonisers are the contemporary purveyors of what Mphahlele called 'a monument to a dead past'. Once a restriction is imposed on what language must be used in a pluralist situation—and pluralism is not just limited to multi-racial societies—the artistic imagination is constricted, if not crippled, in order to meet the requirements of identity, authenticity or whatever other ideological litmus test is on offer. The artist who falls for this seduction, as Mphahlele argues, would see no reason to represent any culture other than the 'traditional or indigenous', and would be inclined to shun 'a wonderful spirit of freedom and display of a universality which could only result from an impact of cultures in the artist'.[33] What is true of the artist can be applied to the scholar. I make the case for this in the next chapter.

The orphaning of significant bodies of thought, not on account of their integrity or lack thereof but purely for reason of genealogy, is unacceptable and it does not advance knowledge. I do not know of any theorist of decolonisation in our time who has addressed Mphahlele's misgivings, especially his 'where do we come in?' question. Mphahlele's question goes to the heart of my challenge to 'decolonise this!' What I mean here is exactly how the discourse has either ignored or refused to take seriously works inspired by Mphahlele's standpoint. I am challenging our younger scholars to become aware of the efforts that the discourse encourages them to overlook. More importantly, our decolonisers need to show what is wrong with works that do not make a virtue of tracking down every slight from colonialism. I refer to works that instead draw from even the colonising countries and from movements that may have originated in these countries but which are not fully constituted within their boundaries, in order to fashion new modes of being human for all of humanity to embrace. Modernity and the elements that issue from it—from the novel as a literary genre to liberal democracy and the scientific revolution—are the most important of these possible sources of inspiration. The decolonising trope constricts the imaginative space within which to work. One consequence of this weight on the budding scholar's imagination is the threat of a very short, limited career. After all, there is only so much that you can do by scouring your inheritance for things that are not 'contaminated'.[34]

I challenge decolonisers to expand their circle of candidates for decolonisation to show what is wrong with African thinkers who do not reject modernity, Westernisation, even, but who elect to borrow from those traditions to construct new theoretical models, new narratives, new dramas, and so on, to enable us to make sense of ourselves and our place in the universe. They should turn their hand to decolonising the specific works of Aimé Césaire, Wole Soyinka, Bessie Head, Derek Walcott, Léopold Sédar Senghor, Flora Nwapa, Mabel Segun, Niyi Osundare, Kofi Anyidoho and so on. Justine McConnell, for example, has shown how various diasporic authors have appropriated for their own purposes one of the founding texts of so-called Western civilisation, Homer's *The Odyssey*, and idiomatised it.[35] The works she discusses range from Césaire's *Cahier d'un retour au pays natal* through to Ralph Ellison's *Invisible Man*, Derek Walcott's *Omeros* and *The Odyssey: A Stage Version*, and Njabulo Ndebele's *The Cry of Winnie Mandela*.

Certainly, these would not be easy works to decolonise because they call for the kind of skills and erudition that decolonising does not cultivate in, nor require of, those who wish to deploy it. This is in inverse proportion to the assiduity with which the writers I have mentioned and others who share similar orientations cultivate their inheritances, school themselves in the artefacts of human experience and seek to write texts that speak to the catholicity and complexity of what it is to be human. Beyond their reaching out to the breadth of the human experience, many of those writers covered by the scope of Mphahlele's simple question also delve deeply into their own inheritances, are very good students of their respective cultures and often have more than a passing relationship with their original languages. One cannot say the same of many who are enamoured of the decolonising trope. Worse still, because they are forever speaking about 'Africa', there is rarely any nuance or differentiation in the discussion of specific authors, works or even regions. Our decolonisers are always talking about Senghor's terrible Francophilia. But when one reads deep studies of Senghor, the complexity of his thinking comes out clearly.[36]

When it comes to polemics on language, the proponents of decolonising evince little knowledge of, much less engagement with, the progress (no matter how small) which has been made in the struggle to promote African languages, and what challenges such efforts face in parts of the continent since independence.

Wiredu on Conceptual Decolonisation

So far, I have tried to show how the call for linguistic decolonisation tends to neglect a significant class of African thinkers. Ngũgĩ's reflections intersect with those of Kwasi Wiredu, who also locates the genesis of the need for decolonisation in the continuing influence of colonialism on the African mindscape, decades after independence was supposed to have been attained. Wiredu explains:

> By conceptual decolonization I mean two complementary things. On the negative side, I mean avoiding or reversing through a critical conceptual self-awareness the unexamined assimilation in our thought (that is, in the thought of contemporary African philosophers) of the conceptual frameworks embedded in the foreign philosophical traditions that have had an impact on African life and thought. And, on the positive side, I mean exploiting as much as is judicious the resources of our own indigenous conceptual schemes in our philosophical meditations on even the most technical problems of contemporary philosophy. The negative is, of course, only the reverse of the positive. But I cite it first because *the necessity for decolonization was brought upon us in the first place by the historical superimposition of foreign categories of thought on African thought systems through colonialism.*

> This superimposition has come through three principal avenues. The first is the avenue of language. It is encountered in the fact that our

91

philosophical education has generally been in the medium of foreign languages, usually of our erstwhile colonizers. This is the most fundamental, subtle, pervasive and intractable circumstance of mental colonization. But the other two avenues, though grosser by comparison, have been insidious enough. I refer here to the avenues of religion and politics.[37]

In a later formulation, Wiredu was more succinct. 'By decolonization, I mean divesting African philosophical thinking of all undue influences emanating from our colonial past.'[38]

I would like to unpack some assumptions underpinning the claims in Wiredu's passage. Wiredu is no less concerned by colonialism's impact on our mindscape in the continent than Ngũgĩ and other decolonisers. Conceptual frameworks are necessarily linguistic. Language is the medium through which concepts are formed and articulated. Concepts are the basic units with which we make sense of our world. It is little wonder that the limits of our language determine the limits of our world. That is, as it is for all peoples, the world is always wider and much more populous than the language with and in which we capture it. What that means is that what we call 'our world' is necessarily an abridged representation of the world that is beyond the grasp of our comprehension. (The philosophical issues that are raised by this simple description, which form some of the perennial questions of philosophy, are not relevant to the present discussion.) When new elements come into our world, we must expand our linguistic framework to accommodate them and, in so doing, expand our world. We do this by turning old words to new uses, thereby extending their semantic fields, or by borrowing concepts from other linguistic registers to capture and make sense of the new reality. In doing so, we simultaneously enlarge our original register by domesticating the new borrowings in it. Wiredu leaves open this possibility. He contends that 'a language, most assuredly, is not conceptually neutral; syntax and vocabulary are apt to suggest definite modes of conceptualization. Note, however, that I say "suggest" not "compel", for, if the phenomenon had the element of necessitation implied by the latter word no decolonization would be possible'.[39]

This relaxing of the connection between syntax and vocabulary and modes of conceptualisation allows us to conceive of a mutual intermingling of the languages of the colonised and coloniser. This has implications that are often unacknowledged by those who call for the decolonisation of language. For one thing, depending on how simple or complex a society is; what kinds of commerce it engages in with its neighbours; how segmented and differentiated it is along ethnic, linguistic, cultural and economic lines, it may not be easy to talk, as Wiredu seems to do in this passage, about 'the conceptual frameworks embedded in the foreign philosophical traditions that have had an impact on African life and thought',[40] as if these frameworks can be easily defined and separated from one another. I will go into this in more detail shortly.

When Wiredu talks of the necessity of decolonisation being brought upon us by the superimposition of foreign categories through colonialism, what are we to make of this? Colonialism is identified as the only agent of causation in the process of superimposition. If this turns out not to be the case, will the need for decolonisation be thereby obviated? And if we grant that this is the case, what then follows? Does it mean that we must remove what was imposed? I hope that I do not have to make a case for how and why this is intuitively impossible. Wiredu himself makes quite clear that this is not an option when he declares, 'obviously, it would not be rational to try to reject everything of a colonial ancestry'.[41] This imposition has also been on 'African thought systems'. Again, we need to make clear what these African thought systems were like before colonialism superimposed foreign categories on them. I hope that the reader begins to see how some of the grand claims made by decolonisation theorists turn out to be quite woolly once we begin to deconstruct them.

'African thought systems' and 'foreign categories of thought' are diverse, multiple and dynamic. The discourse of decolonising seems nebulous unless we make clear which thought systems we are talking about in each case, their historicity and their iteration at any given time. As I argue presently, if colonialism is the key historicity at play here, it may seem that we can easily delineate what those thought systems were like before colonialism. While this looks deceptively simple, it is anything but. To take the example of Wiredu's own homeland, Ghana, not all parts of the country came under the same colonial influences. Nor were these influences felt at the same time or with the same severity. There had also been other foreign influences on the area, and different effects on different groups of people within the area. If we do not impose a spurious uniformity on these colonial influences or on their timelines, it is difficult to even know what the before and after point would be. This is especially the case if, as we just mentioned, not all external influences came from colonialism, nor did they all follow the same trajectory or have the same level of impact. Additionally, the realities upon which colonialism imposed itself were not uniform or at the same level of cultural or ideological development. It may turn out that colonialism is the least important of the many foreign influences at work in those areas.

There are significant differences between Ngũgĩ's and Wiredu's tone and recommendations. Wiredu's domain is philosophy. Philosophy comes with disciplinary peculiarities—e.g., a fundamental concern with the universal—which set it apart from literature, the decolonisation of which Ngũgĩ insists is synonymous with writing or orating in an African language. Unlike literature, which more easily answers to the call of regionalism, philosophy always wears its claims to universality on its sleeve. What this means is that for Wiredu, philosophy may not quite answer to Ngũgĩ's description of what it means for literature to be characterised as African. I focus here on the linguistic element of their arguments, and on politics in the next chapter.

For one thing, unlike Ngũgĩ, as much as Wiredu argues for the importance of language to our relationship to the world, he is less extravagant in asserting the scope of this importance, limiting himself to specific registers—philosophy, religion and politics. Wiredu does not subscribe to Ngũgĩ's notion of the tight fit between our very being as humans and our language. (Though, as we saw above, a careful reading of Ngũgĩ's case reveals some significant ambiguities between language as ethnic register and language as politico-ideological register, language as identity and language as political preference.) For Wiredu, there are no ideological issues involved. The point is well put by Zeyad el Nabolsy:

Wiredu defines decolonisation in *procedural* terms, i.e., for Wiredu decolonisation has been undertaken successfully when the conceptual frameworks which have been inherited from the colonial past have been critically examined. The key point about this procedural understanding of decolonisation is that after critical examination we may decide to keep or abandon such conceptual frameworks. However, in either case decolonisation would have been successfully carried out if critical examination has indeed taken place. Many of those who draw on Wiredu misunderstand this point by taking him to be claiming that decolonisation is defined in *substantive* terms. Those scholars think that what matters most for the process of decolonisation is the *end result*, i.e., the abandonment of the conceptual frameworks which have been inherited from the colonial past. For them, successful decolonisation cannot be said to have taken place if the conceptual frameworks which have been inherited from the colonial past have been retained, regardless of the procedure which led to this decision. This understanding of decolonisation is clearly not in accord with Wiredu's understanding of decolonisation.[42]

The simple fact is that African philosophers labour under the weight of assumptions traceable to 'foreign philosophical traditions'. What is not clear is why this is a significant problem. For it to be so, it must be the case that the operation of these superimposed 'foreign categories of thought on African thought systems' blocks us from gaining insights into the perennial problems of philosophy in African thought systems; or distorts them such that we are hampered in our search for answers to those problems; or, at the extreme, leads to outcomes which are detrimental to our lives. Ngũgĩ was more forcible in this respect. I do not see the same vehemence in Wiredu. Wiredu does not claim that these foreign-derived frameworks alienate us from our very names, history or language. But both share the belief that those frameworks do terrible things to our language. For Wiredu, we end up adopting solutions that we have not critically examined to problems we have identified. Finally, for both, what makes these frameworks problematic is, in part, their colonial provenance. If it turns out that some of them do not have this, the solution proposed to this misdiagnosed problem becomes less viable.

With reference to the linguistic situation, Wiredu asserts that 'By definition, the fundamental concepts of philosophy are the most fundamental categories of human thought. But the particular modes of thought that yield these concepts may reflect the specifics of the culture, environment and even the accidental idiosyncrasies of the people concerned'.[43] How are we to understand Wiredu's point here? Although philosophy is universal and there is an assumption that its perennial questions are similar or the same everywhere, what sets philosophical traditions apart from one another are these 'accidental idiosyncrasies'. Individual thinkers whose philosophical production becomes widely diffused across cultural, linguistic and other boundaries cannot escape the infiltration of their cultural idioms into their philosophical syntaxes. Those who use such idioms as if they are synonymous with philosophy's syntax may end up disseminating 'idiosyncrasies' as universal ideas. The risk is no less present for 'the natives of any given philosophical tradition vis-à-vis their historical inheritance'.[44] From this perspective, one reason to decolonise is for us—as for direct inheritors of the philosophical idioms that we deploy—to seek to separate the wheat of philosophy from the chaff of 'idiosyncrasies'.

What are these concepts which are often contaminated by these suspect idiosyncrasies emanating from specific philosophical traditions? According to Wiredu, there are many of them, but let me mention only the following:

> Reality, Being, Existence, Thing, Object, Entity, Substance, Property, Quality, Truth, Fact, Opinion, Belief, Knowledge, Faith, Doubt, Certainty, Statement, Proposition, Sentence, Idea, Mind, Soul, Spirit, Thought, Sensation, Matter, Ego, Self, Person, Individuality, Community, Subjectivity, Objectivity, Cause, Chance, Reason, Explanation, Meaning, Freedom, Responsibility, Punishment, Democracy, Justice, God, World, Universe, Nature, Supernature, Space, Time, Nothingness, Creation, Life, Death, Afterlife, Morality, Religion.[45]

All the preceding concepts are recurrent themes in philosophies across temporal, spatial, linguistic and cultural boundaries. When we expound the idea of Being, for example, notice that in its very presentation, there are no differentiations, no adjectives, and whatever substantive conclusions we reach can only aspire to enable whoever accesses them to come to a less unclear understanding of the phenomenon and, who knows, guide their relationship with the world accordingly. In elucidating the concept in, say, English, however careful we may be, it is inescapable that the philosopher from England, who is socialised into the fundamental world view that informs what it is to grow up, think and act 'English', is likely to take for granted some elements of the Judeo-Christian tradition, dominant in that country. Between trying to articulate a universal interpretation of 'Being', doing so in English and trying to ensure that the peculiarities of cultural English usages do not contaminate the universal ambition, we have an instance of what Wiredu wants us to be careful of. When we come to engage with this instance of Being, the British person—working in the context of a long history of articulations of this idea in her tradition—must be careful not to take that legacy for granted, and the outsider, say an Akan person, must not assume that the English rendering is universal and erroneously seek to make it emblematic of what Being is, no matter what tradition we are talking about. It is when we do not seek to separate the universal from the idiosyncratic that we slip into a colonial mentality, in Wiredu's view.

According to Wiredu, because many Africans have our education in philosophy in English, French or 'some such language', we are in danger of slipping from 'thinking *about* them [these concepts] in English' into 'thinking in English about them'.[46] The first presupposes that we think in an indigenous language but think about philosophical concepts in, say, English. And when we slip into thinking in English, 'we constantly stand the danger of involuntary mental de-Africanization unless we consciously and deliberately resort to our own languages (and culture)'.[47]

If we do not pay attention to the distinction that Wiredu makes between universal possibilities and accidental idiosyncrasies, it leaves us vulnerable to carrying other peoples' baggage insofar as we are enslaved to the concepts their linguistic and other cultural conventions foster. One cannot overemphasise the importance of heeding Wiredu's wisdom in this respect. For example, many have argued that the reason for the repeated failure of liberal representative democracy to take root in Africa is, in part, the alienness of its package of ideas, institutions, practices and processes. I shall have more to say about this presently. Wiredu would later canvass what he calls 'no-party, consensus democracy' as an option that is more in tune with African temperaments and memory.[48]

To avoid untoward outcomes, Wiredu explains,

> the simple recipe for decolonization for the African is: Try to think them [concepts like Reality, Being, Meaning, Freedom] through in *your own African language* and, on the basis of the results, review the intelligibility of the associated problems or the plausibility of the apparent solutions that have tempted you when you have pondered them in some metropolitan language.[49]

In another formulation, Wiredu affirms that to decolonise African philosophy is to 'try to test philosophical formulations in a metropolitan language in our vernacular to see if they will survive independent analysis'.[50] Only if the conceptual problems involved are independent of the peculiarities of any specific language are we free to adopt them as universals. This is without prejudice, Wiredu insists, to the fact that some problems or ideas may have resonance only in specific contexts. Their not being universal does not detract in any way from their significance in their immediate context. Wiredu does not restrict this injunction to only the colonised. Someone from the coloniser's tradition who is not otherwise invested in a spurious universalism will also be concerned with the same consideration. Hence, the contention in Chapter 1 that a serious commitment to good scholarship from all parties will eliminate a lot of the problems that the decolonisation trope is intended to solve. We cannot afford to farm this responsibility out to the coloniser, and we should not be afraid of calling scholars out when they fall short of this requirement.

Wiredu's simple injunction—think things through in your own African language—is fraught with myriad assumptions that are not always, or for the most part, plausible. He himself immediately warns us that

> [i]t turns out that this form of self-knowledge is not easy to attain, and it is not uncommon to find highly educated Africans proudly

holding forth on, for instance, the glories of African traditional religion in an internalized conceptual idiom of a metropolitan origin which distorts indigenous thought structures out of all recognition.[51]

How easy is it to follow Wiredu's advice to think in your own language? Wiredu assumes that his audience is at least bilingual, knowing both an African language and a colonially imposed one—say English. But given how the scenario is designed, the colonial language is the primary language, the one which triggers thought and in which thought is originally formulated. This is where the problem begins. The thinker here is supposed to 'think through in her own language' the relevant concepts. Why wait to be prompted in the colonial language? Let us try a different approach. Ẹ gba àwọn ọ̀rọ̀ wọnyí yẹ wò: Yorùbá, èdè, àṣà, iṣe, iwà, iṣesí, ìgbésí ayé, ikú, ohùn, gbólóhùn, ọ̀rọ̀, èyà, orin, ọnà, ijó, ilù, èsìn, òrìṣà, ẹbí, ará, ojúlùmọ̀, gbajúmọ̀, òṣèlú, ọba, ìjọba, ìdálùú, ìbátan, ọbàkan, ọmọiyá, ìgbeyàwó, ilémosú, aṣùwàdà, àṣùwàdà, ifọgbọ́ntáyéṣe.

Why not proceed to think through concepts in your primary African language in exactly the way that a speaker of Chinese or Portuguese, for example, would in similar situations, using their own tongue? The answer, of course, *pace* Ngũgĩ and Wiredu, is that we have cut ourselves off from 'belief in our languages' and embraced instead the colonial ones. If this is true, then it is problematic to assume that those who have been thus separated from their languages could simply summon up the requisite facility and grounding in those languages to allow them to carry out the type of recondite thinking associated with philosophy and other advanced modes of intellection.

Oversold Promise: Beyond Linguistic Decolonisation

I cannot speak for Africa as a whole but, as we shall see shortly, in my neck of the global woods, my Yorùbá inheritance, we have not done badly.[52] Maybe that is why, from the beginning, I could not enlist in the linguistic decolonising army. Yet, as I am about to show, even in this area where there is considerably advanced work done on and in the original language, the injunction to decolonise language may be misaimed and its promise oversold because, as I indicated at the end of the section on Ngũgĩ's account, all this cannot be done without more. I will specify what this 'more' encompasses in a moment. I would probably be more impressed by the insistence that our universities operate in our original languages, or that our literature and even our public life be presented in local languages, if our coterie of decolonisers themselves demonstrated some effort to reduce their own reliance on the languages they criticise for their colonial provenance, and acquired some proficiency in African languages for the purposes of intellectual inquiries. It is usually the case that they have little or no ability to speak or write the languages they promote as a medium of intellectual expression, nor do I see any evidence in their writings that they are working to remedy this lack. This is partly why they are unable to acknowledge, much less engage with, works that are being done by others on and in those languages across many different disciplines.

In Yorùbá, for instance, there are institutions where bachelor's degree programmes in the language are conducted entirely in the original language. There are serious records of scholarship and scholarly production in the language: Akínṣọlá Akìwọwọ in sociology; D. O. Fágúnwà, Akínwùmí Ìṣọ̀lá, C. L. Adéoyè, Ọládélé Awóbùluyì, Olúdáre Ọlájubù, Túbọ̀sún Ọládàpọ̀, Lánrewájú Adépọ̀jù, J. F. Odunjo, Ọládèjọ Òkédìjí, Isaac O. Delano, Ọlásopé Oyèláràn, Adébáyọ̀ Fálétí and Ọlabiyi Yáì in literature, language and linguistics; Patricia Olubunmi Smith, G. A. Adeboye, Olu Obafemi, Wande Abimbola, Wole Soyinka, Akínwùmí Ìṣọ̀lá, Ọlanipẹkun Ẹsan, Ọmọtoye Olorode, Baba Omojola, Akin Adéṣọ̀kàn and Adélékè Adéẹ̀kọ́ in Yorùbá–

English, English–Yorùbá, Yorùbá–French and Greek–Yorùbá translation, in areas ranging from the classics to botany to political economy. These are some of the names with which decolonisers should familiarise themselves, in order to consider what remains to be done; how to build upon what has already been done; and, most importantly, to understand why various initiatives have foundered and how to draw appropriate lessons to avoid similar mistakes in the future.

Unfortunately, because I suspect that their audience is elsewhere, away from African institutions and scholars—and that this audience is largely uninformed about African scholarship and, therefore, more likely to be impressed by limited knowledge masquerading as expertise—our decolonisers thrive, but at the expense of the future of the very projects they claim to want to advance. When I insist that we cannot simply deploy our languages for purposes of recondite analyses and explanations without more, I propose to show how even a language with as much advanced work in and on it as Yorùbá still remains very much in the grip of what I shall call 'equivalence-ism'. I will flesh out the earlier remark concerning how flippantly calls to do our scholarship in local languages are thrown out by decolonisers. Familiarity with the research of some African scholars in the field would be helpful. Ayo Bamgbose stands out in this respect. In his assessment of the Algerian government's efforts to legislate for language empowerment, Bamgbose explains it is easy to decree that

> with effect from 5th July, 1998, only Arabic should be used by all public offices, institutions, enterprises, and associations of whatever type in all their activities relating to communication, and all administrative, financial, technical and artistic matters. The use of all foreign languages in all deliberations and debates at official meetings is forbidden. The moment of truth will come when the authorities decide to enforce this law, for they will discover that a large number of functionaries who are expected to carry out the enforcement are

probably more proficient in French than in Classical Arabic. Besides, Colloquial Algerian Arabic, which is in a diglossic relationship with Classical Arabic, is the variety known and used by most speakers of Arabic. For most people, therefore, the high variety is almost like the imposition of another language. In addition, an Arabization law, in effect, discriminates against the minority Berber speakers, who constitute one-third of the population. In fact, with the coming into effect of the law on July 5, there are already reports of protests and demonstrations by the Berber community in some Algerian cities.[53]

The moral of this tale is often ignored by those who too hastily call for the decolonisation of language, without paying attention to some of the difficulties. As I shall argue presently, the closer one looks at the issue of language and the continuing use of colonial tongues in African countries, the clearer it becomes that what is at stake goes beyond colonialism and that, for the most part, the influence of colonialism or imperialism cannot begin to explain the problem in this sphere. The languages are simply not available for the use to which we intend to put them, such as in our insistence that our universities, to be African, must conduct their affairs in autochthonous African languages.

In other words, talking nebulously about using African languages as if they are readily usable for more than colloquial purposes is unhelpful.[54] Language development is important in this respect. As we saw earlier, Cabral had already anticipated this problem. Bamgbose sheds more light on it:

> The constraint of language development is a very real one. It is not possible to use a language in education if that language has not been reduced to writing, described, and materials provided in it for the use of teachers and learners. To say this of course is not to accept that a decision to use a language in education should necessarily await the completion of language development. (In fact, it is doubtful if language development can ever be completed, considering that it is usually an on-going process). The truth is that the language development

constraint is a veritable vicious circle. Unless the language is developed, it cannot be used in education, and unless it is used in education, it cannot be developed. Several agencies and individuals are involved in language development and quite often one group does not know what the other is doing. Unless and until there is a decision to use a particular language in education, it is very likely that we may not know what material is available in it. A logical way to proceed therefore would seem to be a census of languages, including a catalogue of what is available in each language ... Such a census will then be followed by a decision on what language to use for what purpose and at which level. Where materials are lacking, the provision of these will be one of the main thrusts of the implementation process.[55]

A good example of the challenges posed by language development is the Ẹgbẹ́-Onímọ̀-Èdè-Yorùbá (Yorùbá Studies Association of Nigeria). The members of this group were committed to doing in practice what our decolonisers are merely content to talk about (more as a way to shame than to inspire). As Bamgbose again explains, their challenge was to work out what

the medium to be employed in teaching Yorùbá [would be] at the university level. It was generally agreed that English was not the most appropriate medium, yet much work had to be done to evolve suitable Yorùbá metalanguage, in order to make the use of Yorùbá a realistic option. At its Annual General Meeting held in Lagos on April 20, 1974, the Association set up a Standing Committee 'to initiate and coordinate studies on Yorùbá Metalanguage and submit results of same to the Association from time to time.[56]

Their efforts culminated in the publication of two slim volumes of *Yorùbá Metalanguage* (*Èdè-Ìperí Yorùbá*).[57] Their work was motivated by the realisation that when we call for the use of our local languages, there is a lot more to this process than mere rhetoric. The efforts cited here are limited to Yorùbá, as a subject and a discipline. But to do intellectual work at an advanced level in Yorùbá in other disciplines or for theoretical purposes would require a lot more than the creation of metalanguages in the respective fields.[58]

If what we have said so far is plausible, then Wiredu's facile recommendation that we must 'think in our original languages' is neither easy to indulge nor likely to produce the kinds of insights that theoretical explorations are designed to elicit. This is where we must begin to acknowledge the sad fact that as regards complex intellectual activity of the kind that decolonisers do in the university and at academic gatherings, many African scholars are not bilingual in the full sense. Autochthonous African languages are already afflicted with a severe case of fossilisation, which continues to escape our attention. Thinking in a language is much more difficult than understanding a language and using it in everyday discourse. Yes, many of us are fluent in our native languages, and we are ever eager to cherry pick from them to find particular words that we wish—forlornly for the most part—could be used as concepts in theoretical frameworks that we largely construct in foreign syntaxes. Few of us can mentally express in 'our own African languages' deep thoughts about many of those concepts on Wiredu's list. This affliction is not removed or lessened by repeated demands to decolonise our intellectual production. Yes, we use our local languages for colloquial, quotidian purposes. But this misleadingly makes us think that it would be an easy shifting of gears from here to theoretical or philosophical discourse. It only takes a small amount of attention to realise that this is a mistaken assumption. The upshot is that there is little in the way of recondite intellection in many autochthonous languages, especially where research and knowledge production hosted by our tertiary institutions are concerned.

The colloquial register, the most common and general way in which humans use language, is one that is available to many in the African setting. This is not what our decolonisers have in mind when they tell us to think concepts in our own languages. But this is about the only area where we can even say that most of us have fluency in our own tongues. Yet, it is not the one required for academic work. Many of our original cultures also have in them the language of ritual, which can be both complex and obscure. This is not ordinarily available to everybody; only the initiated, after rigorous training, can gain access to and use it. Again, this is not what people have in mind when they tell us to think concepts in our own languages.

What is called for is a register geared towards investigation, analysis and criticism within and across specific practices. For want of a better term, I would call it 'theoretical language'. For this to be acquired, we would need much more than translations or 'equivalence-ism'. Equivalence-ism is the process of spending an inordinate amount of time searching for equivalent terms in our autochthonous languages to show that 'what English can do, we can do in Yorùbá', and so on. The irony is lost on us that this comparison does not allow for original or independent assertions in our languages. That is, our languages and their possibilities become limited by the boundaries set by the external languages. We therefore make no progress in developing theoretical or other recondite thinking, outside of the language of ritual, in autoch-thonous languages.[59] We would need a community of scholars, thinkers, practitioners, students and so on who make it their business to think, speak, write, investigate, report, analyse and debate in our respective languages about our world, our place in it, our social relations—our languages, even—and how we make sense of them. This is the only way to avoid the fate of fossilisa-tion and the ongoing dominance of equivalence-ism when it comes to academic work that incorporates our own languages.

The preceding is not peculiar to African languages and their use in intellectual work. There is a reason why we do not try to make quotidian words in the English language applicable to complex, theoretical thought, for example. Even in academic work, it is no accident that we look to specialised disciplines for theoretical insights and directions in their own domains. We seem to forget this when we talk about intellectual work in our autochthonous languages. As far as I know, and as I indicate momentarily, we do not have Yorùbá theorists who try to populate the language with concepts and theoretical frameworks that can be used in and adapted to multiple different disciplines. We have seen how advanced Yorùbá is in working to create a metalanguage for teaching at all levels of the education system, especially at the tertiary level. And this is what should be happening if we are to do exactly what Wiredu is asking us to do. Incidentally, not even Wiredu has attempted to populate our philosophical sphere with theoretical concepts to aid thinking 'in our own languages'. What he and most of us have done does not rise above the level of equivalence-ism. Might there be a lesson here?

Unfortunately, the lesson is not a favourable one. In many of our attempts to make the Wiredu move, what we have mostly ended up with is equivalence-ism. To limit myself to Yorùbá, which I know intimately, the original work being done at a higher level takes place in sociology, art history, language, and literature and linguistics—and it is no less dominated by equivalence-ism.[60] Equivalence-ism may not be what Wiredu intended but it is what dominates much writing in academic and professional African philosophy. Words are routinely yanked out of their semantic and hermeneutic contexts and made to stand as equivalents for concepts derived from elsewhere. There is hardly any effort to create sustained analyses wholly or even largely in our original language. To the extent that this is the case, the promise of decolonisation in the sphere of language may have been oversold.

Here is why. The academic work carried out in different disciplines often does not cross over or is not disseminated across the intellectual board. Here are two illustrations. The first is the concept of 'paradigm'. When Thomas Kuhn adapted this concept into his explanatory framework for how science evolves over time, he introduced it into a discursive tradition (Anglo-American) in which were operating both those who shared his specific registers of philosophy and history of science and those who used other Anglo-American registers, from literary criticism to economics. It was therefore easy for others outside his specific disciplinary registers to not only read, understand and critically engage with his use of the concept, but, more crucially, to see the explanatory force of his theoretical model, with many of them beginning to explore the possibilities for their own registers of adopting the Kuhnian idea of paradigm. A different but equally illuminating example is the idea of 'civil religion', which has its origins in Jean-Jacques Rousseau's borrowing from religion in the 18th century and adapting it to civil society and the notion of political legitimacy and coherence. Both 'paradigm' and 'civil religion' have become part of the language of intellection in numerous ethnic registers across the globe.

I argue that much of the decolonising discourse barely scratches the surface where the issue of deploying our original languages in literature and philosophy is concerned (to limit myself to my announced foil in this work). I am persuaded that Wiredu did not think of the issue that I raise here. He is too careful and meticulous a thinker to have allowed such a question to go unanswered.

Consider the cluster of words/terms/concepts that we cited earlier in the chapter from Wiredu (see p. 97). It would not be enough for us to think them in our original language. Even if we succeed in doing so, we will merely happen upon their 'equivalents' in, say, Yorùbá or Gĩkũyũ. The register in which they were originally deployed and the discursive tradition within which they enjoyed cross-disciplinary meaning and helped to frame the world are not ours directly, and many of these concepts do not have any clear Yorùbá equivalents. Simultaneously, in the cluster of words that I supplied in Yorùbá (see p. 100), given that some of them, like the example from the English selections, do not have any obvious English equivalents—*ilémosú*, for instance—clearly what is called for here is much more than translation or finding equivalence. The idea of *ilémosú*, as an element of a family form—including marital relations, their associated ethics and the larger social context within which they make sense—would require in-depth analyses and discussions that are not ordinarily available when we incorporate the idea into a discussion in English about feminism, women's status, natal relations and property rights within a family. Only when these have been thrashed out repeatedly in critical engagements among scholars of the tradition, across several disciplines, will we be able to begin comparing them with their 'equivalents' in other discursive traditions. It is only then that we can bring the richness of the discursive tradition from which they have emerged to the attention of the world, not as titillating exotica to be sampled but as serious conceptual categories to be tested in other climes within the overarching framework of a common human understanding.[61]

When we have found equivalents in our languages, to what end shall they be put? Philosophising in our language and explaining the world and the evolution and interconnection of ideas are not tasks that can be done by 'thinking' foreign 'concepts' in our original tongues. I see every day the damage that is done when this difficulty is glossed over. Examples abound. In politics, it is not enough to look for equivalent terms for those derived from English when we wish to do political philosophy in Yorùbá. We conflate, as if doing so is unproblematic, sundry practices in Yorùbá political culture with English formulations, and end up (1) dehistoricising our institutions; and (2) comparing incomparables and, consequently, asserting falsehoods about the character of our indigenous political practices; institutions;

processes; and, most importantly, their theoretical and/or moral principles. Worse still, whatever theoretical insights and frameworks we come up with do not transfer to other registers within the culture.

The most advanced work in Yorùbá has been done in linguistics, literature, art history and sociology. As far as I know, outside of work by a handful of scholars writing in Yorùbá, there is no cross-fertilisation or transference of conceptual discoveries from one register to another. They are not all integrated into a discursive tradition within and from which we pick and choose which terms to develop into concepts and how those concepts might improve understanding in other registers. There is a very real sense in which, when it comes to our indigenous languages and how they are used in various registers, our languages are being privatised. Let me explain. Again, I restrict myself to discussing knowledge production in Yorùbá, which I know well and operate in. Because of the pioneering efforts of the academics at the old University of Ife—since renamed Obafemi Awolowo University, Ile-Ife, Nigeria—the final two decades of the last century saw the injection into our institutions of tertiary-level textbooks in all areas of language learning—from morphology to syntax, semantics and phonology. This was in the wake of the fact that Yorùbá literature already had a solid tradition of written works going back to the late 19th century, following on the heels of the creation of a script for the language under the direction of Christian missionaries. Literature is probably where we have the most output, and in all genres: drama, music, poetry, essays, novels and journalism. Meanwhile, the explosion in radio broadcasting in the 1970s, the deregulation of the industry in the 1980s and the subsequent emergence of broadcast stations devoted solely or primarily to Yorùbá have led to an exponential growth in the Yorùbá lexicon, not to mention in primary materials that could populate a serious discursive tradition at the level of theory-making and philosophical analyses.

With all these developments have also come significant efforts to do academic work in analysis, theory-making, criticism and suchlike in the language.[62] This is where things begin to go south. Despite this effusive output in the language, it is difficult to say that we have a discursive tradition in Yorùbá into which these various discoveries and inventions have fed and within which the members argue, exchange, adapt and generally certify these new usages. No doubt, we have books and papers doing analytical, critical and explanatory work in the language. Àrìnpé Adéjùmọ̀, for example, has written some of the most original articles and book-length studies in Yorùbá on literary criticism, literary history and feminist analysis. She stands out as a scholar who does not just chronicle Yorùbá life and thought or create specific analyses of texts and practices. Before she came onto the scene, there had been analytical and descriptive accounts of aspects of Yorùbá culture, ranging from the usages of the civilisation to discourses on faith and worship, and to critical and analytical works on poetry, prose, music, drama and so on. I will use a specific work of Adéjùmọ̀ to illustrate this point. Given that there is very little linguistic material on which to base herself in some of the registers she works in—feminist analysis, for instance—she has had, like others before her, to invent many new terms and phrases.[63] In the process, she and the other scholars cited here have inserted new words into the language, put old formulations to new uses and, generally, expanded our understanding of the respective fields in which they work. It is her work on satire in historical drama in Yorùbá that I wish to draw attention to here.

In *Ìṣẹ̀fẹ̀ Nínú Àwọn Eré-Onítàn Yorùbá* (2001), Adéjùmọ̀ translates 'satire' as '*ẹ̀fẹ̀*' in Yorùbá. In the 'Summary' in English at the beginning of the book, she anticipates the problems associated with this translation. She explains:

> The work also discovers that the term *ẹ̀fẹ̀* (satire) is interchangeably used for other forms of humour like *àpárá* (jokes), *àwàdà* (jest) and

yẹ̀yẹ́ (ridicule). Thus, the work observes that although a sharp distinction could not be made between these forms, the aim of satire to bring a positive change to the society by ridiculing the fools and the vices in a deviant distinguishes it from the other forms.[64]

Her observation is apt because in *A Dictionary of the Yorùbá Language*, a bilingual volume, the English–Yorùbá section has the following entry: 'Satire, n. arófọ̀; Satirical, adj. ti arófọ̀, bi arófọ̀.'[65] In the Yorùbá–English section, we have: 'Èfẹ̀, n. joke, jest'.[66] Meanwhile, in the only existing monolingual dictionary of Yorùbá, we have: 'Èfẹ̀ n. Apara, ere ti o kun fun apara. A lọ wo iran ere ẹfẹ̀ li Ilaro'.[67] In Roy C. Abraham, *Dictionary of Modern Yorùbá*, we have: 'Èfẹ̀ (1) joking (ẹwọ̀=àwàda=àpárá)'.[68]

Even if we limit ourselves to the domain of language in this context, we can see that simply translating 'satire' as '*ẹfẹ̀*' raises significant questions of meaning and fidelity. The problem is precisely that instead of subjecting *ẹfẹ̀* to analysis in the context of its role in Yorùbá historical drama and framing it in its connection to other art forms, aesthetic theory, literary criticism and so on—as those are to be found in Yorùbá discursive traditions and practices—it is thought of in terms of satire, which, as we can see, does not immediately present itself in Yorùbá. What we have is an attempt to adapt the English concept of satire to the Yorùbá concept of *ẹfẹ̀*, or to conflate the Yorùbá phenomenon with an English concept.[69]

As far as I know, there has not been any debate on the questions raised above. We may not assume that there is a direct correspondence in the semantic fields presupposed by the two words being deployed as equivalents. *Ẹfẹ̀* is an instance of comedy in Yorùbá, and the translations and definitions reported above—especially '*àpárá*' in the monolingual dictionary—do not immediately suggest 'satire'. This does not mean that Adéjùmọ̀ is wrong. It only goes to show that when we do not have a full-blown discourse in Yorùbá, what we end up with is equivalence-ism, which does not really advance any serious debate about the concept as it occurs in different domains of Yorùbá discourse.

The lack of development of a Yorùbá discursive tradition exemplified by the collapse of initiatives to expand the coverage of Yorùbá, both within the academy and as a language of discourse in all areas of intellectual engagement, is symptomatic of another problem to which decolonisers hardly turn their attention. Similar developments to that of language and literature, albeit not as extensive, have been occurring in the areas of philosophy, sociology and art history. In sociology, the late professor Akínsọlá Akìwọwọ spent his career trying to indigenise his field and come up with the tools with which to apply it in Yorùbá idiom. He managed to create a theoretical paradigm, which he named '*Àṣùwàdà*' and which he developed most fully in his inaugural lecture titled '*Àjọbí* and *Àjọgbé*: Variations on the Theme of Sociation', as well as in a handful of significant papers that are now increasingly attracting the attention of young Nigerian scholars (long after they have been recognised and engaged with by academics from Canada, the United States and Australia).[70] And in 2014, art historian Rowland Abiodun, in his instant classic, *Yorùbá Art and Language: Seeking the African in African Art*, shared with us the most original theoretical and analytical framework for understanding Yorùbá art and, by extension, all art. Like the scholars in literature and language, these intellectuals, too, have enriched our language with new terms.

But right there is the problem. Most of what they have created is available only to their students and others who move in the same circles. To put it bluntly, there is no Yorùbá discursive tradition into which these new elements can pour, and where they can become pieces of new syntheses in philosophy, sociology, political science, religious studies, art history or literature. No doubt this is a radical claim, and I do not plan to argue strenuously for it here. I have introduced it to shake up our decolonisers and their all-too-willing fellow travellers, who are driven more by knee-jerk opposition than well-thought-out articulations. More important is that what I have just stated is not a problem of decolonisation. Pre-empting the development of a discursive tradition took more than the machinations of a historical phenomenon that was not even around in most parts of the continent for more than a hundred years. If this is granted, to continue citing colonialism as the cause of this outcome is to fail to appreciate the gravity of the issue and to offer facile solutions to it.

Let me illustrate the point I just made. If Olátúndé O. Olátúnjí, in his study of the poetry of Adébáyọ̀ Fálétí, had appropriated the term '*alóre*' (lookout) and deployed it to capture the function of a poet in society as part of a discursive tradition, there would have been discussions back and forth on the plausibility of the adaptation not only within literary scholarship but beyond, in philosophy, aesthetics, sociology and so on. I included this insight in my analysis of what intellectuals are and what role they play in society.[71] We all remain within the boundaries of equivalence-ism. Neither is there any likelihood that anyone who has not read Olátúnjí's analysis or my adaptation of it for a different end would have any idea of *alóre* or its possible uses in theoretical discussions.

When we do not have a public that discusses, controverts, criticises and expands our diverse usages in our original languages, or even that records and tracks new words, our new coinages, translations, interpretations and so on remain private to those who happen to share the specific universes of discourse where they feature. Each one of us is an authority unto herself on what concepts she isolates from the language and uses in her work, without the usual critical scrutiny of other scholars on the adequacy, correctness or completeness of such coinages and usages. With this we enter the sphere of privatisation, and if that satisfies the requirements of decolonisation, I want no part of it. Such is the disconnection that marks our respective universes of discourse that I cannot vouch for any of our literary theorists in English who mine the writings of their colleagues in Yorùbá studies for insights to help their own theoretical exertions. Nor do I see our philosophers reaching out to insights from their colleagues in sociology or in history to inform their attempts at heeding Wiredu's counsel to think things in their own languages in order to create an interconnected structure of intellectual exchanges.

If history does matter and African scholars are not spared the responsibility for their lousy choices, over 60 years of independence should make us look harder at why, outside of Tanzania and some countries in North Africa, no African state has considered it worthwhile to put in place the infrastructure to deploy their indigenous languages in a way that advances the cause of creating discursive traditions, rather than equivalence-ism. At the outset, Ngũgĩ was aware that the question of language choice in our countries involved a lot more than the preferences of individual authors, be they writers or practitioners in other areas of intellectual pursuits. He knew quite well that it was a matter of political choices and, more importantly, public policy preferences. He made clear he was not interested in this aspect of the matter: 'But in these lectures I am not dealing so much with the language policies as with the language practice of African writers'.[72] What is remarkable about the issue of language policies and their importance to linguistic decolonisation is that many proponents of the trope ignore the matter of policy in their arguments. This is an unhelpful, perhaps strange, position to take.

In a landscape dominated by linguistic pluralism, in which some languages are dominant and others subordinate, the question is not unimportant as to which language should be privileged and why, once we remove colonial languages from the picture. To answer this question would require a good mixture of politics and policies, the latter to develop the preferred language for use in all areas of life, with the concomitant commitment of resources, as Bamgbose indicated earlier in the chapter.

Ngũgĩ's abstention from considering matters of policy in his discourse has attracted criticism from another important African writer, Odia Ofeimun. Ofeimun was willing to overlook it in Ngũgĩ's *Decolonising the Mind*. But he was less willing to accommodate it on the publication of Ngũgĩ's subsequent book *Moving the Centre: The Struggle for Cultural Freedoms*.[73] According to Ofeimun, Ngũgĩ's insistence in *Decolonising the Mind* that 'he was not into the policy implications of his advocacy', that instigating 'a pooling of African energies towards the elimination of the already decapitating impact of European languages', and that 'the concourse of energies would supply the policy arm of the struggle' had left a critical vacuum that had not been filled by the time, 15 years later, his *Moving the Centre* was published. Ofeimun contends that 'if what he calls "my struggle to move the centre of our literary engagements from European tongues to a multiplicity of locations in our languages" was to have meaning', Ngũgĩ could not continue to avoid the challenge of getting 'into the drudgery of practical questions as a means of egging on the muse of the desirable'. Because of Ngũgĩ's refusal to do so, Ofeimun asserts, '15 years after the declaration of the "holy war", and in spite of the general level of awareness about the necessity for the desirable, the issue has not risen above the level of the lament'.[74]

I share Ofeimun's admonition. But I would like to go beyond Ngũgĩ's own share of responsibility. Those who have followed his lead, especially his refusal to address the policy dimensions of his advocacy when it comes to language development, are equally blameworthy. Blindly following the lead of an eminent thinker, especially when it comes to what does not interest that thinker or what he deems unimportant, does not do any credit to either leader or follower. Certainly, it is much easier to paint with broad strokes when it comes to excoriating African rulers for not linguistically decolonising their countries and ensuring that their education systems and other significant institutions adopt local languages for their purposes. This view is quite consistent with, if not necessitated by, Ngũgĩ's identification of the continuing power of imperialism to determine processes and outcomes in post-independence African countries.

By not pausing to ask questions about Ngũgĩ's position and not permitting themselves to reflect on what practical challenges might lie on the path to linguistic decolonisation, many stalwarts of the trope not only fail the simple test of thinking about how to reach their goal but they manage, simultaneously, to make light of the efforts of various African thinkers, scholars and policy practitioners to move their respective countries away from their dependence on colonial languages. Additionally, if you are already convinced that African leaders and intellectuals are still in thrall to imperialism despite flag independence, why would you think that those same characters would enact policies designed to do what decolonisers accuse them of failing to do?

Ayo Bamgbose's book remains an invaluable corrective in this respect. It provides us with the kind of work that shuns ideology (which, I'm afraid, the decolonising trope has become), takes a sober look at the issues surrounding the place of language in African life and engages with the complexities of the politics and policies involved. In his discussion of 'Language Policy and Language Planning', Bamgbose poses questions which every decoloniser eager to advocate linguistic decolonisation should pay attention to or, should we say, decolonise. Bamgbose explains:

> Which languages are to be regarded as 'major' as opposed to 'small group' (or 'minority') languages? Should the imported official languages continue in their current roles? If not, what roles should be

assigned to them vis-à-vis the indigenous languages? What should be the language(s) of national communication? Which language or languages should be declared as the national language(s)? How many languages will a citizen be encouraged to acquire and which? How should this requirement be reflected in the educational system? Are there languages spoken across the country's borders and, if so, how are the potentials of such languages to be exploited in collaboration with neighbouring countries? These issues immediately bring up the question of language policy and, by implication, language planning as well.[75]

Although 'the policy of using African languages as a medium of instruction has been notoriously unstable in several African countries',[76] it would be incorrect to speak as if this has not concerned African countries or as if it was ever abandoned across the continent. On the contrary, one reason for the instability is the frequent changes of regimes and the associated frequent changes of public policy on this subject. Bamgbose cites as instances of this instability in policy-making Ghana, Guinea, Burkina Faso and Zambia.[77] Yet, as Bamgbose explains, there are other examples of countries that use their 'dissatisfaction with existing policies' as a motivation for 'innovations and experimentation ... all designed to increase the use of African languages as a medium. Such experiments are going on in Niger, Mali, Cameroon, Senegal and Nigeria'.[78]

In the final chapter of his study, Bamgbose educates us on language planning and the efforts to break the hold of colonial languages on African life and minds since independence, and the constraints on this. While he acknowledges 'the powerful hold of the colonial tradition' on language planning, he also speaks of other constraints such as 'the language situation, and the language development status of the indigenous languages'.[79] He continues:

The colonial legacy is a recurrent factor in the language policies of African governments. In practically all fields (education, communication, administration, politics and development), the question has always been whether or not it is desirable or even possible to break away from the existing practices, and if so at what cost. This constant pull between retention and change constitutes the major point of departure as well as a dilemma for language policy-makers.[80]

What comes across clearly is that 'the context of language planning' in Africa is not easily assimilable to the sexy but ultimately unhelpful blaming of imperialist and neocolonial machinations. 'Language planning in Africa', Bamgbose explains, 'has to take place against the background of several factors, including multilingualism, the colonial legacy, the role of education as an agent of social change, high incidence of illiteracy, and concerns for communication, national integration and development'.[81]

Our decolonisers will do well to pay attention to this complexity, and permit themselves to grant that Africans may not always be clueless playthings of imperialists as the easy explanation of lazy, unimaginative theorists goes. I have spent an inordinate amount of time on this section because it gets right to the heart of the sloppiness that the decolonising trope licenses. And, it is to be hoped, calls to decolonise may henceforth be accompanied by answers to the questions that we have raised. I suspect that if people are persuaded that colonialism may not be the critical causal factor in language development and deployment, they may well choose to resort to it less easily—or, for the more discerning scholar, possibly not at all.

It should by now be easy to see why I remain unimpressed by our decolonisers who, beholden to their sponsoring audiences in the colonial languages and the honorifics of the academy, show no concern for their preferred languages in articulating their diatribes: their audience, after all, is not really the people of their respective homelands. I shall have more to say about this in the subsequent chapters. I have laid out in considerable detail the difficulties that facile talk of decolonising language hides. Once we drill down to the bottom of these difficulties, it is easier to see how far removed from decolonisation₁ the issue is, and how unilluminating and possibly counterproductive it is when processed from the standpoint of decolonisation₂.

Outside of those cultures that developed their own scripts as part of their historical evolution, all African languages have had scripts created for them either by Islamic (Arabic) or Christian (Latin) inspiration. If we do not separate colonisation from Christianity insofar as decolonisation₁ is concerned, for example, we cannot preserve and deploy its legacy in our alphabetic systems. Indeed, I suspect that part of why the acceptance of European-derived languages in African literature irks Ngũgĩ so much is that he does not leave any room for there to be distance between colonisation and Christianity. It is no surprise that some have questioned his justification for embracing Arabic as an African language, especially given the Arab colonialism along the East African littoral and across all of north and north-west Africa and down into the Sahel, while denying the same consideration to the European languages.

It gets more complicated when we approach things from the perspective of decolonisation₂. It is also where and why Ngũgĩ's identitarian/pedigree-focused approach is most unhelpful. This approach dictates that for literature to be African, it must be written or presented in an African language. This deceptively simple answer may not be as helpful as many have assumed. If we insist that for literature to be African it must be presented in an African language, we must ask what is an African language? This is by no means a simple question. And because many analysts get carried away by superficialities, a number of impossible attributes are imposed to supposedly ensure what Biodun Jeyifo has identified as the 'absolute, originary autochthony' that a language must have to be 'African'.[82] This is the first problem that must be flagged. It is easier when we remain at the level of spoken language. But even then, as many of us who have lived in border-lands know all too well, it is not always clear what elements belong where and to whom when it comes to languages and their dialectal variations. And the longer a language has been in use and in contact with neighbouring ones, the more difficult it is to characterise its identity in a simple way.

The situation is a lot more complicated when it comes to the written versions of our languages. There are few written languages, apart from hieroglyphs and ideographs, original to Africa. And the process of creating scripts for African languages creates a plethora of problems. Because of the impact of post-Reformation Christianity, many Latin-inspired scripts vary the languages in ways that are not always consistent with their oral metalanguages. Additionally, the scripts fell victim to the usages of the European metalanguages of their creators. For example, Yorùbá can be written in Ajami script with Arabic inflection, and French usages of this language yield different alphabetical outcomes to English. The diasporic influences supplied by Spanish and Portuguese come with their own challenges. We often do not invest time and resources in studying the philologies of our languages or their histories. I do not know of a single historian of the Yorùbá language, for instance.[83] We therefore make problematic and often unwarranted assumptions about autochthony and borrowings in our languages. D. O. Fágúnwà and C. L. Adéoyè, for example, both wrote in Yorùbá, but their writings are underpinned by Christian metaphysics.[84] Do we ignore these leakages, or do we just say with Ngũgĩ that, as long as they are written in Yorùbá and their dominant themes and narrative structures are demonstrably (whatever that would mean) Yorùbá, they are Yorùbá works? But this is a pyrrhic victory.

It gets worse. For the most part, outside of the Ajami script, most languages have been rendered using the Latin alphabet. As a native Yorùbá speaker, I know the continuing struggle to get the orthography right and make the written language approximate more closely to the way the language is spoken. More importantly, the expansion of lexicons to include borrowings from the many influences particular cultures have interacted with over the course of centuries is hardly ever traced or researched by our scholars. For instance, many Yorùbá words are borrowings from Arabic, Hausa, Nupe, Portuguese or English, not to mention Edo, Esan and Akan-Twi. So much for 'absolute autochthony'! Because we do not do profound thinking in the academy in our indigenous languages, we do not track their evolution; mark the entries of new words; and usages or, as with other natural languages, engage with their ambiguities and unavoidable polysemy.[85]

There is an additional dimension to the complications with our written languages. Here is a claim that is sure to draw the ire and opprobrium of decolonisers: the entire formal study of the Yorùbá language and of all its theoretical nuts and bolts falls, without exception, under my category of equivalence-ism. If we had language schools that were dedicated to the study of syntax, morphology, semantics, phonology and lexis, we would need to set about the research to give us a better foundation for what the decolonisers want. I confess my ignorance in this aspect. From this ignorance comes my contention that every aspect of our formal study of Yorùbá is based on adaptation from English, French and maybe Portuguese linguistics. Even among the terms we use to capture phenomena in the language—subject, object, predicate, vowels, consonants, diphthongs, phonemes, etc.—not one of them has a Yorùbá source. What does this mean for the integrity and formal study of the language, or for the instruction and reflection that are owed to it? Absolutely nothing!

Given the promiscuity with which human civilisations borrow from one another, and the mutual enrichment and illumination that is the result,[86] a language whose inheritors are too restrictive in opening it up to other influences is a language that is set on a path to ossification and, eventually, death. Indeed, one insight I've had through this realisation is that the many efforts wasted in looking for 'Yorùbá this' and 'Yorùbá that' in philosophy—starting with the fruitless effort to find the Yorùbá equivalent of the word 'philosophy' itself—are an unnecessary expenditure of our intellectual energies. Many other advanced cultures like Yorùbá have no problem turning philosophy into a loan word in their lexicon. These include major European languages: French, English, German, Portuguese and many others all borrow from the Greek original. No informed person would accuse the Arabs of lacking civilisation or not contributing to the march of human progress. But the Arabic word for philosophy is '*falsafa*', straight from the Greek, whose legacy they, the Arabs, secured for latter-day European jingoists who would like the uneducated to believe that the road from Athens to Königsberg did not pass through Baghdad and Cairo. We do not need a literal translation of philosophy. As Souleymane Bachir Diagne makes clear in his 2004 essay, 'Islamic philosophy is not to be understood as philosophy directly coming out of Islam, so to speak. As a philosophical discipline it is, rather, rooted in the classical Greek tradition (hence the loanword "falsafa" which derives from "philosophia")'.[87] We would do well just Yorùbá-ising it—i.e., '*Filọ́sọ́fì*'—and then proceeding to infuse it with whatever empirical analogues we identify in the culture that best answer to that description. The incredible achievements in Yorùbá language studies give us a model to emulate. This is a model for expanding, rather than contracting, the boundaries of knowledge in Yorùbá, which takes full advantage of the sophistication exemplified in the culture's celebrated capacity for domesticating foreign influences and borrowings within its capacious borders.

It then becomes problematic to simply ask us to 'think through' concepts in our 'African' languages, when we are completely oblivious to the not-so-obvious colourations imposed by benign but inescapable intercultural exchanges. To continue with my example, Yorùbá, my 'own African language' is infused with Nupe, Portuguese, Arabic, Hausa and who knows what other borrowings. If, as is usually the case, language is a bearer of cultural values, it would be naïve to insist that the values encoded in these borrowings were discarded when the words were incorporated into Yorùbá. Hence, I cannot think through any concept in it outside of a pattern of interconnected analyses and elucidations in this pidginised language, as is the case with all languages that have been in constant interaction with others. There is no straightforward equivalence, and the effort to isolate particular concepts for discussion in colonial languages turns Yorùbá into a garnish in an otherwise non-Yorùbá main meal. Here I must resist the lure of equivalence-ism which will make one give illustrations from Yorùbá that are yanked out of their original context and made to serve the needs of the English syntax with which one is trying to make sense of the world.

Ngũgĩ and Wiredu both insist that we should deploy African languages to write a truly African literature (Ngũgĩ) and that we should think philosophical concepts through our original languages (Wiredu). Léopold Sédar Senghor's love of the French language, for example, was at the base of Ngũgĩ's brutal takedown of him as a stooge of European cultural imperialism.[88] Ngũgĩ was no less scathing towards Chinua Achebe's pragmatic embrace of English as the language for his writing. He insists that only those works written in African languages can properly be designated 'African novels'. He asserts:

> But some are coming round to the inescapable conclusion articulated by Obi Wali with such polemical vigour twenty years ago: African literature can only be written in African languages, that is, the languages of the African peasantry and working class, the major alliance of classes in each of our nationalities and the agency for the coming inevitable revolutionary break with neo-colonialism.[89]

A few consequences follow from not separating colonialism from other causative agents in the evolution of African phenomena.[90] Leaving aside the problems already identified as regards language, perhaps there is something about the syntax of the colonial languages that makes them impervious to domestication by African thinkers? As a result, no matter what idioms Africans introduce to those languages, they would remain unmistakably, irredeemably alien in the African context. Simultaneously, there could never be a time when we can say that their African users have sufficiently domesticated them to the extent that we can talk of African versions of the relevant languages. As far as I'm concerned, these outcomes are not plausible. Hence, my question: have Africans the capacity to domesticate borrowings—from language to cuisine, from religion to politics, from music to literature—sufficiently to make them unrecognisable to those from whom they were borrowed or, at least, to make their original owners see that African users have brought some creative genius making the end-products distinctive? This will be a sign of agency and creativity that will set such artefacts apart from mere mimicry.

Many proponents of decolonisation₂ seem to assume that it is never possible to domesticate an alien language sufficiently to make its users express fundamental and recondite thought in it.[91] This assumption is possibly false. Outside of an unhealthy preoccupation with origins or an unhelpful attachment to supposed authenticity, while we do not make light of the ravages of colonialism in Africa, there is no reason to lambast Africans for attaining native fluency in a colonial language.[92] What is more, in much of West Africa, as part of modernity, English came with Christianity, and the embrace of this language by Africans was not a product of colonial imposition.[93] We may disagree with the choices that Africans back then made, but we should respect the historical evidence.

AGAINST DECOLONISATION

This, again, is where we come upon the importance of under-scoring the distinction between the two concepts of decolonisa-tion. Many cultural elements that fall within the bounds of decolonisation$_2$ must be dealt with separately from our concerns with the ideological and institutional processes or products cov-ered by decolonisation$_1$. The ex-colonised's choice of language may not be one of which we approve, but it is unacceptable to believe that we know better. We would be presuming to know that just because some artefact has links, strong or tenuous, to aspects of colonialism, it cannot, for that reason alone, be appropriated by the colonised at any later point. Additionally, it is not always the case that the cultural artefacts in question are caused by colonialism. And even if they were, why do we insist that it is illegitimate for the ex-colonised to find something worthwhile in the ideological structures of colonial life, which they not only took hold of in the fight against colonialism but which may also promise better modes of organising life and thought in its aftermath?

Besides berating or pointedly ignoring them, our decolonisers have never been able to carve out a space in 'their' Africa for the category of African thinkers in whose name and on whose behalf Mphahlele (as we saw earlier in the chapter) asks 'where do we come in?' That is, they never engage with Africans who have opened themselves up to new ways of being human derived from the concepts and practices of those who imperialised us. It is remarkable how old this issue is and how uninterested our decol-onisers seem in it. I do not begrudge them their wish to restrict their world. But by the same token, I hope that they do not begrudge the rest of us for preferring a more inclusive world which celebrates the entire range of human possibilities, includ-ing being other than African.

The writers who have chosen the path of inclusivity should be honoured for creating a literature of the universal from their corner of the world—an outcome that is not contingent on their medium of expression. I do not see how anyone who is adequately informed would think there is no difference between the idiom of Léopold Sédar Senghor's writings and that of Michel de Montaigne, for example, even though they both work within the same syntax. Nor would anyone mistake Wole Soyinka's drama for that of Harold Pinter, even though they both write in English. Indeed, one of the most prominent failures of the decolonisation discourse is to ignore the overwhelming evidence of the idiomatisation of colonial languages by colonised users, whether it's the emergence of an Indian-inflected English or of its Nigerian variant.[94] The only difference is that Indians approach this issue with more assertiveness, while African scholars are persuaded to disown any creativity and ownership when it comes to using colonial languages.[95]

Ngũgĩ is wrong. The emergence of 'African literature' did not begin with the emergence of 'African-language literature', if the boundaries of what constitutes an 'African language' are not drawn too tightly. 'African' does not come in only one flavour. So much did Yorùbá usages impact on the translation of the Bible into this language, for example, that latter-day culturally illiterate Pentecostalists resorted to revising the original translation which they thought contained too many 'fetish' references (i.e., borrowings from Òrìsà, Yorùbá religion). If I had to choose between the humanism and sophistication of Soyinka, Achebe and Senghor's articulations and their 'Africanness', I would willingly give up the label and keep the works.[96]

3

DECOLONISING PHILOSOPHY OR EMBRACING NATIVISM/ATAVISM?

ON THE LIMITS OF PEDIGREE ARGUMENTS

We will not be like Africa of years past. Africa will not go back. We are moving forward like any other people. It's not a question of catching up with the West. We have to take care of our development by ourselves, step by step. But I carry on my work under very difficult conditions.

Ousmane Sembène[1]

Homogeneity of African culture is nothing more than a myth. I will even go so far as to say that we do not have a homogeneous culture in Senegal. At present the different ethnic groups that make up Senegal are in the process of interpenetration, of levelling out, and creating a new culture. The collage that is the sum of all the differences between them will lead to a culture that geographically speaking we can call Senegalese. As it is today, all the population lives in the same economic situation but in different cultures.

Ousmane Sembène[2]

We saw in the last chapter that the threshold Wiredu sets for decolonising philosophy is much lower than that of Ngũgĩ wa

129

Thiong'o for decolonising literature or the mind. For Wiredu, an English person who does not subject her intellectual heritage to critical scrutiny and who merely uses elements of that heritage in her scholarly work would be just as guilty of exhibiting a colonial mentality as a Yorùbá philosopher who uncritically deploys materials from German philosophy. Wiredu's version of decolonisation is therefore less exacting and does not require a different name for what good scholarship should entail. Regrettably, this aspect of Wiredu's thinking is hardly ever noticed, and his followers read him as if he and Ngũgĩ held the same views. As a result, the misguided search for uncontaminated philosophy in our autochthonous languages or the insistence on thinking philosophical concepts in 'our own languages' has produced some grotesque outcomes.

The focus of this chapter is the case made by philosophers for decolonising their discipline, and the seemingly unintended consequences of this demand: replacing critical thought about philosophy with equivalence-ism and an uncritical embrace of whatever is dredged up from the depths of indigenous African life as exemplars of philosophical thinking (as long as it pretends to be untouched by colonialism). Once we accept false binaries like 'the West' (an idea) versus 'Africa' (a place), 'Western/modern' versus 'African/traditional'—with one shunned and the other embraced—the road leads us directly to nativism and atavism. Much of what is produced under the rubric of decolonising is either dedicated to exposing slights or is busy entering into the record crude formulations masquerading as philosophical insights. And these are rarely called out by other scholars because concerns over identity preempt serious critical engagement. But a more catholic approach will likely enable us to find sophisticated syntheses stemming from critical agency by African thinkers.

Given how zealous our decolonisers are when it comes to freeing the colonised from the continuing stranglehold of colonial hangovers, there is some irony in the fact that they may be guilty of condescension towards the colonised, refusing to take seriously the choices that some colonised make when exercising their subjectivity and the autonomy that comes with it. Beyond the woolly but ultimately empty rhetoric, I do not see a clear way charted by the decolonising discourse out of this predicament. Yet, I hope that part of what comes out of this book is a renewed interest in and appreciation of the many different ways in which African thinkers have responded to the colonial experience and to the other outside influences which have, over time, shaped the life and times of the continent. The importance of this line of thinking cannot be overemphasised for younger scholars who, at present, continually react to slights by denizens of 'the Global North' against them in 'the Global South' (their preferred designations). A better way to engage with African thinkers is not only possible, but it is made necessary by the availability of a huge intellectual legacy, on the basis of which young scholars can bring substantive ideas to the table and escape being caught between atavistic rehashes of ideas that are best forgotten and dubious syntheses that peddle distortions of their cherished thinkers. Frantz Fanon is probably the most bastardised in this respect. You would think, to read some of them, that Fanon was a 'Black thinker'![3]

We would all do well to pay attention to Ato Sekyi-Otu's reminder that it is a gross distortion of Fanon's philosophical work to list it in the ranks of race-based identity ideologies or undiscriminating collectivist dogmas that refuse to take the individual seriously. In a chapter titled, aptly enough, 'Individualism in Fanon and After', Sekyi-Otu contends that

> the burden of the entire critique of racism in Fanon's oeuvre is that it is radically inimical to individuality, and that the *raison d'être* of antiracism as a generative principle of postcolonial political morality is precisely the vindication of the person. What else can we call this vindication but *individualism*, individualism born of the inferential

logic of antiracism, from refusal of racist culture's constitutive collectivism? ... Against the metaphysics of colonial occupation and the 'racial polity' with its contempt for 'independence of persons,' against the ordinance of race and its practice, according to *The Wretched of the Earth* of placing 'all blacks in the same bag,' Fanon asserted the principle of individuality.[4]

There are other points of Sekyi-Otu's work with which it is well worth serious engagement for those who are inclined to use the decolonising trope. This is particularly so given that part of what motivates the well-meaning among our decolonisers is to free the colonised from the continuing (as far as they are concerned) effects of colonialism.

In its preoccupation with exposing slights, cataloguing wrongs and bringing to book colonialists, decolonisation₂ has descended into vitriol and name-calling. For contemporary thinkers like Tsenay Serequeberhan and John Ayotunde Isola Bewaji, any colonised people or their intellectuals who find anything of value in the ways of their colonisers remain locked in a colonial mentality. Coming to this realisation has enabled me to see why proponents of decolonisation₂ do not argue with those of us who continue to insist on the continuing relevance of modernity's tenets to Africa's situation today. It explains their almost primal hostility to significant philosophers like Léopold Sédar Senghor, and their almost complete avoidance of other African thinkers who embrace modernity and seek to remake their societies in its image. Given that, as I have continuously pointed out in this book, our decolonisers are convinced that there is no distinction between colonialism and modernity, it is no surprise that their project is defined by negativity. For Serequeberhan, Africans like Senghor, who liken the course of colonialism in Africa to the unfolding of History in a Hegelian sense, are a problem. Serequeberhan cites the following passage from Senghor's writings as proof of this sin:

When placed ... in context, colonization will appear to us as a necessary evil, a historical necessity whence good will emerge, but on the sole condition that *we, the colonized of yesterday, become conscious and that we will it.* Slavery, feudalism, capitalism, and colonialism are the successive parturitions of History, painful like all parturitions. With the difference that here the child suffers more than the mother. That does not matter. If we are fully conscious of the scope of the *Advent*, we shall ... be more attentive to contributions than defects, to possibilities of rebirth rather than to death and destruction. Without ... European depredations, no doubt ... Negro Africans would by now have created more ripe and more succulent fruits. I doubt that they would have caught up so soon with the advances caused in Europe by the Renaissance. The evil of colonization is less these ruptures than that we were deprived of the freedom to choose those European contributions most appropriate to our spirit.[5]

Here is Serequeberhan's take on the passage:

What speaks in and through Senghor is the stern educational-cultural formation of the colonial period, whose destructive effects are here presented, by a brilliant pupil, as the conditions of the possibility for future beneficial effects—provided that 'we, the colonized of yesterday, become conscious' that to secure 'the advances caused in Europe by the Renaissance,' such 'death and destruction' was necessary. If only that were the case![6]

I should point out that before quoting the passage from Senghor, Serequeberhan had insisted the former was an example of

the formerly colonized, who have internalized the colonial model of human existence and history, into permanent supplementary appendages of the West. Such persons, grounded not in an indigenous history or tradition but in the vestiges of imperial Europe, have as the yardstick of their existence an exteriority that has to be constantly emulated. ... Existence for such persons is an ongoing process of self-nullification. Like Kafka's ape, biological life is sustained by the never-ending nullification of its indigenous ethical-historical ground.[7]

Serequeberhan then segued into how Senghor was an exemplar of this parody.[8] This is not the place to get into a full discussion of Serequeberhan's criticisms of Senghor and others who take similar positions to his. It suffices to say that as scholars, we know that there are alternative readings of this passage. It says more about Serequeberhan that he makes no attempt to nuance his assessment of one of the most complex thinkers of the 20th century.

The position articulated by Senghor was not peculiar to him, nor was it ever intended by him to justify colonial pillage. His position as regards what the colonised ought to do in the aftermath of colonialism corresponds to my call to take the agency of the colonised seriously and to pay attention to what they do with the legacy of colonisation. The italicised section of Senghor's passage speaks to the will of the colonised in wringing some good out of the tragedy of colonisation. And, far from expressing the opinion that colonisation was good because it was designed to lead Africans to progress, Senghor's point was that even if colonisation had done that, it still would have fallen short of the ideal by having 'deprived the colonized of the freedom to choose those European contributions most appropriate to our spirit'. Additionally, because the protagonists of the decolonisation discourse do not pay attention to debates among Africa's thinkers unless they are to their ideological liking, Wole Soyinka's own analysis of Senghor's humanism has largely gone ignored. Soyinka provides a scholarly and sophisticated response to Senghor in his analysis of the latter's poem, 'A Prayer for Peace'.[9]

Finally, as those who seriously consider the work of African thinkers know, Senghor's orientation is very similar to the model of 'Providential Determinism' promoted by many returnees from the Americas, who interpreted theirs and their ancestors' enslavement as God's way of bringing them to the light of 'Civilisation' (Christianity), which they were then duty-bound to take back to heathen Africa to free their people from backwardness. Again, we do not have to share their perspective but, I argue, good scholarship requires us to debate with its proponents. When prominent intellectuals present one-dimensional interpretations of complex thinkers, they foreclose interest from other scholars who, for whatever reason, follow their lead.

Having apparently shown Senghor to be an example of 'Kafka's ape', Serequeberhan proceeded to use Julius Nyerere to counter what he takes to be Senghor's lauding of colonialism, citing Nyerere's damning balance sheet of how colonialism ill-served colonies like Tanzania, Kenya, Zambia and the Congo. He then goes on to tie colonialism to the 'ultimate source and authorization—its metaphysical anchoring-stones—in the thinking of the icons of the modern tradition of European philosophy. The great minds of this tradition—including Locke, Hobbes, Hume, Kant, Hegel, and Marx—all had access to, and utilized, this "storehouse of lurid images"'.[10] This is how he links colonialism and modernity. You cannot have one without the other, on this reading.

Another of our preeminent philosophers, John Ayotunde Isola Bewaji, has an even more frightening warning to the colonised to steer clear of, in his words, 'Western modernity'. He argues that his Yorùbá people and culture do not need and cannot draw any lessons from modernity, because 'modernity had existed in Yorubaland before the contract theorists who were mainly motivated by greed, private property and oppression of the poor devised the theories of governance based on the worst elements in the depraved human'. It gets worse because, according to Bewaji, modernity's base in the 'worst elements in the depraved human' explains its emphasis on absolute rights. He writes:

Let me use a stark example, earlier hinted at, that I find most appo-site here. Part of what constitutes Western modernity and European civilization is the substitution of domesticated animals and pets for the friendship and sharing of space with other human beings for love, affection, intimacy and pleasure because, with modernity and the inordinate claiming of absolute rights against the other equally self-centered and hedonistically inclined persons, it imposes the impossible situation on Western humanity where each human becomes an unnecessary encumbrance on the other. This then sup-poses that animals are better companions than siblings, off-springs, parents, relatives—especially when they reach a certain age, because each person must covet their space, protect it, and ensure that it is not shared by anything that has the capacity to talk back at one, unless invited and with time limit for departure. Two consequences flow from this: while on the one hand there is now a reduction in the potential for incest, there is the pervasive, though unquantified upswing in bestiality; while on the other hand, we find the tolerance level of other humans to have reduced, because we find it very diffi-cult to communicate effectively with each other, as the pets though they may suspect what we are saying to them, could not respond back to further aggravate our pleasure.[11]

Among two of our top contemporary philosophers, for whom modernity and colonialism are two sides of the same bad coin, decolonising cannot be a positive project. The concern of the decolonisation discourse is to ferret out the continuing influences of modernity and colonialism in our practical and intellectual lives. Serequeberhan captures it succinctly: 'This is our contem-porary inheritance. How then do we purge the colonial residue that still controls—from within—the actuality of the present?'[12] I read this as an affirmation of the continuing presence of colo-nialism in our lives. And I do not see any sign here of Wiredu's conception of decolonisation, which asks us to critically pick apart whatever idea or practice we might like to embrace, whether from our own inheritance or another's. For Serequeberhan, what he calls the 'critical-negative project' is a crucial component of intellectual decolonization. For in spite of the fact that colonialism has ended, its cultural and intellectual residue still endures and is utilized to perpetuate the political-economic submission of the formerly colonized. Intellectual 'housecleaning' is thus an indispensable supplement necessary for the completion of our political self-liberation. Just as the political and armed struggle ended the de facto actuality of colonialism, the critical-negative project of African philosophy has to challenge and undo the de jure philosophic underpinnings that justified this now defunct actuality and still today sanction Western hegemony. And this, by extension, is applicable *grosso modo*, to all intellectual work in Africa.[13]

I know better now why many who deploy the trope never bother to respond to the arguments of those of us who find something worthy of appropriation in our colonisers' repertoire of ideas. If our colleagues do indeed believe the ideas I described, on what basis could one expect them to engage with those who embrace this wrong, or even evil? On my part, I would not know how to persuade them that my position makes sense. As we say in Yorùbá, the sky is big enough for all birds to fly without touching wings. My concern is that by shutting the door to the possibility of learning from our conquerors, the ideas of some of our most profound thinkers, including Senghor, are cut off from the coming generations. Many are therefore misdirected into what I shall identify as atavism by following the injunction that our thinking, to be authentic and liberatory, must forever be wary of continuing colonialism or modernity-inspired ideas and formulations.

My goal in this work is to offer an alternative path which takes the ideas of African thinkers seriously, regardless of how and where they are sourced. By doing so, I seek to help create the much-needed, but sorely lacking, critical engagements with the originality, complexity and sheer variety of African thinkers and their ideas. When this is done, as we saw with Fanon and

Cabral in the previous chapters, we find that their thinking is multi-dimensional; sophisticated; and, quite often, evolves throughout their lives. For example, even as Nyerere condemned colonialism, he did not therefore shun liberal representative democracy and the 19th-century philosopher John Stuart Mill who inspired him. This was a commitment that Nyerere shared even while he presided over a one-party state, and which he never abandoned till he died. Nor did his justified hatred of colonialism make him give up his cherished Catholic faith or his love of William Shakespeare, which led him to translate *Julius Caesar* and *Macbeth* into Swahili as part of his contribution to the development of culture in his country and the world at large.

I am inviting interested scholars to join me in exploring the channels that our thinkers created to help them make new syntheses informed by both their autochthonous inheritances and those borrowed from other sources. These channels remain largely unexplored, to the detriment of scholarship in and on Africa. This is why people do not know that Kwame Nkrumah went through a phase in his philosophical evolution when he was a stout defender of liberal representative democracy and of precisely the kinds of rights that Bewaji would like us to believe promote bestiality.

Colonialism—the common anchor for Ngũgĩ, Wiredu, Serequeberhan and Bewaji in their cases for decolonisation—is problematic. There is a near absolutisation of the concept in the literature such that little care is taken to acknowledge its complexity and historicity, nor to investigate the distinct paths of colonialism and modernity in different parts of the continent (not to mention in other parts of the world, especially Latin America, where decolonisation$_2$ has birthed a whole new academic approach called 'decolonial theory').[14] The same people who hector us to decolonise are the ones who absolutise modern European colonialism and turn it into the single pole for plotting

African phenomena, no matter how removed in time those phenomena are from the colonial period.

What is problematic about it is not easy to see. Allow me to explain. Decolonisation, as Fanon points out, is a negation of colonialism/colonisation. The central significance that is given to colonialism in the discourse is not justified by the historical evidence nor by the different experiences of colonialism across the continent.[15] It also does not produce insights into phenomena. That is, it does not aid the development of appropriate explanatory methodologies for historical events and their evolution in Africa. What's more, the obsession with decolonisation has the unintended consequence of misconceiving the trajectory of the continent's historical evolution and of turning scholars away from embracing, engaging with and explaining ideas, movements, practices, processes and institutions. In short, it renders illegible to undiscerning scholars an awful lot of the intellectual products of the African mind, awareness of and engagement with which the continent sorely needs.

If we accept the Manichaean binary represented in the 'Western' versus 'African' model, and insist that any element of the 'Western' in the 'African' (whether inspiration or content) taints the latter as colonial, it is easy to see how such a model is likely to block us from taking seriously the dynamic evolution of social phenomena in any given context. Borrowings in one direction are delegitimised and in the other are labelled thefts. The mutual learning that is standard fare in human interactions, especially among civilisations, is almost legislated out of consideration. In reality, especially in Africa, colonialism is neither as powerful nor as profound in its impact as our decolonisers proclaim.

Against a Bastard Periodisation

It was the late doyen of African historians, J. F. Ade Ajayi, who, in 1969, inaugurated a debate on this matter by arguing that colonialism was a mere 'episode' in African history and experience, and that the continuing talk of it having enacted an epochal break is not justified by the evidence. He argued that African history is to be noted more for its continuities than any discontinuities attributable to colonialism.[16] Ajayi's essay, short and pithy, deserves the serious consideration of decolonisers. I shall presently be looking at a rare example of such an engagement. But, first, let us examine the case that Ajayi made. The immediate motivation for his reflections was the imperious arrogance of Sir Harry H. Johnston who, as Ajayi described,

> was one of the most sophisticated of the builders of European empires in Africa. He saw the European invasion and conquest of Africa in the late nineteenth century not as an isolated event but as the last of a whole series of invasions following after those of the Phoenicians, the Greeks and Romans, the Arabs, the Turks and others from the Middle and Far East. He envisaged it, too, as a culmination of the activities of Europeans in Africa which began with the Portuguese explorations of the fifteenth century. His *History of the Colonization of Africa by Alien Races* was a pioneering effort to view the partition of Africa in a time perspective, and is therefore a useful starting-point for this discussion of the significance of European colonialism in African history.[17]

Ajayi had good reasons for making this the foil for his case against the 'epochal impact' thesis regarding colonialism. To begin with, Johnston had a grand, possibly exaggerated, view of European adventures in Africa, wishing to dress them up as later examples of the civilisational impact associated with some of the invasions in the above quote, and not just with the rapine and dehumanisation that the European slave trade, the trans-Atlantic slave trade and its successor, European colonialism, represented on the continent. Sophisticated thinker that he was, Ajayi was careful to separate colonialism from the other aspects of European intervention in Africa across time.

Notice that, for Ajayi, European colonialism commenced with the partition of Africa at the fateful Berlin West Africa Conference, from November 1884 to February 1885. This is not an unimportant point. There had been European colonisation efforts in North Africa in the late 18th and early 19th centuries, but they had not been fully successful. There had also been sporadic European attempts to colonise select patches of land in West Africa beginning in the 15th century and accelerating with the success of the abolitionist movement in the early part of the 19th century. The latter was the period that historians have identified with 'informal empire', and their control was mostly in Sierra Leone; some parts of coastal Ghana and, after 1874, Ashanti territory in that present-day country; and, from 1861, Lagos in today's Nigeria. The French had only just mastered the Four Communes of what is now Senegal, and were still fighting sporadic wars with assorted potentates in what would later become Guinea, Mali, Burkina Faso and Côte d'Ivoire. We must also remember that before 1866, there was no 'Italy' as we know it today, and, until 1871, there was no 'Germany'. So, it is easy to see the conceited arrogance that projected a complete makeover of Africa at the hands of Europeans, even as the designers barely knew the territory, had not attained significant statuses themselves and had conquered mere slivers of the land. As I point out momentarily, making European colonialism the singular axis for plotting African historiography effectively awards the Johnstons of this world the prize they wished to have but never really earned.

Ajayi had no use for such a conceptual and historiographic framework. Johnston, he pointed out, 'believed that Europeans were the harbingers of a new civilization, and that they were destined to leave their mark on the physical and mental nature of man in Africa'. It is this vaunted ambition to do in and to Africa what had been done 'in the Americas and Australasia, involving significant European immigration, settlement and miscegenation' that Ajayi called into question.[18] In short, the claim that in the aftermath of colonisation Africa would be fitted with a new human, fashioned in the image of Europe, would be the ultimate demonstration of the power of colonialism to effect an epochal change in the continent's historical trajectory. Ajayi argued that this never happened, contending that the evidence does not support this 'epochal change' thesis. 'We know that his [Johnston's] analysis must be faulty because the European intervention has proved far less permanent than he had thought it would be', Ajayi explains. He continues: 'A full assessment of the impact of colonialism on Africa and on African peoples must, however, be made in a historical context ... But the proper historical context is not *the history of the colonization*, but *African history as such*'.[19]

This distinction between the larger situation of 'African history as such' and the much narrower scope of 'the history of the colonization [European colonisation, specifically]' is one that much of the decolonisation discourse neither recognises nor takes seriously. Once placed within this larger context, Ajayi asserts, '[i]t is now possible to write the history of the conquest and the establishment of European rule in Africa in terms of the interaction of two sets of human beings rather than in terms of the contemporary view of Europeans "as gods dealing with sub-human natives"'.[20]

I argue, following Ajayi's lead, that the absolutisation of European colonisation is an oblique affirmation of what Ajayi condemned: turning Africans into permanent subalterns in their own history. That this is being done by those who claim to be combatting colonial arrogance is the ultimate irony. I refuse to place colonialism on such a pedestal, and not out of racial pique. Ajayi cleared the path. He contended that the framing of Africa's history primarily, if not solely, in relation to colonisation led to the privileging of the 19th century and the coding of the history of African activities during the period as a direct reaction to the increasing pace of European activities prior to the partition. This argument exaggerates the extent to which the activities of Europeans can be seen as the central events of African history from which all others derived. It equates the reactions of Africans to European activities with the totality of African history or, rather, it neglects African initiative throughout African history.[21]

This last charge is one that should give us cause for pause. We should not even allow the appearance of 'neglect[ing] African initiative throughout African history'. Periodising African history around the point of colonialism does exactly what Ajayi cautioned against. I believe that Ajayi's long-ago essay anticipated the current career of decolonisation discourse here. One would think that colonisation by Europeans is the single most important event in African history rather than 'an episode' in it, as Ajayi urged us to designate it. He did not deny that colonialism wrought significant changes on the African land- and mindscapes, 'the most fundamental ... [being] the loss of sovereignty, which it entailed for practically every African people'.[22] There were changes in African social life, too, especially in the areas of marriage and family life, and in the economic sphere. But despite these consequences, the overwhelming impact of colonialism was 'to put a brake on historical change'. Ajayi explains this in more detail:

Far-reaching as these changes might have been, their impact on Africa was very uneven. While the lives of some communities were profoundly affected, others had hardly become aware of the Europeans' presence before they began to leave. What is more, colonial régimes were far from being uniformly radical. Just as the boundaries of colonial territories tended to put a brake on historical change, so the colonial régimes themselves tended to ally with the most conservative elements in society and to arrest the normal processes of social and political change. Once conquest had been achieved, it was the submissive chiefs, the custodians of law, order and hallowed custom, rather than radical educated élite, who became the favored agents of European administration. No colonial régime would have hesitated to ally with the most conservative forces to topple a hostile but progressive and modernist leader. After all, the main preoccupation of those régimes was not to carry out social reform but primarily to control and to maintain law and order so as to facilitate economic exploitation.[23]

There are two aspects to Ajayi's challenge. There is the empirical dimension which is easily refuted by showing that the historical details do not match Ajayi's report. I am persuaded that his analysis is not vulnerable in that regard. There is enough evidence to buttress Ajayi's claim that many of the positive outcomes that are erroneously attributed to colonialism were obtained in spite, rather than because, of it. The more important dimension is the logical one. If, indeed, a phenomenon that is held to have brought about an epochal change 'tended to ally with the most conservative elements in society and to arrest the normal processes of social and political change', it stands to reason that there is an inconsistency, possibly a contradiction, here that needs to be ironed out.

Our decolonisers have rarely responded to Ajayi's challenge. Eghosa Osaghae is an exception. In his 1991 article 'Colonialism and African Political Thought', Osaghae argues that treating colonialism as an episode rather than an epoch in Africa leads to distortions in naming and accounting for African political thought. Although he agrees with historians from the Ibadan School that 'colonialism in Africa was not a case of total European domination',[24] he contends that the 'colonialism-as-an-episode' thesis (1) ignores the Atlantic slave trade and its effects; (2) is overly defensive vis-à-vis European distortions of African history; (3) relies excessively on oral history; and (4) romanticises African history.[25] He instead embraced social scientist Peter J. Ekeh's argument that colonialism was an epochal moment in African history. For Osaghae,

> Since colonialism, 'things have fallen apart', and post-colonial Africa bears little or no qualitative resemblance to the pre-colonial past. This certainly has to be the case, because with colonialism came the sacking of empires, segmentary and non-centralized societies, and their replacement with new states which were mostly artificial creations of the colonial masters; with colonialism came the introduction of western institutions and processes of government, Christianity, the one-man-one-wife maxim of western societies, the monetization of the economy and attendant capitalism which emphasizes the exploitation of raw materials for the colonialist metropoles, and, of course, the underdevelopment of Africa in the world capitalist system. Surely, with all these transformations which constitute the realities of post-colonial Africa, colonialism cannot be just one of those other episodes in African history.[26]

Osaghae's final claim here can only stand if there are no alternative or better explanations for these historical outcomes. My interest in this piece is limited to the philosophy of history to which he subscribes. There are other issues it contains that cannot be dealt with here. How does one move from talking about political thought to talking about Africa in general? Or it may be that the argument is that political thought instantiates the general collapse? But, as I argue, that notion cannot be supported. As I develop below, even if it were true that colonialism explains some aspects of African political thought, it is an overreach to argue that the other phenomena referenced in the quoted passage can be accounted for in the same way. Neither Christianity nor 'monetization of the economy' can properly be traced to colonialism. And it is established that colonialism prevented the development of capitalism in Africa.[27] Of course, Osaghae could always respond that the failure to install capitalism is yet another iteration of the impact of colonialism. But his language suggests that he thinks colonialism installed a type of capitalism in Africa, a position which is not supported by the historical evidence. To the extent that there are alternative explanations, we cannot remain satisfied with Osaghae's rejoinder.

He concludes that this view of colonialism as a cause of radical change best explains the nature and trajectory of African political thought which, in its modern iteration, was and is deeply determined by its 'colonial milieu'.[28] However much African thinkers insist that 'the roots of virtually every conception of thought in Africa [are] to be found in the indigenous pre-colonial African society',[29] he argues, the truth is that their thought is a product of and is bound by its colonial inspiration. It is the failure of African thinkers to acknowledge the indelible stamp of the colonial epoch on their thinking and colonialism's limitless reach that has 'led to the denial of whatever was alien, and therefore, European',[30] for example, the concept of class struggle, and its abrogation in African socialism.

What follows is a discussion of only that part of Osaghae's essay which deals with the place of colonisation in Africa's history and thought. I am only concerned here with the need to endow colonialism with what are unheard of causal powers in order to make his case plausible. Contrary to what Osaghae claims, Ajayi never 'romanticised African history' or relied excessively on oral history. And, according to my reading at least, Ajayi was not even minimally defensive in his call for a much-needed balance and recognition of complexity in our narrative of African affairs. Unfortunately, Osaghae has ignored Ajayi's cautionary note and, in his eagerness to seal his case, he retroactively made colonialism causally responsible for events that even temporally predated it. He completely missed out on the tightly delimited boundaries for colonialism—post-Berlin Conference—that Ajayi marked out. In Osaghae's less careful exposition, the Atlantic slave trade became part of the colonial narrative even though colonial rule was not an element of it;[31] and the introduction of Christianity and the changes in social philosophies it brought in its wake also became effects of colonialism's causal prowess, even though, again, many of the critical events happened before colonialism was entrenched in West Africa. I am surprised that he did not attribute the social and political experiments under the inspiration of Islam similarly to colonialism. Osaghae completely ignored the fact that many of the new state forms incorporated by Islamic social-movement leaders in the Sahel, from Mauritania to Sudan, were actually stymied by colonialism.

Had Osaghae paid close attention to Ajayi's call for us to take 'native agency', as he called it, seriously, he would have saved himself from error and unclarity. Ultimately, the fundamental problem with his analysis and those of other decolonisers is their insistence on inflating the causal power of colonisation beyond what its history and temporal boundaries would support. Even in those contexts where colonialism was efficacious, the influence of 'native agency' must not be discounted and, more importantly, the creative adaptation by local peoples of institutions and practices with colonial provenance must not be ignored. I conclude that the case for regarding colonialism as an episode, not an epoch, in African history remains solid.

For example, to go back to the story I told at the beginning of this book, in spite of the colonial boundaries imposed on our minds and spaces, Yorùbá culture and its usages on either side of Nigeria's border with Bénin have persisted, and the narratives that supply their agglutinating element continue to mark life and thought. This includes, but is not limited to, indigenous modes of governance, rules of succession, grounds of legitimacy and so on, even though the Yorùbá people are now Nigerians and Béninois(e).[32] Furthermore, the connection between colonialism and continuity was not a noble one. Ajayi made the historical case and I will now offer a philosophical explanation of the continuity that colonial authorities imposed on Africans against the normal evolution of social formations and against the clamour of the colonised to enact their own changes in their lives, institutions and practices. I style it 'sociocryonics'.[33]

Sociocryonics is a term I have coined to describe the range of policies that colonisers put in place across the whole continent—except in the settler colonies, under which social and political institutions were frozen in time and place, and Africans were forced to operate in them whether they wanted to or not. This was because, as far as the colonial administrators were concerned, those institutions and practices were 'African', and Africans were not permitted to aspire to living outside of their parameters. Sociocryonics is the resulting ignoble science of the cryopreservation of social forms without paying any attention to whether those to whom they belong wish to preserve, modify or eradicate them. This is consistent with Ajayi's declaration that colonialism was a brake on change, not its accelerator.

If what I've just said is true, then to turn colonialism into the most important or even the only element in explaining social phenomena in Africa cannot be plausible, adequate or correct. This is, for me, probably the most vexing aspect of the decolonisation trope. Because colonialism is adopted as the single or dominant axis on which to plot the continent's history and events post-colonisation—and no serious attention is paid to the fractures, cleavages and different historicities as colonialism evolved—the many divergences that characterise it are glossed over in most analyses. The Manichaean division of which Fanon spoke is taken out of the spatial context that he originally indicated, and the metaphysical zones (in the coloniser's mind, at any rate) in which the being of the colonised was a nullity are considered a firm scaffolding on which analyses can be built. That is, the decolonisation trope persists in treating the African moment as completely unimportant and the colonial world and its artefacts as the only things that matter.

Fanon, Cabral and other sophisticated theorists of colonialism knew that, despite professions to the contrary, the inevitable communion of human interaction, no matter within which hierarchies, will always result in pairings, influences and exchanges—in short, a trading of ideas and practices which can make it difficult to ascertain the authorship of specific products. And in those societies where modernity was midwifed by Christian missionaries, most of whom were themselves Africans, it is easy to see how late-arriving colonialists would have had to contend with Africans who had already begun to appropriate for themselves and their societies some of the principles that colonisers wished to deploy as justification for their plunder. In other words, the Manichaean discourse of decolonisation theorists—who see only colonisers and their local collaborators on the one side and resisters who gallantly fought the colonisers and these collaborators on the other—does not account for those Africans who saw a promise of better ways of being human in the modernity that they knew from experience was not produced by colonialism. Ezekiel Mphahlele's question (see Chapter 2) continues to haunt the decolonisation discourse, even when its proponents are either unaware of or choose to ignore it.

Here, I hope, is an apt analogy.[34] Moorish rule in the Iberian Peninsula and much of present-day France lasted for over 700 years. Does anyone periodise the history of Spain or Portugal according to that long history of colonial rule? Or do we wish to deny that it was an instance of colonialism? Meanwhile, nowhere in Africa (except South Africa) did European colonialism last for over 100 years. Writing about the history of Mozambique, for instance, Elísio Salvado Macamo asserts,

> History books tend to claim that Mozambique, a southern African
> country on the Indian ocean, was a Portuguese colony for five cen-

turies. It is an exaggerated claim, which neither the Portuguese nor the Mozambicans themselves seem interested to correct. ... Whatever the case, the historical evidence indicates otherwise. ... The period from the end of the fifteenth century to the second half of the nineteenth century can hardly be described as one of Portuguese colonization of Mozambique. It was, on the one hand, the Berlin Conference of 1885, which saw the partition of Africa among European colonial powers, and, on the other, renewed Portuguese attempts at establishing themselves in the territory that mark the beginning of colonialism.[35]

Yet, we periodise African history with colonialism as its singular pole. That cannot be right. For one thing, we would be making dangerous assumptions regarding African and European societies, the solidity of their cultures and institutions, and their capacities to resist colonial makeovers by their conquerors. We would be assuming that the practices and institutions of Iberia's inhabitants were resilient while those of Africans in the time of European colonialism were weak and easily altered. For example, when we look at the phenomenon of chieftaincy in different parts of Africa and Asia, and its career under British colonialism, its survival or abrogation in either place is not a simple story to be told with reference to colonialism alone. And Andalusian Spain has turned its Moorish past into an integral piece of its cultural narrative without periodising its entire history by it.

I do not need to provide numerous examples. It should not matter how often this way of proceeding is repeated; it cannot be right. How often in the literature do we encounter the following phrase: 'precolonial Asia'?[36] The truth is that we have allowed ourselves to be driven into holding on to the African continent as a gross, almost undifferentiated unit for analytical purposes, based on our reaction to the discourse of our racist detractors. The time has long since passed when we could allow our engagement with the world, especially the African world, to be determined by a negative relationship conditioned by the ignorant denials of our very being by global white supremacy. No one looks at Asia, nor do Asians look at themselves, as one homogeneous bloc. This has not stopped Asian countries, too, from working towards pan-Asian solidarity and, on occasion, even toying with the idea of unity. The failure to achieve such unity has only allowed Asian genius to effloresce in diverse ways that have resulted in some of the miracles of human development, miracles which no part of Africa—burdened by the deadweight of seeking an elusive unity with no serious coherence of developmental paradigms—has ever arrived at.

To stay in Asia, it is instructive that South Korea, instead of using Japanese colonialism as a significant or defining element in its history, treats it as a mere unfortunate interlude, maintaining a periodisation that is indigenous to its dynastic history and to its religious and intellectual movements. It used the collaboration, even though it was coerced, of its monarch with Japanese colonialism as a reason for not restoring the monarchy in its post-independence history. We, on the contrary, have made a virtue of the collaborationist and distorted chieftaincies in many African countries, and continue to accept their existence in the new political systems we are trying to install, despite these nominally being defined by the equality of all. But many of our decolonisers, in the name of identity and authenticity, embrace these backward institutions and practices almost without criticism. Like South Korea, India also refuses to periodise its history by prioritising British colonialism, despite the fact that it lasted longer in that country than in any part of Africa and had a much more lasting impact on Indian life and thought. Chieftaincy is no longer part of India's governance, for instance, and Indians are now some of the principal scholars of modernity in English.

I suggest that the preoccupation of many Africans with decolonising is inseparable from our placing colonialism as the

AGAINST DECOLONISATION

defining framework within which to understand and narrate African life and thought. Our past—designated 'precolonial'—is understood in terms determined by colonialism, and our future—postcolonial—is tied to our obsession with leaving it behind. How we expect to do the latter while privileging colonialism in our own understanding of our history and letting it characterise our discourses beats me. This is where the wisdom of heeding Ajayi's caution is clearest. If we proceed to study African history with colonisation as a mere chapter within it, however significant it may be, we are immediately enabled to see all the other pieces available to play with, including, especially, comparative colonialisms within the continent and between the continent and the rest of the world. Think of Arab colonialism in East Africa and the emergence of polities like Zanzibar, the Comoros, Dar es Salaam and other Islam-inflected societies there. Nor do we have to keep colonialism in view every time we talk of African phenomena. The history of eighth-century Africa, for instance, will include the rise and fall of the ancient Empire of Ghana, while studying the 10th century on the continent will bring into focus the Almoravids, and so on. It would not be 'precolonial history' because, even if we extend European colonialism back to the period of the trans-Atlantic slave trade, it would still be quite a stretch to find the slightest connection between ancient Ghana and European colonialism. In fact, if any colonialism is involved, it would have more to do with pressures from the north-west, the Iberian Peninsula, or from the north-east, the Mediterranean Sea. This is the kind of sophisticated analysis that shrinking the influence of European colonisation in African history is likely to enable.[37]

Now, our relationship with colonialism is necessarily and justifiably negative. That is as it should be. But European colonialism was not the sole alien movement that had a significant role in Africa's evolution. We also have Christianity, from its very origins; Islam, soon after its founding; and motley other interactions shaping African phenomena. And while we are fixated on modern European colonialism, we neglect that much of North Africa was victim to Roman, Byzantine and Ottoman colonialisms before the modern European; and Arab colonialism was present on the East African littoral since medieval times. Simultaneously, North Africa was for many centuries the base for African-derived colonisation that subdued many parts of southern Europe and the eastern Mediterranean all the way to Syria. If there was never a time when any part of Africa was hermetically sealed from the rest of the global exchange of human discourses and ideas, then to suppose that what needs to be changed or made sense of in our current experience is best traced to modern European colonialism is at least implausible and possibly wrong. Those who take this route must show us their case for privileging modern European colonialism in the philosophy of history in Africa.[38] They must make clear the causal lines between the phenomena they wish to decolonise and this specific colonialism. This does not seem to be the case, for the most part.

What needs to be explained is much more than can be accommodated within the decolonisation discourse. If you are Sahrawi, for instance, which colonisation should you be pushing against: Spanish or Moroccan? And why did Morocco seek membership of the European Union rather than decolonising and shunning Europe? In any case, Morocco combines in its history both coloniser and colonised moments. Talk about complexity!

We must separate, and do so meticulously, that which pertains to colonialism from other influences that we all too often lump together with it. For, given the justifiable hostility of Africans to European colonialism, if we were to see it as the herald of other phenomena that we believe to be part of our 'colonial mentality', as Fela Anikulapo Kuti would put it, it stands to reason that we would also be dubious of those inheritances, too. This is why modernity continues to evoke negative responses from African scholars. Yet, again, as I have argued in *How Colonialism Preempted Modernity in Africa*, at least in West Africa, contrary to accepted wisdom, modernity came *before* colonialism, and the imposition of formal colonialism put a brake on the transitions to modernity that were taking place in the region at the beginning of the 19th century through the agency and under the direction of African converts to post-Reformation Christianity. Because neither Ngũgĩ nor Wiredu considered these possibilities, many scholars of decolonisation influenced by them are unable or unwilling to contemplate that a lot of what they associate with colonialism and, therefore, which deserves to be shunned, can actually be fruitfully examined, for good or ill, independently of colonialism. I return to this point presently.

From Bad Historiography to Erasure of Native Agency

Let us recall and address another of the problems we identified earlier with how the obsession with decolonisation renders illegible to undiscerning scholars many of the intellectual products of Africans, engagement with which and awareness of which the continent sorely needs. I take philosophy as my exemplar. I begin with Wiredu's case for decolonising philosophy, and argue that his recommendations, probably unwittingly, end up erecting a wall between the present—dominated by the zeal for decolonising—and a much longer history of philosophising on the continent that has absolutely nothing, or very little, to do with colonisation. Wiredu's work is particularly instructive in the present case because he is a philosopher whose theoretical sophistication has few equals anywhere, yet he ends up with characterisations that he would have objected to in others.

As I have already outlined, Wiredu argues that because African philosophers do not think their concepts in their original languages, 'we constantly stand the danger of involuntary mental de-Africanization unless we consciously and deliberately resort to our own languages (and culture)'.[39] This specific strand of Wiredu's argument raises different conundrums when it comes to philosophy in general and to political philosophy and ethics in particular. I examine these points one at a time. First, philosophy. The idea that we suffer from a condition called 'mental de-Africanization' that has its roots in alienation from our own languages, and which can be ameliorated by a reconnection to them, has behind it some very dangerous assumptions. This is where the identitarian foundations of the discourse of decolonisation become worrisome to those of us who venture beyond the surface appeal of working in our languages and with materials derived from our culture. It is assumed that what is or is not 'African' is simple to ascertain. As someone who once suffered the sting of being accused of belonging 'to a small band of the well-urbanized, westernized, de-Africanized Africans who tend to think that the African would be reckoned with, only by renouncing himself and whatever is "African"',[40] I know a bit about how this works. Generally, rules about what counts as 'African' are deployed to delegitimise uncomfortable challenges to usages like 'mental de-Africanization' or 'the African legal tradition' (the issue between my interlocutor, who called me those names, and me).

What does it mean to be mentally African? That one uses African languages? But African languages are many and varied, and many non-Africans use African languages. We already saw in the last chapter a significant divergence between Ngũgĩ and Cabral on the nature and function of language. African languages, like many other natural languages, are heavily creolised. Must it be the case that whatever is supposedly African persists over time and can be easily separated from non-African equivalents and, most importantly, be conceptualised in an African language? Such is the anxiety induced by possible mental de-Africanisation that otherwise sophisticated thinkers allow themselves to be goaded into embracing a flattened-out, dehistoricised Africa that is limited to uninsightful characterisations like 'precolonial philosophy', 'traditional statecraft' or even 'traditional religion'. This is where the influence of atavisms and atavistic responses to the predations of European colonialism is most pronounced.

Once we stop making European colonialism the pole around which we build our explanatory and narrative structures, it is easy to see that even just to take the 19th century as our time frame and West Africa as our location, there is a lot more philosophical material to work with and a lot more complexity to unravel than would be the case if we assimilate the area and its ideational processes and products to some precolonial designation. If, indeed, time answers to the dynamism that we suppose of it, a description of any part of Africa or of African phenomena that implies we cannot talk of eras, fashions or movements which evolve from one period to another cannot aid our understanding. Worse, it would hearken back to the racist characterisation of Africa as a place that never changed!

If we take this issue of change as given, it means that 19th-century African philosophy must necessarily include the contributions of the many participants in the intellectual life of the period. And there were different conceptions of 'African' at the time. (1) There were the returnees from the Americas and other places in the growing African diaspora who had had enough of the restrictions on their life chances in the lands to which their forebears had been forcefully taken as enslaved persons, and therefore repatriated to Africa to build better lives for themselves and their progeny. They were Africans and their efforts were towards the advancement of the Africa they called home/fatherland/motherland. (2) There were the 'recaptives', Africans who were being taken to slavery in the Americas but whose ships were intercepted by the British Navy on the high seas after the abolition of the slave trade in Britain, and who were then liberated and returned to Freetown. Freetown was a port city specifically chartered to serve as a receptacle for such freed persons, as well as for former enslaved persons from any of the British territories, who wished to go back home to Africa. They, too, were Africans. (3) There was Liberia, a creation inspired by the American Colonization Society but brought to fruition by the physical and intellectual labour and the capital of former enslaved persons in the Americas, whose desire was to realise the utopia announced at the founding of the United States of America but from which its American originators had shirked in order to continue enjoying the profits of slavery. They undertook their brave but perilous project as Africans. (4) There were the indigenous Africans who from the late 18th century had become dissatisfied with the version of Islam they had inherited and who wished to establish Islamic societies that were closer to ideals of the faith and, to that end, prosecuted social movements for change. They were no less African. I am sure there are more different varieties of being 'African' than I could ever identify, but that is not necessary now. It should also be clear that, given these complexities, many Africans of the period subscribed to heterodox beliefs about philosophical anthropology, social ontology, family systems and ethical systems. Last, but certainly not least, were the native inhabitants who were all part of diverse intellectual traditions, some of which were written and all of which were undergoing both palpable and often imperceptible transformations at the time. And this is just in West Africa.

It is from this patchwork of African-nesses that our decolonisers wish arbitrarily to select some pristine 'African' way of being, identified only by the fact that it is articulated 'in our own languages' and those marked by Jeyifo's 'absolute autochthony', or that it emanates from some nebulous 'African culture and tradition' spread over a vast continent and which almost certainly excludes all the categories outlined above. Additionally, none of the typologies of African that I have mentioned owed their emergence, their allegiance or their political socialisation to European colonialism. So, they and their ideas cannot be candidates for some spurious decolonisation. A trope that promises to expunge so much of a complex reality from its purview, I argue, cannot be geared towards explanatory adequacy, completeness or correctness.

When the writers of the Liberian constitution made it a close relative of that of the United States, they were not mimicking the Americans. On the contrary, they were indicting the United States for not living up to its idealistic proclamations and for thereby forcing them from the land of their birth to seek to realise those ideals in the land of their forebears' birth. What's more, beyond their own fortunes, they processed their exertions as being their contribution to the advancement of the African homeland which had been degraded by the European slave trade. Writing several decades after the founding of this country, Alexander Crummell was fulsome in his praise of the impact that Liberia was having on surrounding communities so soon after its creation. There is a lot of philosophy waiting to be engaged with in the accounts of our thinkers who did not permit themselves to be limited by the exigencies of identity considerations. They were not identity-less, of course, but it was their primary identity as humans that they saw as their ticket to roam the entire human landscape for usable ideas to be applied in their respective communities, while condemning in the strongest terms the arrogance of white supremacy.[41]

What is the significance of all that I have said so far in this section? For anyone who is seriously interested in what Africans have thought, when they have thought it and with whom they have thought it, the more inclusive the boundaries of the discourse the more likely it is that what comes forth from it is closer to the truth. Furthermore, the landscape of African philosophy, for example, would then have more than the usual limited offering of 'traditional thought' with absolutely no attention paid to time and only very sketchy attention paid to place, and nary any interest in who thought what. All areas of thought will be on display, from the history of philosophy from ancient times to the present to the philosophy of history, ethics, sociology, political philosophy, philosophical anthropology, philosophy of race, theories of nationalism, philology, philosophy of culture, philosophy of art, philosophy of education and so on.

We will then find out why, even though he was no fan of his thought, Emmanuel Ayandele called James Africanus Beale Horton 'the father of modern African political science'. We will discover that while the likes of Horton's contemporaries Edward Wilmot Blyden and Alexander Crummell shared standpoints as regards Africa that were not too dissimilar from those for which we excoriate the 'problem-moderns',[42] in no way could we say that they did so for the same reasons or that they shared the thesis of the absolute alterity of the African relative to common humanity, a standard fare in racist discourse. We are sure to discover how the history of Euro-American philosophy cannot continue to be told as if it was constructed solely by people who look a certain way. We can then appreciate the debates in African discourses and cease to be satisfied with merely descriptive narratives of what is to be found in our spaces. I present all this as a clear payoff from abandoning the sterile obsession with decolonising. The further back we go and the more complexity and the bigger the wealth of ideas we will encounter, the fuller the narrative landscape of African thought will become. There can be no better way to cut European colonialism and the overblown claims of its principal ideologists down to size and to restore the integrity of our history, expansively conceived.

As is standard in the history of philosophy, the presence of a plurality of modes of being human, of movements, persons, groups and ideas in the slice of time and sliver of space that we highlight here means that there are a lot of materials from that time—ranging from pamphlets to books, private journals, newspapers, travelogues, sermons, etc.—with which we can craft philosophies. This is the treasure trove that is hidden from a purview limited to only looking for 'traditional', 'precolonial' or whatever can be deemed 'native'. The latter is an invitation to embrace nativism and succumb unwittingly to the lure of atavisms. It is why our history of African philosophy is so parlous in its offerings.

The opportunities for philosophical engagements being ignored here include themes in the philosophy of history respecting the question of historical change, to which Alexander Crummell, Edward Wilmot Blyden and James Africanus Beale Horton contributed; the preference for liberal education expressed and justified by Blyden and Horton; contributions to theology and the philosophy of religion by Philip Quaque, Usman dan Fodio, Nana Asma'u, Ahmed Baba, Samuel Ajayi Crowther and James Johnson (remember this was the period that saw the inception of African-instituted churches as well as Islamic movements for social renewal); the preoccupation with freedom found in the thought of S. R. B. Attoh Ahumah, Joseph Ephraim Casely Hayford and William Essuman Gwira Sekyi; and the first theoretical studies of indigenous languages in West Africa—for example, by Samuel Ajayi Crowther, Thomas J. Bowen and others. Decolonising here tends to misdirect the energies of our young scholars into less-productive but easier channels.

Against Atavism/Nativism

It is time to consider how the demand for decolonisation stunts knowledge production in the sphere of politics and philosophy.

I continue to use Wiredu's discussion as the foil for my argument. According to Wiredu, 'involuntary mental de-Africanization' is demonstrated in the sphere of politics. There, Wiredu claims, 'many contemporary African leaders of opinion' have suspended 'belief in African political traditions'. He continues: 'Many African intellectuals and politicians' evince a 'visible enthusiasm ... for multiparty democracy. Indeed, to many, democracy seems to be synonymous with the multi-party system'. What is wrong with this enthusiasm, Wiredu explains, is that it is driven by 'foreign pressures' and there is 'little indication, in African intellectual circles, of a critical evaluation of the particular doctrine of democracy involved in the multi-party approach to government. Yet that political doctrine seems clearly antithetical to the philosophy of government underlying traditional statecraft'.[43] On Wiredu's reading, Africans are embracing multiparty democracy because (1) they have their wills bent by 'foreign pressures', or (2) they have not decolonised the idea, as is attested by their embracing this option with little 'critical evaluation of the particular doctrine of democracy involved'. Here Wiredu is accusing African political thinkers of forgetting their traditions, while, as we saw earlier, Osaghae accused them of falsely tracing their ideas to the same traditions. Of course, because decolonisers do not often debate with one another, it would be too much to expect them to square their stories. Clearly, Wiredu does not make a case against the doctrine of multiparty democracy on the basis of pedigree: its provenance does not seem to bother him. This is quite consistent with his version of decolonising. It does not matter where an idea comes from as long as it is put through our critical wringers before we adopt it.

Is Wiredu right? We already anticipated above what might be wrong with Wiredu's designation of 'traditional statecraft'. Whose tradition is he referring to? And what time frame is involved? This is another dehistoricised usage. Did this statecraft unfold within any temporal horizon? Did it evolve in terms of changes taking place within it, driven by both internal factors and opening to external pressures and influences? We know that historically African polities, big and small, were not unlike their counterparts in other areas of the world, and evidence abounds of the evolution of political structures and their underlying legitimating ideological principles. This makes it difficult to talk of statecraft even in one single complex political tradition, never mind doing the same for a whole continent.

For Wiredu, 'thinking through the concept of democracy in our own African language' yields an awareness that multiparty democracy 'seems clearly antithetical to the philosophy of government underlying traditional statecraft'. The issue is not what it would mean to think about democracy in our own language. It is the justification given by Wiredu for his opposition to democracy that is of concern. Second, he seems to be assuming, again, that we cannot sufficiently domesticate a foreign idiom enough to make it our own. This is where the difference with Ngũgĩ becomes important. Wiredu must insist that there is no critical evaluation because, as we pointed out above, to him, embracing practices or ideas based on critical evaluation is equal to decolonisation. On this score, he is more open to possibilities. I argue that African thinkers already answered that question before Wiredu posed it. And they have been answering it since Prince Sundiata Keita adopted Alexander of Macedon and the Prophet Mohammed as his models of leadership in medieval Mali; since the Fanti and the Egba decided to embrace liberal democracy and since Usman dan Fodio chose to substitute Islamic theocracy for Hausa indigenous modes of governance in 19th-century West Africa.

Here are some questions for Wiredu and other decolonisers. What informed his conclusion that 'there is little indication, in

African intellectual circles, of a critical evaluation'? It definitely did not come from any awareness of or engagement with the robust debates in African political thought going back (to limit ourselves to the modern period) to the mid-19th century in West Africa, before formal colonialism was imposed, and continuing into the period in which Wiredu wrote. Examples abound.

In the 19th century, as the movement towards empire was gathering pace and Britain was dithering over whether to proceed with the formal colonisation of its West African territories or to prepare them for self-government, the Fanti of coastal Ghana—led by graduates of the missionary school of modernity—set about moving their political, economic and social institutions forward along modern lines. Their most significant accomplishment was the issuance of a written constitution that ranks alongside the Polish constitution of 1793 as one of the earliest attempts at liberal constitution-making in the world. That this continues to be illegible to generations of African philosophers is a scandal, but it is also a reflection of the barriers that decolonisers have erected on the path to a greater appreciation of African genius in social and political thought. The effort of the Fanti involved the newly educated class and the indigenous rulers who owed their legitimacy to autochthonous sources and immemorial usages. The indigenous rulers were the embodiments of what I take Wiredu to be referencing in his phrase 'traditional statecraft'. They who were living it and knew what embracing change would mean for their power were open to change. Wiredu—more than a hundred years removed from it but motivated by identitarian pressures and the need to push back against the white supremacy that was no less present when the Fanti made their constitution—is more reconciled to stasis. It is a testament to the Fanti's use of the 'critical evaluation' which Wiredu complains does not exist that they looked closely at their situation and decided that they could use new modes of governance borrowed from elsewhere. They chose to combine the best of the old with the best of the new.[44]

The new proposed confederacy was to be led by a figurehead 'King-President', a nod in the direction of their indigenous mode of governance as well as incorporating new elements. The executive would be headed by a vice-president, who would come from the ranks of the newly emerged Christian, educated class. But, ultimately, and this is the most radical of their proposals, *all* offices would be elected and no ascriptive qualities would be allowed to trump achievements based on criteria open to everyone willing to strive for them. Here is the constitution's Preamble:

> To all whom it may concern
>
> Whereas we, the undersigned kings and chiefs of Fanti, have taken into consideration the deplorable state of our peoples and subjects in the interior of the Gold Coast, and whereas we are of opinion that unity and concord among ourselves would conduce to our mutual well-being, and promote and advance the social and political condition of our peoples and subjects, who are in a state of degradation, without the means of education and of carrying on proper industry, we, the said kings and chiefs, after having duly discussed and considered the subject at meetings held at Mankessim on the 16th day of October last and following days, have unanimously resolved and agreed upon the articles hereinafter named.[45]

The Fanti were not alone. In Abeokuta, modern-day Nigeria, a similar movement was under way which led to the formation of the Egba United Board of Management (EUBM), which later metamorphosed into the Egba United Government (EUG), the dissolution of which was the first act of the imperialist regime of colonial administrator Frederick Dealtry Lugard when he first brought Nigeria together in 1914.[46] And we should not forget the Liberian constitution, either, in this respect. Among individual thinkers, James Africanus Beale Horton was very sophisticated in his analyses of various communities in British West

Africa, recommending new political systems according to how advanced their current political systems were at the time of his writing in the mid- to late 19th century. In the late 19th and early 20th centuries, opinions varied from the more liberal Joseph Ephraim Casely Hayford to the more conservative William Essuman Gwira Sekyi (a.k.a. Kobina Sekyi), and later in the 20th century, to the ever-evolving relations to modern liberal democracy in the writings of Obafemi Awolowo, Kwame Nkrumah or Sylvanus Olympio.[47]

To assume, without evidence, that African thinkers uncritically embraced liberal democracy is wrong and dangerous. What is even more significant is that from the Fanti Confederates to the Egba United Board of Management, to individual intellectuals like John Mensah Sarbah, Joseph Ephraim Casely Hayford, Kwame Nkrumah, Julius Nyerere, Sékou Touré, Nnamdi Azikiwe and Obafemi Awolowo, a critical evaluation of the doctrine of democracy condemned by Wiredu did not lead them to embrace 'traditional African statecraft'. Each one of these individuals and movements, at certain periods in their respective evolution, embraced variants of liberalism—a fact that is often unacknowledged in African discourse.[48]

I will cite only two examples to illustrate the wealth of ideas from which our decolonisers—encouraged by Wiredu, Serequeberhan, Bewaji and others—are alienated when they conflate liberal representative democracy with Westernism. Firstly, I am convinced that Kwame Nkrumah could not have been uncritically accepting liberal democracy, as Wiredu accuses, when he wrote

> In our struggle for freedom, parliamentary democracy was as vital an aim as independence. The two were inseparable. It was not our purpose to rid the country of the colonial régime in order to substitute an African tyranny. We wanted to free our people from arbitrary rule, and to give them the freedom to choose the kind of government they felt would best serve their interests and enhance their welfare.[49]

The second illustration comes from Obafemi Awolowo, one of Africa's foremost philosophers. In 1960, he wrote:

> As we planned for Nigeria's independence, we were fully conscious that freedom from British rule does not necessarily connote freedom for individual Nigerian citizens. I and most of my colleagues are democrats by nature, and socialists by conviction. We believe in the democratic way of life: equality under the law, respect for the fundamental rights of individual citizens, and the existence of independent and impartial tribunals where these rights could be enforced. We believe that the generality of the people should enjoy this life and do so in reasonable abundance. The most detestable feature of British administration was that the governed had no say in the appointment of those who governed them. A Nigerian administration by Nigerians must be erected on the general consent and the united goodwill of the majority of the people. In my view, there can be no satisfactory alternative to this. At the same time I fully recognize that the healthy growth of a democratic way of life requires the existence of an enlightened community led by a group of people who are imbued with the all-consuming urge to defend, uphold and protect the human dignity and the legal equality of their fellow-men.[50]

As far as I know, not a single proponent of decolonisation in African scholarship has evinced any awareness of or engagement (critical or otherwise) with these thinkers and their works. This is part of what I mean by a walling-off of Africa's intellectual heritage by privileging colonialism and by focusing on decolonising in our philosophical and other theoretical exertions. My hope is that bringing their work forward may help those who wish to break down that wall and engage with the richness and complexity of African intellectual history, outside of simply excoriating colonialism and global white supremacy.

Ironically, Wiredu's evidence for his preference for 'traditional statecraft' derives not from African scholars such as those I just mentioned, but from the same foreign pressures he admonishes us to critically evaluate: the colonial anthropology of Meyer Fortes and E. E. Evans-Pritchard and, in later works, Kofi Abrefa Busia.[51] If I may say so, Wiredu and those who follow his lead are the ones who need to critically evaluate anthropological sources and their static representations of African life and thought. I dare our decolonisers to delve into works like those I just cited and to try to show why they ought to be discarded. What's more, given that, as we have seen, for Wiredu, decolonising may mean no more than a critical evaluation of what we wish to embrace—be that from our culture or another—the fact that Nkrumah and Awolowo had done so before 'decolonising' came into vogue supports my contention that the trope may be irrelevant. And to the extent that decolonisation$_2$ blinkers its followers when it comes to taking seriously the breadth, depth and complexity of the African library, it may also be pernicious.

I do not begrudge our decolonisers, including Wiredu, their political-philosophical preferences. But by seemingly asserting that there is an essential conflict between African ideas and practices and those of foreign provenance, on account primarily of their alienness—especially if those concepts are from our former colonisers—Wiredu and other decolonisers are not improving our understanding. I don't want to be misunderstood. I argue that the alienness of an idea or practice, by itself, cannot be a disqualifying attribute. If we wish to point out its inappropriateness for a particular location, there must be more to it. In other words, unless we assume that any one African society, never mind Africa as a whole, is monolithic or characterised by some measure of unanimism in its institutions, practices and ideas, we must be able to show through our exploration of life in that community that there are no local nodes of these alien practices. We must be able to show that there is no plurality of social and political forms, such that our singling out of 'no-party consensus democracy' as the sole mode of governance in this community becomes plausible. Neither Wiredu nor any of the other defenders of the 'African modes of governance' that they counterpose to their favourite bugbear, liberalism, has ever made this case.[52] On the contrary, they studiedly, often crudely, ignore contrary discourses evidenced by the availability of a long tradition of engagement by Africans with alternative forms of political organisation. Yet, they persist, in a backhanded manner, in placing more value on democracy by comparing—at grave risk of distorting their preferred modes of governance—their preferences to it, thereby turning liberal democracy into a measuring standard.[53]

I argue that all attempts to reimagine our monarchies and other forms of non-democratic rule as 'democracies' are vulnerable to this criticism. African scholars, driven by the need to combat global white supremacy, allow themselves to be goaded into defending African institutions as if Africa had been left out of common humanity or of the general movement of history across all humanity. This is too heavy a price to pay for an outcome that is better secured by doing solid, sophisticated analyses of our institutions with an eye to understanding their relative strengths and weaknesses and, most important, their historicity. I can only hope that works like this inspire our scholars to let go of their anxieties about white supremacy and focus instead on telling our stories in ways that do credit to our place in the evolution of ideas.

As far as I know, these atavistic responses are meant to show that we have democratic equivalents in our indigenous institutions. Yet, none of our decolonisers have ever campaigned for the restoration in today's world of these former modes of governance and their substitution for those of exogenous provenance. And when they speak as if these old monarchical/aristocratic/oligarchic structures were democratic, too, one is right to seriously question their understanding of these concepts and practices. I do not see anyone seriously arguing that Chinese imperial systems or the British monarchy were ever democratic. Here I see evidence of what I called elsewhere 'occident anxiety'.[54] These are all moves that obscure rather than illuminate our understanding.

Just as decolonisers assume that no amount of fluency in the acquired tongues would suffice to domesticate them, this same attitude is applied to political structures. The suggestion is that there is an essential incompatibility between multiparty democracy and so-called traditional African statecraft, because something about Africa, its peoples and histories makes it impossible for liberal representative democracy to be domesticated there. Do African institutions grow? Do African societies evolve? Should we even enquire into whether those institutions and practices we celebrate as 'African' are in fact native to the places and peoples we claim are their authors? In short, does history matter? Of course, once you embrace the static idea of a 'precolonial Africa', all the preceding questions are peremptorily excluded. When in doubt, identity and pedigree always seem to triumph. I believe that contentions like Wiredu's lead to a persistent but wrong-headed search by African scholars for African equivalents of 'democracy', 'rule of law', 'modernity', 'knowledge' and so on. It is as if these concepts are so foreign that it does not matter what level of fluency we attain in the foreign languages, we can never domesticate them unless we think them in our own languages. Worse, they, too, are evaluated in static terms. It is why an ideal like the 'rule of law' would be considered outside of its history and treated as if it could be found throughout it.

Of Confidence and New Syntheses

The preceding are problematic claims. This is where, I am afraid, proponents of decolonisation$_2$ have simply constructed a new wall in place of the ones that decolonisation$_1$ was designed to tear down. Once everything is defined by its relationship to European colonialism, whatever has even the faintest scent of colonialism becomes tainted and, therefore, unworthy of further exploration—not just in terms of its provenance, but, more significantly, in terms of its integrity as a part of a body of ideas. The canvas on which to paint African ideas becomes increasingly small, and a false 'originality' rules the roost of African philosophy, for example. A trope that is supposed to break away from the imperialist domination of our knowledge production ends up being even more limited in its own scope. That cannot be right.

This wall blocks interest in African discourses which engage with the 'foreign' ideas that have made their appearance in and impacted on African life and thought over time. Because of the insistence on decolonisation, Africa's long history with the core tenets of modernity, dating back to Napoleon Bonaparte's arrival in Egypt in December 1798, commands no attention from our contemporary philosophers. Of course, this is to be expected once one accepts the racism-inspired ideological separation of North Africa from the rest of the continent. The many African contributions to the discourse of civilisation going back to our participation in the Mediterranean societies of antiquity are increasingly lost in the vapid references to 'precolonial Africa'. This ill-advised manner of proceeding means that many now think there is nothing to be found in terms of Africa's engagement with modernity and interactions with other civilisations, and what they must do instead is to look for 'African things'— understood as those that do not have anything to do with the supposed colonial legacy. This needs to be reversed both for theoretical and practical purposes.

Scholarship in contemporary Africa is not just lacking critical engagement with political philosophy of foreign provenance, but there is also next to no interaction with liberal representative democracy and its pertinent ideas—beyond the ritual denunciations of its so-called colonial roots. Instead, the focus is almost entirely on the need to find practices of African provenance or which are more attuned to African history and culture. The wall built by decolonisers is holding up too well, ensuring that a younger generation of scholars never read their African predecessors as complex thinkers—especially those of them who embraced, with varying levels of intensity, the modern inheritance in the 20th century. Obafemi Awolowo, Kwame Nkrumah, Julius Nyerere, Sylvanus Olympio, Léopold Sédar Senghor and Fatima Mernissi all, at different times in their intellectual careers, embraced liberal democracy, and even those who did not—like Kenneth Kaunda, Sékou Touré, Jomo Kenyatta and Ndabaningi Sithole—all had serious arguments for their positions which went beyond identitarian justifications.

This abandonment of serious intellectual engagement comes at precisely the time when Africa needs determined education about the philosophical foundations of the entire system of governance in place across much of the African continent. Other than Eswatini, which has the last absolute monarchy in the world, most countries in Africa have some form of liberal representative democracy, along with associated ideas like the rule of law and the dominance of rights discourse. Whether it is in Morocco or Egypt, Guinea Bissau or South Africa, the cry is the same: rights, freedom, governance by consent and inviolate human dignity. It is very difficult, if not impossible, to successfully operate systems with underlying philosophical foundations which are not part of our own intellectual orientation. There is an assumption that being alienated from our traditions is, by definition, bad. But the late Abiola Irele thinks otherwise. He explains:

> Our present experience of alienation stems directly from our historical encounter with Europe, and from our continuing relationship with a civilization that, in its present form, was forged in that continent, and which therefore, holds out a special interest for us. We

cannot ignore the fact that the transforming values of contact with this civilization have produced the present context of our collective life, if we are to get a mental handle upon the process of transition in which we are involved. The very tensions and conditions of stress of this process would have been beneficial if they helped to concentrate our minds both wonderfully and intensely upon the nature of our alienation.[55]

The above lines were published in 1992. Of course, as Irele is another self-confessed Europhile, had our decolonisers looked at his work, they would have thrown the same barbs at him as they do at the rest of us who share his standpoint. Indeed, by practically delegitimising certain thinkers for not sticking with their African heritage—as if the meaning of 'African heritage' were easy to ascertain—attention is directed away from exploring their works; debating their ideas; and, on occasion, showing what is wrong with their positions, as I have tried to do in this work. African scholarship is therefore impoverished. Our decolonisers open the door to atavistic preferences, unexamined affirmations and an uncritical embrace of things for the simple reason that they are 'African'. We can and ought to do better.

Incidentally, long before Irele's call for us to work with the changes shaped by our engagement with modernity and with the various external influences which have made their mark on the continent, earlier intellectuals who had become aware of the same problem had some insightful responses to the challenge. It is part of the problem of the decolonising forces that—outside of their fixation on Senghor—they hardly ever pay attention to what Africans who do not buy into their ideology wrote or are writing. Again, the issue is not whether the thinkers concerned are necessarily right. Rather it is a question of embracing the breadth, depth and complexity of the African library over time. It is a matter of heeding Kwame Nkrumah's injunction in his investiture speech as First Chancellor of the University of Ghana, at its inauguration as an independent institution on 25 November 1961. In his account of the intellectual history of Africa, Nkrumah did not limit himself to only autochthonous contributions, nor did he deploy the bastard periodisation criticised above. He went back to what he called 'the great mediaeval civilizations of Africa' and the role that 'higher institutions of learning played in them'. Speaking about Africans who attained distinctions as intellectuals even while slavery lasted, he said:

> In our endeavour to organise and promote researches into the African background and history and to assess the full structure of this period, I have asked Mr. William Abraham, a product of this university and a Fellow of All Souls, Oxford, to work on the life, times and philosophy of Anthony William Amoo [Anton Wilhem Amo]. I could mention also Mensah Sarbah, Attoh Ahuma, Casely Hayford, Phillip Quarcoo [Philip Quaque], and our own Aggrey. I could continue to speak of Africans capable of repeating the whole of the Koran from memory, Africans versed in Latin, Greek, Hebrew, Arabic and Chaldaic, celebrated Africans who were corresponding members of the Academies of Science of Europe and America.[56]

I wish that we, their successors, would be as committed as Nkrumah and those in his list to being excellent students of Africa's past in all its bewildering complexity! What Nkrumah and those whom he insisted must be studied never evinced was any discomfort at being denizens of modernity, and they were dedicated to creating a knowledge society as Africa sought to recover from the predations of the trans-Atlantic slave trade and march in tandem with the rest of humanity to a better life. They were ever conscious of and ready to acknowledge the state of their continent and its peoples. They never papered over them.

I cite below the work of Ladipo Solanke, one of the most important stalwarts of the pan-Africanist movement and a leading light in the efforts to form a West African federation. He was also a distinguished lawyer, legal scholar and overall brilliant and influential public intellectual. On 10 April 1930, Solanke deliv-ered a public lecture in which he, as with many of that genera-tion of African intellectuals, dwelt on how African societies were to move forward in the aftermath of the trans-Atlantic slave trade, of European colonialism and of the impact of Islam and Christianity on their indigenous institutions, practices and pro-cesses. I will let him speak directly:

> Dear Countrymen, it seems to me that the right and correct view we should take together with the course we should adopt as regards the progress of our country towards the attainment of modern political Self-determination should be first of all to admit that it is impossible for us to make any progress through developing solely upon our ancient laws, customs and institutions.

> Perhaps this would have been possible had foreign peoples such as the Europeans, the Asiatics, and such like not yet come among us to earn their livelihood. But since their advent, new conditions, new modes of life, and new problems for which no remedy or remedies may be discovered out of our ancient laws and customs, have not only made their appearance but have also continued to increase in number, strength, and variety. For instance, the custom of preparing annually estimates of the revenue and expenditure of the Administration, is a new and modern one which conditions impose on every Administration to adopt. It is not native .... In the next place, whilst it is true that a good deal of our laws, customs, and institutions have become archaic or are either crude, barbarous, harsh, inhumane, insufficient or inadequate, there is also a large amount of others that are good, sound and more suited to our condi-tions than any that may be substituted for such. The right course to adopt under the above circumstances, seems to be the process of elimination by substitution i.e. to abolish and scrap up, root and branch, all those customs, laws and institutions which have become useless but retain those that are still good and sound. The laws, customs and institutions abolished and scrapped up must be replaced by modern and sounder ones. But the only source from which mod-

ern and sounder laws, customs and institutions may presently be drawn is British or Western civilization, and before these can be properly and firmly grafted into our life we must have them thoroughly assimilated.[57]

I am not going to comment on Solanke's ideas. I have quoted them here to show the kind of nuanced and complex thinking that earlier generations of intellectuals brought to their study of the relationships between what they inherited from their autochthonous cultures and what was of foreign provenance, however it came to them. Unfortunately, our decolonisers evince little knowledge of or interest in the intellectual history of the continent. Now that I have brought it to their attention in this book, I hope that scholars who would like to seriously engage with the complexity and heterogeneity of African thinking find direction for better analyses.

How much more insightful would it be to have today's philosophers grapple with the Solankes of our intellectual heritage (even if we find their understanding erroneous), who had no qualms about recognising the shortcomings in their culture and about seeking to remedy such by exercising that all-too-human facility: borrowing? Curiously, other than thinkers like Wiredu and the late Kwame Gyekye, it is rare among academic philosophers to find proponents of decolonising who lay out defects in their indigenous heritage and how such are to be resolved. Nor is there an acknowledgment of the complexities of contemporary societies, the heterogeneities to be found therein and how such are to be accommodated by so-called 'indigenous' processes, practices and institutions. Additionally, how might these ideas instruct and guide humanity elsewhere, or are they content to have their ideas applicable only to their societies? It is even more curious that many of their offerings are limited to descriptions, and they never explain how their concepts could be incorporated into existing societies.

Of greater importance and relevance is that Solanke and many of his contemporaries were doing exactly what Irele asked of us in his lecture: coming to grips with the alien influences that have shaped our lives and refusing to pretend that we can somehow separate 'our' inheritance from these influences, especially modernity.[58] Despite what decolonisers might eagerly seize upon as a denigration of his African inheritance, Solanke actually went on to defend what we criticise here. He insisted on the generally democratic nature of indigenous modes of governance, usually headed by monarchs, even as he argued that these institutions needed to be supplemented by borrowings from the British and the West, particularly in matters of policing and prisons.

As a matter of fact, Solanke's reflections are not so different from what we find in the writings of some of the thinkers that decolonisers love to parade about as authorities for their positions. Amílcar Cabral is a notable example. But, again, if only our decolonisers would properly embrace Cabral's complexity and sophistication as a thinker they would find that a straight line ran from Solanke through Cabral to Irele. Here is a sample of Cabral's writing on the subject:

> If you see a film about the Vikings of olden days, you can see them with great horns on their heads and amulets on their arms, setting off for war. And they would not set off for war without their great horns on the head. No one should think that to be African one must wear horns on one's chest and an amulet around one's waist. Such persons are individuals who have not yet properly understood the relationship between man and nature. The Portuguese did the same, the French did it when they were Franks, Normans, etc. The English did it when they were Angles and Saxons, voyaging across the sea in canoes, great canoes like those of the Bijagos.[59]

Decolonising theorists make it easy for scholars not to engage with this literature at all and, in so doing, gloss over the contributions of African thinkers to the domestication of these ideas going back to the 19ᵗʰ century and earlier, especially in West and North Africa. The proponents of decolonisation are largely uninterested in the efforts of African thinkers to adapt foreign ideas for their own purposes. Many African intellectuals have critically engaged with both foreign and indigenous ideas in trying to work out the best form of government for the flourishing of human life and societies in the African context. Unfortunately, so thick is the wall erected by our decolonisers that, to continue with the example of politics, many of them would be hard pressed to name any serious political philosophers outside of Nkrumah, Fanon, Cabral and Nyerere from any time other than the present day. And they hardly ever grapple with even those thinkers in their full complexity. Of course, none of our decolonisers thinks to engage with the robust defence of liberal democracy by Obafemi Awolowo or by Abiola Irele in his 'In Praise of Alienation', or with Paulin J. Hountondji in his argument for liberal individualism.[60]

Most frightening of all, because Africans can only be resisters or victims of modernity according to the decolonisation trope, we are unable to come to terms with the philosophical genius of African thinkers who are disdainful of decolonising and who find it worth their while, after critical evaluation of course, to appropriate the core tenets of modernity as fundaments of their own thinking, both in politics and in moral philosophy. The latter approach is as it should be because, again, in Irele's words,

> We must not forget, too, that African labor and resources went into the building of the material prosperity of the West. In many ways, therefore, we have a claim upon Western civilization, as well as a considerable stake in it, as the instrument for the necessary transformation of our world. It is in our interest to make good that claim, to adopt strategies that will make our stake in that civilization pay handsome dividends. We cannot do this if we continue to be burdened by the complexes implanted in us under colonialism, and which are only

intensified by cultural nationalism. If the Japanese had been deterred by the insults constantly hurled at them by the Europeans during the last century, they would not have been where they are today: as we all know, the yellow peril has become with time the yellow paradigm.[61]

But because of the penchant for nativism in African scholarship, buoyed by a crude conflation of colonialism with modernity, we ignore Irele's wisdom. We are not able to engage with the eminently modern appropriations of a Fanon, a Robert Gardiner, a Cabral, a Fatima Mernissi, a Saad Eddin Ibrahim or an Abdullahi Ahmed An-Naim.[62] When Nelson Mandela put his prosecutors on the back foot at his treason trial in 1961, he was not channelling some 'traditional' legal philosophy; nor was Martin Luther King Jr. in his famous 1963 'Letter from Birmingham Jail'. Both marshalled the modern liberal political philosophical principles that our decolonising scholars love to defame. I present all of them for decolonising! Mphahlele's question: 'where do we come in?' deserves serious answers, not dismissal.

It is time that African scholars of the humanities and social sciences, especially up-and-coming ones, stopped wasting the riches that have accrued in African intellectual history from the earliest times till the present. And I do not see us making any significant progress in this direction until we quit our fascination, even obsession, with forever chasing down the last traces of a colonial presence in the framework of our world. We will not make any significant progress until we distance ourselves and our intellectual exertions from permanently trying to catch errors, flag slights and denounce those whose only interest in our criticisms is as a source of amusement. In short, I am saying that it is time to give up 'the critical-negative project of decolonization', as Serequeberhan has dubbed it, and open our intellectual horizons, in order to move our societies forward and educate, rather than titillate, the world with our critical offerings—both original and borrowed.

In his 'Address to Court Before Sentence', Nelson Mandela may have referenced the tales told by his royal uncles about how their forebears 'lived peacefully, under the democratic rule of their King and their "amapakati", and moved freely and confidently up and down the country without let or hindrance'. But when it came down to what kind of country should be built in South Africa, Mandela and his compatriots in the African National Congress (ANC) had no hesitation in declaring that the country they sought to incorporate would be unlike any that their traditions had anticipated:

> [The ANC] policy was one which appealed to my deepest inner convictions. It sought for unity of all Africans, over-riding tribal differences among them. It sought the acquisition of political power for Africans in the land of their birth. The African National Congress further believed that all people, irrespective of the national groups to which they may belong, and irrespective of the colour of their skins, all people whose home is South Africa and who believe in the principles of democracy and of equality of men, should be treated as Africans; that all South Africans are entitled to live a free life on the basis of fullest equality of the rights and opportunities in every field, of full democratic rights, with a direct say in the affairs of the Government.

> These principles have been embodied in the Freedom Charter [a prime candidate for decolonising], which no-one in this country will dare challenge for its place as the most democratic programme of political principles ever enunciated by any political party or organisation in this country.[63]

The principles espoused in his address may be dismissed as a tactical move on his part, in the context of a criminal trial. Surely he could not have been invested in a legal system and its founding principles that came straight out of the colonialist playbook (given that our decolonisers do not separate modernity from colonialism)? But there is a reason why the proponents of decolonisation conveniently sidestep the works of those, like Mandela, who found the core tenets of modernity an adequate guide for creating not the best society possible, nor even a particularly good society, but at least a just society where no individual must bear any burden to which her fellows are not also subject. It is because these principles are not regional, ethnic or adjectivised in any way; they are genuinely universal and have been used, over time, by Karl Marx at his own trial in 1849, Fidel Castro at another trial in 1953 and Martin Luther King Jr. Of course, our decolonisers are probably convinced that Mandela and King Jr. are easy dupes or even running dogs of imperialism for finding modernity and its tenets to their liking even as colonialism and slavery had tainted its packaging.

Insofar as we do not see beyond a superficial understanding of the many possible responses Africans have had to colonisation across time and space, we are not able to have a robust representation of the ethical debates in the African world, such as those between Senghor and Soyinka on the ethics of reconciliation.[64] This is a debate that, when engaged with by our scholars, is sure to extend the frontiers of knowledge in ethics, both substantive and theoretical. Senghor was also a significant philosopher. His creative amalgamation of his Serer inheritance, his adherence to the Catholic Church—the contribution of Africans to the growth of which cannot be downplayed—and his immersion in and embrace of modernity, modulated by his French identity, not only produced great poetry, it also created one of the most sophisticated philosophies of humanism. Wole Soyinka, too, has combined his Yorùbá inheritance, his education in the classics—another field to whose constitution Africa was integral—his prowess in the English language and, as with Senghor, his embrace of modernity (tempered by a deep immersion in Òrìṣà, Yorùbá religion) to not only produce great drama but also to create an equally sophisticated philosophy of humanism.

They are both humanists. But while Senghor subscribed to the need for forgiveness and reconciliation, consistent with his Christian faith, Soyinka advocates the necessity of justice and restoration. Incidentally, knowing that the original culture that Soyinka comes from had possessed, at certain times in the past, sophisticated models of reconciliation, including ways of expiating guilt, it is noteworthy that he does not base his commitment to justice on such grounds. And while he has, at various times in his repeated denunciations of Islam and Christianity in Africa, referred to the humanist impulses in Òrìṣà, he has never established this as an uncomplicated justification for his humanism. This is the sophisticated discussion from which the world can benefit, coming from a continent with many horrific unique experiences, including the shipping of significant percentages of its population to chattel slavery in the United States and the continuing scourge of global white supremacy. How do we restore the world, our world, in the aftermath of such crimes against humanity perpetrated by some humans against others?

Much of the debate about politics and its requirements in contemporary Africa unfolds almost without reference to theory or to the philosophical foundations of the institutions of representative government, impartial judiciary, the rule of law and the separation of powers that we seek to install in our various countries. Thus, it often seems as if our political operatives are building without any understanding of the discourses that underpin our institutions. Scholars and practitioners alike are working with significant knowledge deficits. This is despite the fact that, as I argue in the next chapter, the continent has been grappling since colonial days with the challenge of redeeming the promise of modernity for its own citizens. Its philosophers have been singularly neglectful of this, and it has consequences for the design and operation of our political system. Africa cannot afford to continue proceeding the way it has until now, building modern institutions without deeper knowledge of the philosophical templates from which they were forged. We should stop shooting darts in the dark. I know that most people rarely consider in tandem the elements that I have in this work. But my hope is that this book, at least, encourages more people to take another look at the allure of decolonisation.

At a time when Africans are prosecuting their second struggle for freedom, it does them a disservice to keep reinforcing the wall which separates them from the full spectrum of African engagements with colonialism and its aftermath. A genuine commitment to human liberation cannot afford anything less.

4

DECOLONISE THIS!

TAKING HISTORY AND AGENCY SERIOUSLY

Liberty is not unilateral. It does not merely mean freedom from European domination.

Ousmane Sembène[1]

I have argued in previous chapters that putting colonisation at the centre of ex-colonised lives is historically suspect and has the unintended consequence of making less legible, if not rendering completely invisible, the autonomous lives (despite colonisation) led by the colonised even while colonialism lasted. It eviscerates the lives they led before colonialism was imposed on them, and the lives they have crafted since they threw off the colonial yoke. Opposing this does not mean a denial of the impact of colonialism on the life, times and thoughts of the colonised. But it surely means, and I cannot emphasise this enough, refusing to define the colonised strictly by the colonial experience, however profound colonialism's impact may have been on them. Hence, I insist that the ultimate problem with decolonisation discourse is its oft-unapprehended failure to take seriously the complexity of

African agency and the many ways it has grappled with both colonialism and its legacy—ranging from wholesale embrace of colonially derived languages, ideas, institutions, processes and practices to attempts at wholesale rejection of the same. We need to engage with this complexity. In this final chapter, I focus on a problem in political science and political philosophy that is often zeroed in on by African and Africanist scholars in their strident call for decolonisation: the central political philosophical problem of who ought to rule when not all can rule, and the related question of the fate and career of liberal representative democracy and the form of governance it underwrites on the continent. Consistent with the tenor of the rest of this work, I direct our attention to a problem that goes to the heart of the decolonising discourse but can be shown to have little, if anything, to do with colonisation. If we do not buy into the idea of the near permanence of colonialism and its continuing impact more than half a century after independence—i.e., if we accept that decolonisation$_1$ has been won—the discourse about the fate of the state, questions of legitimacy and suchlike must be beyond the ken of decolonisation$_2$.

The importance of complexity and the agency of the ex-colonised cannot be overstressed. Many aspects of life in contemporary Africa are intimately connected with material and ideational structures that are framed by the dominance of modern governance, legitimated by and founded on the consent of the governed. What is even more significant is the repeated elision in discourse and in practice of the underlying metaphysical grounds of the modern state: the principle of subjectivity, the centrality and inviolate status of the individual. While the state and its allied institutions like the judiciary are built on this principle, some areas of life continue to be structured by other, not necessarily compatible, ideas and associated beliefs—ranging from at what age girls can marry to what rites widows must undergo at the passing of their husbands, to age-grade member-ships that are not voluntarily chartered.[2] This is not to mention the continuing distortions of governance by the presence of chieftaincies in many countries on the continent. None of the fundamental human rights that our polities enshrine in their constitutions and pledge under numerous international conventions to observe owe any of their legitimating foundations to autochthonous cultural and political ideas and practices.

As I always insist, if we decide to eliminate these externally derived structures, processes and ideological practices, there would be no need for us to argue about their provenance or their place in our societies. This is a vital point made by those of us who embrace modernity and would like to see our societies embody its core tenets, and which is often a source of rancour between us and our opponents.[3] But the point I just made is separate and separable from my preference for modernity as a principle of social ordering and a mode of social living. The issue at stake here is this: since independence, Africans have been free to rid their polities of the empirical analogues of the modern, consent-based governance that was a nominal legacy of colonialism. It is no answer to say that this has not been done because our erstwhile colonisers would not let us. The political history of the continent is instructive in this respect. From absolute monarchy in Morocco, Ethiopia, Swaziland (now Eswatini) and Libya to one-party socialist experiments, military rule of various flavours and even an ill-fated empire in Central Africa, Africa has been a veritable workshop of political experiments. Through it all, one thing has remained constant: the persistent effort by all our countries, outside of military dictatorships, to accommodate our modes of governance to respect for the dignity of the individual; the rule of law; the independence of the judiciary; and, for the most part, multiparty elections that must be free and fair to be legitimate.

This is the crucial question here. Nothing stops any of our countries from severing ourselves and our polities from the dominance of the modern form of governance dominated by liberal representative democracy and its related institutions and lifeworlds. Certainly, the response to my challenge will require more than supplying equivalents from our culture, continentally conceived, or making imprecise statements about how our autochthonous modes of governance embodied all the attributes I just laid out. Care must be taken to show how those principles emanate from specific cultural formations or particular theories, following the pattern of works such as Obafemi Awolowo's *The People's Republic*, Kwame Nkrumah's *Africa Must Unite*, Julius Nyerere's *Ujamaa* or Joseph Casely Hayford's numerous speeches in support of liberal democracy.

My argument is that if Africans, organised in their polities as we currently have them, keep the institutions of modern governance or fail to found them on autochthonous philosophical foundations, they owe it to themselves to realise these borrowed institutions in their best incarnations and ensure they are operated in such a way as to get as close as possible to the best life that they promise. That is, if we continue to privilege them, organise our lives around and within them, the call to decolonise them misses the mark unless decolonisation's proponents can show that these institutions are inseparable from colonialism and that there is no conceivable way for Africans to embrace them of our own accord other than under the continuing domination of our former colonisers. The entire purpose of this book is to show the errancy of both approaches.

Africa is a continent in which we are insisting that parents should no longer be able to marry off their female children under the guise of religion or culture, where we are delegitimising certain widowhood rites and where we are demanding that law-enforcement agents respect the inviolate dignity of the individual and take seriously the presumption of innocence when someone is alleged to have committed a crime. Even if all the protocols that inform and legitimise our actions are not derived from our original philosophies and traditions, how useful can a trope be that asks us not to dig deep into the traditions and philosophies from which we have borrowed?

I wish to restate the key point in this chapter. African countries are like other countries across the world—from Japan to Argentina, Pakistan to Spain—which are struggling to come to terms with modernity. In the African case, outside of Eswatini, there is no single country that is not genuinely working to install or is at least paying lip service to the key elements of a modern political system—representative democracy, governance by consent denominated by party politics and free and fair elections, an independent judiciary and a government that is subordinate to the wishes of and serves those that charter it. No amount of dithering or double-speak in the name of so-called homegrown ideas and practices will wish that away. Here is the challenge to decolonisers: if liberal representative democracy is inseverable from colonialism, why do you not just reject it outright? Why waste your energies on 'decolonising' it? Those to whom you have surrendered their authorship and ownership—the so-called West, Global North, etc.—have no anxieties about liberal representative democracy outside of continuing to acknowledge how far their countries remain from realising it in the best possible form, and 'Western' intellectuals never shy away from making the improvement of it their daily preoccupation.

Given the richness of cultures and relevant forms of governance across Africa, it would be more efficient and would answer more to anxieties about racism and identity to turn our backs on these colonial relics and install novel (even if they are retrieved from our authentic, autochthonous past) political arrangements that better suit our heritage and our needs. Why are we so invested in forcing other people to reconfigure their inheritance for our convenience and why do we get mad when they do not? Here is the deal: the world, the so-called West or Global North, does not owe Africa. And I fail to see—unless we grant that white supremacists are right and we are permanent children whose will is forever at the mercy of our erstwhile colonisers— why after 60 plus years of independence, Africans are willing to accept that we are still colonised and that we have no will or strength to defeat our oppressors and, therefore, do not have the wherewithal to expunge modern institutions and practices inspired by the so-called West from our lives.

If the call for decolonising amounts to no more than we saw in the last chapter, with other people asking that whatever is foreign be domesticated for use in a different culture, then there really is not much, beyond fad, to the decolonising discourse. Furthermore, if African scholars are not willing to eradicate all the ideas, practices, institutions and processes that they believe are colonial, it is their responsibility to become good students of the intellectual (especially philosophical) and theoretical foundations of those phenomena, as a prerequisite for making them deliver as they do in other countries such as South Korea and Japan. This is where we should aim our intellectual energies, and striving for the best life for humans in our communities should be the touchstone for judging what matters. All else is show, and I am arguing that much of the current decolonising discourse in and about Africa is exactly that—and not a very good show either.

Here is the evidence. African scholars have no problem appealing to the United States to put pressure on the Nigerian government to stop its police from killing the people they are supposed to be protecting. Does imperialism stop being imperialism when it serves our purpose? What principles does the United States use to enable it to have the moral authority to censure the Nigerian state for treating its people like sub-humans, but which escape the opprobrium of colonialism? Or France when Ivoirians call on French President Emmanuel Macron to intervene to stop their country's president, Alassane Ouattara, from succeeding himself in an illegitimate third term? If those principles are of use to us when we reach an impasse in our polities, why are we wasting so much time denigrating the same principles when we fly the decolonisation banner? We can and must do better.

We saw in the last chapter how the need for decolonisation has led to (1) the preference for atavistic appropriations from the African past which do not take account of the passage of time and the inescapable hybridisation of life and thought in a complex world peopled by creatures who have never remained separate from one another or one another's practices; (2) the erection of a wall between what took place and what ideas had been incubated and disseminated in that mythical, ahistorical world dubbed 'precolonial Africa', and current attempts at formulating ideas and creating institutions which would enable Africa to move in tandem with the rest of humanity towards a better future. In this chapter, I take a comparative turn to look at other communities with historical and, more crucially, racial trajectories and profiles similar to our own to show how the decolonisation enterprise can not only be misleading but may in fact have harmful consequences for Africans; their lives; their societies; and, most importantly, their capacity to domesticate borrowed ideas and institutions.

Decolonisation$_2$ has built a wall that is qualitatively different from the one its proponents sought to break down or thought they were dismantling. If the idea was that we should clearly demarcate events that took place under colonialism and their consequences from what came before it and what we should be doing in its aftermath—because the decolonisers have made colonialism the main axis for plotting Africa's history—the unwanted outcome is that what came before is flattened into a nondescript 'precolonial' era that encompasses anything from the beginning of time to whenever colonialism irrupted into the lives of Africa's indigenous peoples. Even then, if what I argued in the previous chapters is plausible, short of looking for 'authenticity' uncontaminated by any part of colonisation (expansively conceived to include Christianity), there is still a renunciation of a great deal of ideas and practices that are thereby shut off from our critical exploration. When we are not deploying this drumhead historical periodisation, we are busy conflating modernity with colonialism and both with Westernisation. They make for a trifecta of errors and unhelpful explanatory models.

Certainly, everyone is at liberty to insist that there is no real distinction between colonialism and modernity, and between both and Westernisation. Unfortunately, for some parts of Africa, that conflation is not just a wrong interpretation but it is historically unsupportable. We should stop allowing Euro-American racists who claim that Europe has always been modern while Africa was 'traditional', and that Europe owns, absolutely, the very idea of modernity, have their way. In the 18th and 19th centuries, not even Georg Wilhelm Friedrich Hegel, one of the principal philosophers of modernity, could deny that Europe was not conscious of itself, as such, until it came to the 'New World'. That the new world was eventually subjugated was not the same as saying that it was annihilated. As any dialecticians worth their salt know, a sublated moment remains a defining part of a new whole, the absence of which would make that whole a different entity. What this means is that no account of modernity's formation would be complete if it makes it a solely European phenomenon with sole European authorship. In other words, as some of us have argued, modernity may have originated in Europe, but there is no way that it could be said to be fully constituted there. (This is almost like saying that because Black people were enslaved for much of the existence of the United States, they played no role in the constitution of the history and thought of the country.)

If our argument is correct or, at least, plausible, it means that the conflation that dominates much of decolonisation discourse, especially in Africa, must be eschewed. To this end, we do not need to multiply entities by designating modernity in terms of regions—as if 'European modernity' is qualitatively distinguishable from 'African modernity' rather than both being styled instances of modernity, construed as a genuine universal, each trying to realise the concept with different degrees of adequation. If this universality is true, there is much that unites efforts at realising modernity in southern Italy and northern Nigeria, and in the Fanti Confederacy of 1871 and the Polish constitution of 1793.

Here is one implication of the failure to reject this conflation. If we let it stand, it would mean that to embrace modernity and its tenets is to seek to 'Westernise' or to find something to be recommended in colonialism. Or, we would have to invent, and some current thinkers do, an 'African modernity' which, I insist, is not a helpful notion if by this we mean anything more than the engagement with and adaptation of modernity within African contexts. When it comes to the matter of politics and what kind of state to install, post-independence, if we choose liberal representative democracy, unless we can identify a local—or, better still, autochthonous—provenance for it, we would have failed to 'decolonise', almost by definition. If, on the other hand, we accept the claim of the colonisers that part of their justification for colonialism was to move the colonised to modernity, then decolonisation discourse must pose a paradox: if liberal representative democracy, a tenet of modernity, is a Western contraption, then post-independence political arrangements must not include democracy or, at least, that version of it which has a Western provenance. But if democracy is a core tenet of modernity, but the latter is not Western, then what decolonisation calls for, post-independence, would be the deepening of democracy, not its overthrow. The tragedy of decolonisation$_2$ is that it cannot condone the idea of any Africans embracing modernity as their own and seeking ways of redeeming its promise for their societies. Perhaps the most pernicious wall erected by decolonisation is the truncating of the history of Africa's rich and long engagement with modernity.

In the remainder of this chapter, I provide evidence of Africans' striving to redeem the promise of modernity for their societies before, during and after colonialism. I also, for comparative purposes, show that preference for and success at manipulating the institutional and ideological artefacts of modernity have nothing whatsoever to do with the inheritance of the people concerned, only with historical contingencies. That is why we have a lot to learn from our kin in the Caribbean. Meanwhile, I am leaving out the contributions of African Americans in forcing the United States to move closer to its founding liberal ideals and, in so doing, ensuring that the country continues to bridge the chasm between ideal and reality as a modern state. I am also leaving out the role of African-descended intellectuals in ensuring, post–Second World War, that France was saved from fascism and its republican ideals were upheld.[4]

I would like to end on a positive note. Here I take a deliberate risk that, I can only hope, the reader will, in the end, find worth taking. I am acutely aware of the many failings of the state in post-independence Africa, from Cape to Cairo and all points in-between. I do not exaggerate that an overwhelming percentage of the discourse on the state in post-independence Africa, conducted by African and Africanist scholars alike, is devoted to its failings. I question how right their descriptions are and how plausible or adequate their explanations are. I challenge our decolonisation theorists to decolonise what is offered in this chapter and show what the aftermath might be in terms of advancing our knowledge and the quality of our lives when it comes to installing a modern system of political governance in our respective countries.

When all is said and done, it is plausible to contend that, given its many challenges and disabilities, the state in post-independence Africa has been incredibly resilient. Yes, there are areas, many of them, that need significant improvements. And one must not make light of those deficiencies. But we should not exaggerate them, either. Despite the gloom and doom that is routinely predicted of the state in Africa, especially its 'postcolonial' exemplars, and which is used as justification for seeking 'African' substitutes, it is remarkable how successful that much-maligned institution has been. This success is best understood as the product of the continuing striving of the state to reduce the distance between what it ought to be and what it is at any given moment. That is, Africans have never given up on the objective of redeeming the best of what the modern state promises. It is what makes them fight and never reconcile themselves to manifestations of the state that fall too far off the mark. It is what they are all striving to install for the umpteenth time in the current attempts at democratisation across the continent. This is why I have called it Africa's second struggle for freedom.[5]

During the first struggle for liberty identified with decolonisation$_1$, Africans wanted the freedom to order their own affairs as they saw fit; they did not want to be ruled by any government that they had had no hand in installing; they wanted their human dignity restored from the battering it had taken under colonial rule; they wanted governments that were responsible for and responsive to them. Above all, they wanted to be FREE. But, as we found out from Awolowo in the last chapter, as he and some of his colleagues 'planned for Nigeria's independence,' they 'were fully conscious that freedom from British rule does not necessarily connote freedom for individual Nigerian citizens'.[6] Only those who care to drill down to the granular would discover that the obstacles to the realisation of individual freedom that Awolowo had in mind had little or nothing to do with colonisation, but with the internal dynamics within their countries related to cultural practices, indigenous political institutions (especially chieftaincy), religion and its sociological implications, and the like. The first struggle was to create the conditions for the second freedom, something that was neither synonymous with nor the automatic result of independence. After colonisation, the problem of freedom is a different order of questioning.

Unfortunately, once independence was obtained, Africa's rulers—including Kwame Nkrumah in Ghana, Sékou Touré in Guinea and Félix Houphouët-Boigny in Côte d'Ivoire—decided that the struggle for freedom was over and done with. They proceeded to put in place numerous political contraptions—all designed to subvert and deny the freedom of their people—to turn their citizens into subjects and to substitute their own wills for those of their people when it came to the installation of governments all across the continent. Did they have any more truck with freedom? No, they had their coats of arms, their flags, their national anthems and so on. It was almost as if they thought that the struggle they had led for independence did not include the freedom of individual citizens to have, hold and seek to realise their own conceptions of the good life. The proverbial freedom to be left alone, especially by their governors; the impermissibility of governmental interference in the details of their daily lives; limits on the powers of government; and the sanctity of their dignity and their life were all cast aside by their leaders. In other words, the promise of independence was never redeemed for ordinary Africans at the micro-level of their quotidian lives.

Watching the images in the media from Egypt; Tunisia; Libya; Malawi; Uganda; and, in the mid-2000s, Ethiopia and Zimbabwe—and, as I write this, in Eswatini and Sudan, in the interviews at the barricades with young and old, men and women, from all walks of life—it is clear that, much more than the chronic economic and other problems of their daily lives, their main demand is that THEY MUST BE FREE! When street vendor Mohamed Bouazizi committed the brave act of self-immolation in 2010 that triggered the Tunisian revolution, he was not dying for country, ethnic group or religion; he could no longer take the repeated assault on his freedom and dignity, as well as on that of his countrymen and women. Therein lies the ultimate lesson of the current movements for change in both Africa and the Arab world.[7]

Let us begin with a few uncomfortable facts for those who think that the ongoing struggle for individual freedom is an anti-colonial one. Except for Ethiopia and Egypt, all countries in Africa are the results or creations of the machinations of foreign mischief-makers or, in the case of Liberia, seekers after freedom. This explains why it is standard fare in discourse about Africa to remark on the artificiality of African boundaries. That African countries are artificial creations is not—repeat, not—anomalous: most countries in the world are.[8] This is a fact that is often lost on African scholars who have become convinced beyond all doubts that the manufactured nature of African borders is exceptional and a source of unresolvable conflict. What is anomalous in the African context is that they were all created at the whim of outsiders and for the convenience of those same outsiders, with scant respect for the preferences of Africans. But, again, we come up against the reality that this latter quality is not peculiar to African countries: India and Pakistan were no less created for the convenience of the British. In the same way that Pakistanis decided to separate and create Bangladesh (formerly East

Pakistan), first Eritrea and later South Sudan have shown that there is nothing set in stone where African geopolitical boundaries are concerned. Nigeria ceded the Bakassi Peninsula to Cameroon in 2008, for example, in the aftermath of a judgement by the International Court of Justice at the Hague guided by the same principles that are the object of the decolonising animus. Simultaneously, I hate to think that Africans should not be held responsible for accepting these artificial boundaries and consecrating them for the over half-century that much of Africa has been independent.[9]

Think of the eagerness and, dare I say, murderousness with which African governments—Cameroon is the most tragic example as I write this—defend the same borders that they blame on colonial adventurers. We know how many millions perished in Nigeria's civil war (1967–70), in Sudan's ultimately unsuccessful bloody efforts to keep South Sudan from seceding in 2011 and in Ethiopia's ultimately failed bid to keep Eritrea as part of the country until 1991. And we have Ivoirian intellectuals and politicians defending the bogus concept of 'Ivoirité' based, again, on the same boundaries that they are all too eager to condemn for being imposed on them. At different times, African politicians from Nigeria to Zambia have had no difficulty disenfranchising their citizens and making certain citizens ineligible to stand for elections as a result of their parents not being born in the same 'fake' countries that they want the world to believe they would rather not have. Yet, they never make any serious efforts to redraw those boundaries. If people want to interpret the instances just cited as reflecting ongoing colonialism, they are welcome to. But, simultaneously, as we keep repeating, they must grant that Africans have no will and no subjectivity—exactly how our racist denigrators see us. We cannot have it both ways. The preservation of colonial boundaries after 1960 is no longer a colonial issue, period. The single outstanding colonial issue in the continent as of this writing is the unresolved one of Western Sahara, and it involves an African principal: Morocco.

There is one crucial difference. While colonialism lasted, Africans were not trained in the statecraft required for the successful operation of the new state form inspired by modernity, which our colonisers had falsely claimed that they wanted to share with us. This point is often misunderstood. The modern political system comes with philosophical underpinnings with which we must engage at an intellectual level. Their associated institutions, practices and processes require work towards perfecting them over time. It is not an accident that the United States, one of the pioneers of the system, continues to strive to create 'a more perfect Union' after more than 200 years of efforts. The presidency of Donald J. Trump between 2017 and 2021, and his attempt to engineer a coup to stay in office beyond his time on 6 January 2021, having lost his bid for re-election, is no different from what Awolowo identified as part of the bane of Africa's rulers after independence: 'tenacity of office'. So, it is nothing to lament, much less apologise for, that Africans, because they were prevented from it, came out of colonialism unpractised at working the modern institutions bequeathed to them at independence. Worse still, Africans who made themselves excellent students of modern statecraft—we already made their acquaintance in previous chapters—were not merely discouraged by their rulers; they were severely punished and denigrated for daring to proclaim themselves worthy successors to the lofty principles, practices, institutions and processes that were supposed to define the state forms foisted on them. Incidentally, it was the failure of those who baited them with a transition to modernity to deliver on that promise that triggered the 'reactive nationalism' of many African thinkers, who began to define their identity and preferred modes of being human in opposition and hostility to modernity and its ways. Much of the decolonising animus is captive to this opposition. It is time to let go of it.

Across the continent, while colonialism lasted, Africans fought the scourge with many weapons and from varied ideological angles. One angle was particularly prominent and was more widespread in West Africa: that of modernity. Because, in that region, colonialism was confronted with the unusual situation of Africans who had been schooled in the ways of modernity and had chosen to embrace its core tenets. When colonial administrators began to play fast and loose with those principles, African thinkers and activists accused them of bait-and-switch. They could do so only because they accepted the main elements of modernity and they wanted to see their societies manifest those ideas and embody the relevant institutions. It did not matter whether it was French, Portuguese or British colonialism. Meanwhile, the founders of Liberia had exited the United States precisely because their white compatriots kept racialising the idea of modernity[10] when it came to the latter's commitment to the universalism that was supposed to mark the principles undergirding their republic.[11]

When our forebears accused their colonisers of bait-and-switch, we must make sense of their argument or show that they were wrongheaded. When, on the eve of independence, either in Africa or Asia—Hong Kong being the last example in the 20th century—the colonisers started handing out constitutions with Bills of Rights, we either dismiss such as shams and our leaders who accepted them as easy dupes or we take them as they are: the late realisation of the promise of modernity which colonialists had falsely used to justify their plunder.

I would like to suggest that the residents of Hong Kong—who are fighting tooth and nail against the rollback of the modern ideas, institutions and practices enshrined in their Basic Law literally on the eve of the handover back to China—illustrate the argument of this book: that the failure to separate decolonisation₁ from decolonisation₂ and to have a more complex understanding of the place of modernity in the ex-colonies results in confusion and unsophisticated analyses. Why would Hong Kong's citizens by their hundreds of thousands risk life, limb and personal freedom to defend a way of life and its founding principles, which only became reality for them post-1997, if those are no more than the ways of colonialism? Why are they not marching in the name of some modernity of Asian vintage, properly decolonised? I think there is a lesson here for African intellectuals who are all too eager to embrace intellectual fads that hardly ever shed light on the issue at hand. Interestingly, the failure of post-independence regimes in Africa to consummate this promise of freedom (of conscience, expression, association, etc.) and to install their associated rights—the very objects of movements across the continent right now—is what shows the limits of the decolonisation trope.

Where this issue is concerned, we do not need any new term to capture the simple reality under reference: *freedom is not a cultural thing; it has no byline; it does not answer to the dictates of geography.* Whether in the Central African Republic or in Hong Kong, in South Korea or in China or Russia—or lately in Belarus, Myanmar and Thailand—when people march for the freedom to be the authors of their own scripts, the freedom to believe or not believe in any faith, the freedom to determine who rules over them and to set limits to that rule, they are one and all channelling the gains of that human inheritance: modernity, *sans differentiation!* To fail to acknowledge, much less engage with, this long history and salute Africa's singers of freedom's song over centuries is simply bad scholarship. It is unacceptable. Let us stop walling away this genealogy and obscuring from our students and fellow scholars significant contributions to political philosophy from the continent. African thinkers deserve to be argued with, not ignored.

AGAINST DECOLONISATION

Black and Modern: Learning from the Caribbean

Let us draw what I am persuaded is an instructive contrast, by travelling to the Caribbean. Few would deny that the postcolonial countries of the Caribbean share a lot in common with African countries, not least of which are their common colonial heritage and the fact that most of them have majority African-descended populations, with the exception of Trinidad and Tobago. And we need make no exception for whether they were colonised by the British, the French, the Spanish or the Dutch. Those differences are of no consequence in the present discussion. As different parts of Africa with different colonial traditions currently work to create republics of free citizens associated with the political discourse of modernity, they are all in agreement on what the goal is: states that are subordinate to their citizens, that respect the person of the individual and all the rights that we are quick to accuse neoliberalism of infringing, that have an independent and impartial judiciary charged with holding everyone equal under the law and arbitrating between the state and the citizen and among the citizenry, and so on.

Of greater significance is that many countries in the Caribbean share state forms with most African countries. We often read of the incompatibility of African conditions and cultures with liberal democracy. In fact, it is standard fare in political science to speak of the disabling elements in African culture that make it impossible for liberal democracy to thrive there. Until the 1990s, messy apologias were always on hand for strongman rule, military rule, one-party rule, misbegotten socialist regimes and numerous other forms of misrule. Then, suddenly—yes, suddenly—in 1991, the people of Bénin removed a military regime from power; and in 1993, the Nigerian people forced a military dictator out of office. His successor, who unleashed a regime of terror on the country, fared no better, with the military being forced out of power again in 1999.

Examples abound. All of these movements, in one form or another, sought to put in place a socio-political order founded on the very modern principle of governance by consent, sovereignty of the subject and the rule of law. Nowhere has anyone, even in the shape of political parties—and the political space is open to all and sundry in those polities—canvassed for the restoration of chiefly rule,[12] even as some people have, in the name of their African tradition and the identity associated with it, called for its inclusion in some form in their governance system. Nor have even our decolonisers campaigned for alternative forms of political ordering that are antagonistic to this. This is the basis for the claim I made in the last chapter that decolonisation$_2$ does a disservice to the need of African people to know at a deep level and engage critically with the underlying philosophical principles of the institutions they are enshrining in their communities, and the forms of life that they enjoin for everyone. This education is being scuttled by our decolonisers without anything of comparable value being substituted. This, to me, is unacceptable. Collapsing Westernisation and modernity into 'Western modernity', and treating the rights and forbearances it brings as harbingers of unspeakable evils or proclaiming the project of contemporary African philosophy a 'critical-negative' one, do nothing to help establish across Africa regimes and modes of social living that respect the inviolate dignity of the lowliest Africans and promote their capacity, and right, to be the authors of their own scripts. I perfectly understand if scholars who are opposed to these options in Africa have no more than excoriation and refusal to engage with the situation that we describe here.

If, indeed, it is the case that modern liberal representative government, for whatever reason, is incompatible with African traditions, as Wiredu argued in the previous chapter, and if one is not suggesting that this has anything to do with geography, then one must ask why the same failures do not come with its use in other jurisdictions populated by similar peoples and with sufficient convergences in their historical experiences, as in the Caribbean. Given that colonialism is the singular pole in the formulation of much of decolonisation discourse, one would expect that the career of the state in the postcolonial histories of the Caribbean would mirror the dismal record of that in African countries. The fact is, that is not the case. I limit myself here to the operations of the state and its associated institutions.

An incident happened in Kingston, Jamaica in 2010 that offers a good illustration of the larger point I am trying to make here. It took place at the residence of the Jamaican reggae star, Luciano. A combined army/police operation was under way to apprehend a suspect wanted for murder and believed to be hiding in Luciano's home. A resident heckled a female police officer on the street. An army sergeant intervened and asked the man to back off. When the heckler would not, the sergeant slapped him. It later turned out that the man had some mental health issues. I watched the whole episode unfold on live television. I recall my shock at the sergeant's behaviour and its utter unacceptability in the context of the modern state. Apparently, the Jamaican authorities, both the executive and the legislature, thought the same of the incident. The matter was on the front page of Jamaica's newspapers, was much commented upon by pundits and was discussed in the Jamaican parliament. The army authorities disciplined the errant non-commissioned officer involved shortly thereafter. In using this example, I am not suggesting that all the ills that we associate with misconduct by state agents and the violation of citizens' rights are either absent or rare in Jamaican society. The comparison is meant to show a distinction between what happens in some jurisdictions when misbehaviour has been established as compared with others. One way to understand the comparison made in this section is to assess the ease or difficulty of escaping with impunity when it comes to the behaviour of state agents and their accountability for their actions in the performance of their duties.

Contrast all this with what routinely occurs across much of Africa when similar situations occur. We have witnessed the world protesting against the tradition of police brutality against Americans of African descent in the United States, more recently triggered by the wanton killing of George Floyd by officers of the Minneapolis Police Department on 25 May 2020. It is also a time dominated by news of the ravages of Covid-19, which has necessitated lockdowns of whole countries and cities across the world since its beginning in 2020. What was remarkable was the number of Africans killed by state agents in Nigeria, Kenya and South Africa in the name of enforcing lockdown rules during this time. I did not see a requisite level of outrage on the part of our lawmakers or any repercussions for the perpetrators of those acts. In Nigeria, as one example, although things are slowly changing when it comes to punishing state violence against citizens, it is still the case that the officer would have to have killed the civilian and, even then, there is no guarantee that he would ever be punished for his action.[13]

The #EndSARS protests that put the Nigerian state, at all levels, on the back foot would change that. In October 2020, after officers of the Special Anti-Robbery Squad (SARS) of the Nigeria Police Force allegedly chased a young man to his death in Warri, Delta State, Nigerian youths who had borne the brunt of the unbridled brutality of the unit had had enough. They launched a series of protests calling for the squad to be disbanded; for offending officers to be brought to book; for victims to be compensated; and, above all, for an end to police brutality. Although the peaceful protests would be taken over by hoodlums and other lumpen types after protesters were attacked, with some killed and others injured, by Nigerian soldiers at the Lekki Toll Gate Plaza on the night of 20 October 2020, there is no doubt that something is afoot on the path to change. But it is the change that is being demanded that is of interest to us here. All the rights that are being demanded—the changes to the operations of law enforcement and criminal-justice administration, as well as the demand for respect by the state and its agents—are quintessentially modern tenets and they are exactly the same demands being made today by young people in the United States, Hong Kong and in China at Tiananmen Square in 1989.

In the specific case of Nigeria, protesters wanted to put a stop to warrantless searches, under which police and other state agents would harvest victims' phone contacts and bank-account details from their phones and extort them by threatening to arraign them for money laundering or for engaging in internet fraud, and so on. For those of us who take seriously modern tenets regarding respect for the dignity of the individual and the exclusion of the state and its agents from infringing upon the body and property of the individual without serious grounds to believe that crimes have been or are being committed, such warrantless interferences with the privacy of the victims should be cause for alarm. This recognition of the individuality of the puny subject and demands for the individual's protection from the all-powerful modern state are the centrepiece of what I have called the second struggle for freedom in Africa. Those who think that this does not matter are welcome to their opinion. But I contend that directing fire at colonialism in this setting is misaimed. Given that there are African thinkers who have made the case for these rights to be actuated in our land beyond their mere enshrining in our constitutions, those who think there is nothing to this owe a duty to good scholarship to make the opposing cases. In other words, Mphahlele's question comes up again: where do those African thinkers who see worth and the possibility of a better life under this new dispensation come in? Away from the decolonisers' 'critical-negative project', I hope that others begin to see the possibility of much more fecund scholarship around these issues.

As ex-British colonies, both Nigeria and Jamaica inherited empirical analogues of the modern state which was implanted in them. This means that the principle that no one should be accuser and judge in her own cause is present in both their politico-juridical systems. This principle was breached when the army sergeant slapped the heckler. That slap represented punishment. It was summary punishment that ran counter to the presuppositions of justice within the system. It meant that the officer had decided that the man had committed a wrong that warranted sanction. This extends to all instances of extra-judicial actions against suspects or anyone alleged to have committed a crime. The only thing the system permits the law enforcers to do is to *allege* wrongdoing and, in argument before a magistrate (an impartial arbiter), to try to establish the suspect's guilt or innocence. The entire purpose of the presumption of innocence is to ensure that no-one is unduly or unjustly punished before their guilt is established by a properly constituted tribunal. Only then is punishment imposed, if guilty is the verdict. This is the involved process that the officer's single slap abridged. Again, this is just an illustration of a principle; it is no endorsement of the operation of the larger law-enforcement system in Jamaica. But this much can be asserted: the principle involved has more purchase in Jamaica than in Nigeria, and the reason for this is stated below.

Again, I am not suggesting that this is the best possible system or that Africans and their intellectuals may not come up with better outfits to ensure respect for human dignity and the protection of the individual from both the state and her fellow citizens. My argument is that this is the model in place, and I am yet to encounter a positive programme of how things would look in the aftermath of decolonisation$_2$, or what decolonising these phenomena might entail. I do not think that even if we could say that these principles came with colonialism, or that they had their genesis in Europe, we should reject them only for that reason. If we keep these political structures, we should operate them with some fidelity to their grounding principles. If we are unable and or unwilling to do so, we should expunge them from our polities.

We must wonder then why there is such a wide divergence between the realisation of the modern state in Nigeria and Jamaica, where respect for the citizens' right not to be summarily punished by the state or its agents is concerned. It surely is not the case that the kind of overreach involved in the incident is limited to Nigeria or Jamaica or other countries of Africa and the Caribbean. Such behaviour occurs everywhere in the world including, say, the United States, the country which some look upon as epitomising the best that the modern state has to offer as regards the protection of civil rights. Indeed, it was the repeated failure to take seriously the universalist precepts of its founding that delayed its entry to full democratic status till the last third of the 20th century, and it is the repeated divergence between those ideals and its unequal treatment of its African-descended citizens that moves it further away from living up to its founding utopian declarations. It is at the base of the Black Lives Matter movement and the global response to it in the aftermath of the killing of George Floyd. In other words, contrary to the affirmations of our decolonisers, we can think about these discrete movements together not on account of race, even if race were a factor in certain situations, but on account of the failure of different states to take seriously and abide by the core tenets of modernity that give them their peculiar hue in the evolution of political systems.

It is noteworthy that our decolonisers—who mostly live in the old colonialist redoubts of Europe and America, or are forever addressing their main audience there—think nothing of encouraging distortions of the history of modern institutions and of the fact that concern on behalf of the puny individual in the modern state is often the biggest protection of the dignity of the poor in many countries around the world.[14] What we need is not to muddy the waters as regards the core principles of modernity, but to shed light on them. And while we seek to transcend the boundaries of modernity to a more humane society, we should not allow the denial or the erosion of the gains that its core tenets have represented historically for common and oppressed humanity. I cannot think of places that need this reminder at the present time more than in Africa, eastern and central Europe and in Asia—particularly, China, Myanmar and the Philippines. And the citizens of Hong Kong, by their protests against the despotic inroads into those rights and privileges, showed us how and why they matter.

It seems as if only intellectuals suffer from a lack of interest in these matters. Ordinary people from the colonial period up until now, even in the bleakest days of military rule, never relented in their commitment to the fundaments of modernity and the demand to have constitutional rule: government with limits and whose operatives serve at the behest of the citizenry. Certainly, for those who wish to congratulate themselves on the United States' 'democraticness', the only warning they need of the dangers of complacency is to look at the erosion of the fundamental human rights of all citizens, especially Black citizens, as a consequence of the ascendancy of the right on the Supreme Court and its slim law-enforcement jurisprudential majority.

Are African operators of institutions that are not too dissimilar to those of Jamaica unaware of the limits on their powers in their own jurisdiction? Or, if they are aware, are they unable to recognise that there is something amiss when that limit is breached? My contention is that only if one is persuaded that Africans do not know or do not care about limits on the power of the state would one make light of both the expectation and the aspiration that the officers of the state would not act in flagrant breach of these limits—that is, with impunity. I argue that even under the worst instances of executive lawlessness, Africans—state agents and ordinary citizens alike—have persisted in seeking to reduce the distance between their aspirations and their momentary reality. The rogue states favoured by some in the literature dare not announce themselves as such and then still expect to remain in power for too long thereafter.

I am, of course, neglecting those who facilely claim that original African societies had the rule of law and checks on the exercise of power.[15] Indeed, the entire purpose of many who warn us away from modernity is to argue that it was a colonial import, and whatever different modes of social living and principles of social ordering it brought were inferior to, or at least no better than, what Africa already had. We have seen some of our most important thinkers shun this approach. On my part, anyone who is willing to argue that societies that historically had monarchs with powers of life and death ascribed to them, where humans were sacrificed, and where children were used to cement friendships and political alliances were rule-of-law societies must show how these practices accord with the principles that I am urging us to take seriously. I do not see the scholars of other societies in Asia, Europe or the Americas that fit the model I just described blithely arguing for the 'democraticness' of their past arrangements.

What we know from the empirical records of the state in much of Africa is that Nigeria is not atypical of the dominant situation on the continent. Neither is Jamaica atypical of what transpires in the Anglophone Caribbean where the operation of the state in the postcolonial period is concerned. Were we to accept the philosophical groundings of the modern state and their diffusion in the ex-colonies of Africa and the Caribbean, one plausible explanation immediately suggests itself. It is the significant differential in the penetration of the philosophical discourse of modernity in Africa and the Caribbean. The evidence is unimpeachable. I question the easy but unilluminating binaries that make it almost impossible for African scholars to take seriously our struggles with and the strides we have made towards redeeming the promise of modernity for our long-oppressed fellow Africans. No, we do not have to think that everything about modernity is fine or that it is the only model that we should consider. What is unacceptable is to continue writing as if empirical evidence makes no difference and as if all that matters or should matter are our fanciful, even if relentless, bromides against modernity, colonial modernity, coloniality... the list goes on. I am often flabbergasted by the refusal to engage with, beyond bland generalities (often couched in indigestible highfalutin jargon), the desperate lifeworlds dominant in African countries and the denial to millions of their basic dignity as humans in these countries—and not all of this is traceable only to the depredations of colonialism.

Many proponents of decolonising often use variants of communalism as a counterpoint to modernity and what they consider its unrelenting commitment to individualism. What I do not see them doing is grappling with the underbelly of our so-called communocratic traditions, or how we square the suffocating demands of communalism with the welfare and dignity of gay, lesbian, transgender and queer Africans, for example, or of young girls suffering from vesicovaginal fistulae as a result of being made to bear children before their bodies are developed enough, and so on. This is without prejudice to the support of other decolonising theorists for the recognition of LGBTQ rights in various jurisdictions across the continent. I am happy and proud to report that some African countries are now following the example of South Africa in extending to LGBTQ people the legal and political recognition of their right to the respect due to their inviolate dignity as persons and to order their lives as they see fit, insofar as they harm no-one or otherwise infringe on the rights of their fellow citizens to the same consideration. In 2019, the High Court of Botswana struck down a law criminalising homosexuality, and in 2020, the parliament of Gabon also altered a similar law. In fact, given that the laws being changed now are part of the colonial legacy in all our countries, one would think that decolonising them would involve the restoration of the humanity and dignity of our LGBTQ brothers and sisters. Unfortunately, homophobia continues to stalk our societies on both sides of the Atlantic Ocean! I am arguing that we do not have to compare our countries with those in the so-called West for us to see where we fall short. Countries with which ours share affinities, and peoples with whom we share histories but have been on different trajectories as regards engagement with modernity, offer us more effective, more illuminating comparisons.

When we do that in the sphere of politics and the state, this is what we find. Outside of a hare-brained attempt by a group of Islamist jihadists, known as Jamaat-al-Muslimeen, in Trinidad and Tobago on 27 July 1990, and the self-destruction enacted by Grenada's revolutionaries on 27 October 1983 (subsequent to their original military take-over of the island on 13 March 1979), no country in the West Indies has experienced a coup d'état. This is remarkable given, for example, Jamaica's history of violent civil wars, called elections, between its two 'tribes': the Jamaica Labour Party (JLP) and the People's National Party (PNP). Few African countries got anywhere close to civil war before 'saviour' soldiers would insert themselves into the political sphere in the name of 'saving' the polity. Despite the considerable progress that the continent has made, we see the recent setbacks of military misadventures in Guinea, Mali, Chad, Sudan and Burkina Faso. In Jamaica's case, that history has never provoked a military intervention or even an attempt at one. That is, the principle of civilian control of the military has never been at issue in Jamaica. Although there are continuing problems with police brutality and gang violence, there has been no coup attempt. And the judicial system has never been called in question. The party system works. The judiciary works. The key to everything is that the Jamaican people—legitimisers of the system according to the principle of governance by consent—take their sovereignty seriously, and are insistent and boisterous in holding their elected representatives to account by tossing out one party and installing another at regular intervals.

The countries of the Caribbean are mostly dominated by African-descended peoples. And this is not in name only. Many of them take their cultural antecedents very seriously. Curiously, I do not know of any serious thinkers there, including decolonisers, who think that so-called traditional modes of governance are an appealing option for remaking their polities. That is, for them, 'African pride' does not include going back to 'consensus democracy' anchored on 'monarchical democracy' or any version of chieftaincy. Most scholars in the Caribbean do not evince any of Wiredu's anxieties regarding the incompatibility of liberal representative democracy for them. Yet, they have not only had to deal with colonialism which, for them, had followed on the heels of slavery perpetrated by the same people who authored the philosophies on the basis of which they fought for and obtained their freedom, and who inspired the institutions which remain the framework for life and thought across the Caribbean. There is an object lesson here for us, Africans, on the limits of pedigree and identitarian arguments.

Why do Black people in the Caribbean, who also are inheritors of 'artificial' countries and state forms, have a better record of running the institutions that also make up the state in postcolonial Africa, the career of which on that continent is generally regarded as an unmitigated failure? This is where the differential penetration of modernity provides us with a better explanation. What would this situation look like were we to decolonise it? Of course, as I pointed out in previous chapters, on Wiredu's account, unless we have reason to believe that the countries concerned and their intellectuals have embraced this outcome uncritically, we can say that they have decolonised the institutions and their associated practices. But I think this is not an insightful response to our challenge. Of course, if we insist, as our decolonisers do, that these institutions, practices and processes are an inherent part of the epistemic, ideological and practical structures of colonialism and/or Western imperialism, there must be some fundamental variation in them, beyond mere critical adoption, to make them acceptable to us. I am suggesting that I fail to find such clear directions in much of the literature.

Regardless of their racial inheritance, African-descended peoples of the Caribbean had a singular socialisation into the politico-philosophical discourse of modernity. This, for me, is the critical difference: there were no policies of indirect rule or association to defeat, as there were in West Africa. Chieftaincy was not present in the Caribbean to push against, nor for colonial authorities to exploit to crush the ambitions of the colonised, independently of colonialist machinations (and most likely despite such), to reorder their societies along modern lines. There were no retrograde ideologists like Frederick Dealtry Lugard to force so-called character education on the colonised. The battle was joined on the grounds of modernity, and colonisers had no hiding place, no place for sociocryonics (see Chapter 3)—the preservation of African customs whether Africans wanted such preservation or not—away from answering those they dominated, who issued their indictments of colonial rule on clearly modern principles.

The paradox that decolonisation actually means a deepening of the rights subverted by colonialism, rather than their abandonment (as I identified earlier), had no place in this setting. Post-independence, countries across the Caribbean set about realising the promise that the colonial state could not deliver; their intellectuals did not permit themselves to think that the core tenets of modernity—the principle of subjectivity, the centrality of Reason and the idea of progress—were a European or Caucasian inheritance. They sought to deepen their commitment to the inviolate dignity of the individual and the equality of all, ideals to which the colonial state could only pay lip service. It was in the name of its principles that they fought slavery. And it was the only philosophical currency they dealt in, post-emancipation.

But they did not merely parrot their masters on this score. On the contrary, they became freedom's philosophers and poets in their own right. Indeed, it was through the exertions of Caribbean poets of freedom, in part, that the discourse of modernity was introduced to West Africa long before formal colonialism became a fact there.[16] Colonial administrators in the Caribbean could not limit the aspirations of those African descendants to only a bastardised culture that they were not permitted to alter or abandon (if they so wished to), as was the case in Africa's colonies under the guise of indirect rule or association and its associated *Code Indigénat*, as the French styled it. There were no indigenous modes of governance—the original peoples of the Caribbean islands were marked out for extermination and those that survived had their culture devastated—that could be exploited to frustrate the ambitions of Caribbean freedom fighters to have modern institutions installed in their societies. It was modern institutions or nothing. West Indians grew up with no idea besides the principle of governance by consent and the unacceptability of unauthorised interference by the state with the person, space or property of the individual who is invested with absolute protection of her human dignity.

And African- and Asian-descended peoples in the Caribbean have, especially post-independence, used their subjectivity to inscribe into their cultural institutions, including their universities, their cultural heritages and promote them as part of their identities. Here think reggae in Jamaica, calypso in Trinidad and Tobago, Orisa in Grenada and Trinidad and Tobago, and Vodun in Haiti—not to mention Lucumí and Erindinlogun in Cuba and Puerto Rico, even though, at various times in the past under the brutal sway and ignorance of colonial rulers, all those practices were criminalised, and their adherents hounded by the authorities. They show that you do not need any new inventions to redeem the promise of modernity while preserving your most important and humane cultural values. Indeed, insofar as the modern principle of subjectivity is concerned, being the author of your own script requires that you live your life from the inside guided by the requirement of freedom of conscience, of association and so on.

Towards a More Hopeful Future

Given the preceding, the challenge to decolonisation is to show what is wrong with this picture and how decolonising might correct it. Maybe there is no unmitigated failure after all when it comes to the operations of political modernity. A better way to look at this is to see the business of installing modern forms of social ordering and social living as works in progress, and this would be as true for Africa as it is for the rest of the world including, crucially, those countries like the United States that are in the grip of premodern backlashes in their politics.[17] For all the prattle about the utter failure of the state in postcolonial Africa, outside of Ethiopia, Guinea-Bissau and Cape Verde, and Sudan, *all* the 'artificial' countries have survived. Nigeria endured a brutal civil war prosecuted by the same state that is all the terrible things scholars talk about, and still managed reconciliation better than the United States did in the aftermath of its own civil war in the 19th century. The Nigerian state, under its admittedly worst ruler, managed to end the first civil war in Liberia in 1997, at the head of the Economic Community of West African States Monitoring Group (ECOMOG) forces. Both Liberia and Sierra Leone are now on the mend after their brutal civil wars.

The total collapse of the state in both cases did not generate any serious calls for some sort of 'African' democracy. On the contrary, both countries are working hard to perfect their adaptations of the modern state structured by liberal representative democracy. This is why I insist on a granular approach, away from the nebulous, often global approaches taken by many in the decolonising literature. The Tanzanian state helped Ugandans to get rid of the murderous rule of Idi Amin in 1979; the Ugandan state, in turn, provided the beach head for the Rwandan Patriotic Front to put an end to the genocide prosecuted by the Hutu-dominated Rwandan state in 1994. And the secessionist struggle in Casamance has not resulted in the collapse of the Senegalese state, nor has it become for that reason a police state; on the contrary, it has made giant strides towards greater democracy. The Ghanaian state, which hit rock bottom in the 1970s, did not dissolve or degenerate into chaos. In fact, despite Wiredu's disquiet, it has instead become a model of political succession by alternate parties over the last 30 years.

Here are a few other examples of progress in Africa towards working the principles of modern governance and creating the accompanying temperament in ruler and ruled to ensure that all forms of extra-constitutional rule never again bother the continent:

(1) Presidential elections were held in Ghana in December 2008. The two leading candidates in the first round had a run-off that was won by the man who until July 2012 was president of Ghana, John Attah Mills. That by itself is no cause for

215

comment. But he won by a slight fraction of 1 per cent of all votes cast. Initially it sounded like the losing candidate was going to ask for a recount or even go to court to contest the outcome. Ultimately, he chose to accept the results: that is, no recount, no challenge, no acrimony. According to him, he and his party have four years to undo the results and he chose to gear up for that next election against the incumbent. Contrast that outcome and the losing candidate's equanimity with the sordid record of Florida in 2000 or Donald J. Trump's continuing refusal, abetted by his Republican Party, to acknowledge that he lost the November 2020 presidential elections by a wide margin to President Joseph Biden. I do not recall Ghana's successful elections attracting much coverage in the American press.

(2) Presidential and parliamentary elections were held in Kenya in December 2007, which led to inter-ethnic violence, rioting and looting in their aftermath. Some of the leaders who were identified as sponsoring the mayhem had indictments brought against them by the International Criminal Court at The Hague. When it happened, news of this unrest was widely reported. Unfortunately, those indictments could not proceed to trial because witnesses refused to testify. But that is not what is of significance to me. In the aftermath, reforms were made to the constitution and the independence of the judiciary was enhanced, making it worth the while of the losers in the elections that followed in 2011 to take their case to court and who, having lost, accepted the outcome and the country remained calm. That is, where people are persuaded that the rules have been followed scrupulously and have affected all parties equally, there would be no reason to take their grievances to the street. This is why an independent judiciary, and the rule of law are a *sine qua non* for a workable modern politico-legal system.

(3) Zambia held presidential and parliamentary elections in September 2011. The incumbent president, Rupiah Banda, was defeated and the ruling party he headed lost control of parliament. Banda promptly relinquished power, saying that 'We just did not reach the voters this time around'. Another point about the Zambian election: the vice-president on the winning ticket was a white Zambian. The last time I checked, no doubts have been raised about his Zambian citizenship. This is not to say that Zambia has not had its share of the latest refuge for scoundrels, birtherism. A former president of the country did question the citizenship of the founding president of Zambia, Kenneth Kaunda. This only goes to show that hatred is an equal-opportunity employer. If you do not see the convergence in the systems that dominate Zambia and the United States, you are unlikely to catch the commentary on human nature that their contrasting outcomes represent. This pattern was repeated in Zambia in the 2021 elections, with the incumbent president yielding office after being trounced by the opposition candidate.

(4) In 2011, the Senegalese went to the polls. The then incumbent president, Abdoulaye Wade, had decided to 'grandfather' himself into an exception from constitutionally mandated two-term limits. He obtained dubious legal cover for this from the Constitutional Court. But he was massively opposed by the Senegalese voters. Against a united opposition and a determined electorate, he limped into the run-off elections which eventually terminated his political career. As usual, the experts on Africa in the United States were sure that Senegal would descend into chaos since, it was held, the incumbent would not quit even if he lost the run-offs. But he did leave, and Senegalese democracy, one of the oldest and most continuous in the continent—originally curated by Senghor—delivered on its promise. Nothing extraordinary

there for those of us who know the history. Again, compare this with the recent experience in the United States.

(5) And then there is Malawi where, in 2020, the judiciary stood up to the executive in annulling presidential elections held in 2019 which it found were riddled with irregularities. In the fresh elections on 22 June 2020, the electorate chose the opposition leader as the new president with absolutely no drama.

The list goes on. What would decolonising involve in these situations? The more I think about it, the more convinced I become that it is either a solution to a non-existent problem or a misdiagnosis of an existing problem. What is becoming clear is that Africans are increasingly confident that the modern political institutions they inherited at independence will work for them as long as everyone is committed to playing by rules agreed to by all parties, the independence of the judiciary is maintained and judges do due diligence in performing their role as impartial arbiters. In Guinea and Côte d'Ivoire, where incumbent presidents engineered constitutional changes to prolong their tenures, their citizens deployed peculiarly modern ideas and practices—legal challenges and, in the Ivoirian case, 'civil disobedience'—to push back against their rulers. Unfortunately, in Guinea, Mali, Sudan and Burkina Faso, opportunist military adventurers have short-circuited the process of popular opposition to unpopular regimes to install themselves as 'saviours' of their polities. It is significant that their neighbours in the Economic Community of West African States have, unlike in the past, imposed punitive sanctions on the regimes in defence of constitutional rule.

Most important, as in other societies, liberal representative democracy in Africa is a self-correcting mechanism, as long as no-one takes power and uses it to make it impossible for them to be removed, as did the Nazis in 1930s Germany and as Trump attempted in the United States in January 2021. The electorate can always correct course at the next election if they discover they made a mistake in the previous one. John Mahama in Ghana and Goodluck Jonathan in Nigeria were both one-term presidents because their respective electorates frustrated their bids for re-election. The same applies to Trump in the United States. Decolonising has nothing to contribute to this discourse, from my experience.

In all African countries, regardless of the challenges faced by the state in them, people go along with the craft associated with all state forms. They get married under state auspices, they ask that the state treat them with respect, they cooperate with law-enforcement authorities, they protest when they think that the state has failed in discharging its primary responsibilities and they demand that the state deliver to them the promise of independence. In jurisprudence, for example, there are robust debates about varying the elements of the modern legal systems in different countries to suit local needs, even as other elements of the debate turn on the meaning and relevance of diverse jurisprudential principles ranging from legal positivism, the place of the *grundnorm* in constitutional adjudication, the importance of Miranda rights and the presumption of innocence. And we are finding that concern for the dignity and independence of the legal subject in modern law has enabled more and more women to obtain just outcomes in divorces, both in terms of marital property and child custody, as well as criminalising or, at least, delegitimising child marriages in our various cultures.

For us to make sense of the resilience of the state in postcolonial Africa and come up with real research designed to improve our understanding, rather than titillate our prurient desires or feed the imperious arrogance of racism towards Africa and Africans, we need to make sense of the state, *simpliciter*. We need carefully to monitor the nodes of possible transformation in order thereby to realise what gains have been made and safeguard them, while we work to bridge the gap between the current reality and the philosophical idea of the state bequeathed by modernity. The embrace of rules, adherence to the principle of meritocracy in allocating public offices and the rule of law under-pinned by the independence of the judiciary are institutions and practices that need to be brought into closer alignment with their founding philosophical ideas. It remains unclear to me what the decolonisation trope contributes to the elucidation of these issues or their attainment in real life.

In this chapter, I have argued that it is insightful to process current events across Africa and events throughout the post-independence period as attempts—sometimes deliberate, other times inchoate—on the part of Africans, rulers and ruled, to undo the pre-emptions that colonialism enacted as regards the transition to modernity. That is, in the area of politics and implanting principles of social ordering dedicated to securing for the lowliest Africans the promise of independence, African coun-tries are striving to create modern polities, in the same way that several other countries across the globe are. African countries are not different from others in recent history which, guided by their divergent historical experiences and cultural specificities, are fighting to create and install empirical analogues of an ideal type: the modern state. In this struggle, the principles we appeal to (for example, human rights), the benchmarks we deploy to assess how far along our polities have come, the limits that we demand our rulers observe in their rule and that our fellow citizens rec-ognise in our interactions—almost without exception—all hear-ken back to those principles traceable to the philosophical dis-course of modernity.

We call for our governance to be legitimised by our consent, for our governors to be subordinate to and bound by the same laws that they enact for the rest of us, for the power of the state to be curbed by the rule of law, for a government of law and not of humans, and for recognition of the inviolate dignity of every person. These demands are not peculiar to Africans and they were all in play while colonialism lasted, even as colonial authorities thought their subjects were unworthy of their observance. Africans share similar struggles with other regions of the world, as I have argued throughout this book.

If the preceding is correct, it means that the more education we have in the philosophical underpinnings of the institutions, practices and processes that dominate our social and political lives, the greater the likelihood that we will infuse our leaders and their followers with the appropriate temperaments required to achieve the maximal outcomes for all concerned. In directing attention away from this engagement, decolonising discourse does palpable and long-lasting damage. Contrary to this, I insist that we need to get back to philosophy. I have seeded the discussion in this book with thinkers that remain unknown to many in and out of the decolonising industry, and who have engaged with and sought to adapt the principles and practices of modern governance to their different societies and times.

I do not ask us to embrace these thinkers because they are right. I ask us to challenge them because that is the only way we expand the boundaries of discourse in our neck of the global woods, away from the constricting, almost sclerotic offerings of our decolonisers. Simultaneously, because I have already made my case for why Africa must be modern in a separate work, I do not make the case for engaging with the political and philosophical discourse of modernity on the grounds of personal preference or that it furnishes the best of which humanity is capable. No, I am arguing that other countries that have chosen to be modern in our time have exited the 'misery corner' of the globe that they used to share with us. Now, they have become givers of alms to Africa. And Africans are happy to stretch out our arms to them while fulminating against the same principles whose adoption enabled them to overtake us.

At a time when Africa is in the thick of the second struggle for freedom, philosophy must lead the charge. I see no place for the decolonising trope in this daunting but exciting challenge. I rest my case.

NOTES

PREFACE

1. Táíwò, 2019b.
2. Appadurai, 2021.

INTRODUCTION

1. Táíwò, 2019b.
2. For a similar caution, see Sekyi-Otu, 2019.
3. Ibid., pp. 14–15.
4. See Waterman, 1990, Chapter 3.
5. Chinweizu et al., 1984.
6. Dominique-René de Lerma, commentary included in the album notes. *Black Composers Series*, vol. 7, stereo album M 33433, Columbia Masterworks, 1975.
7. I am deliberately making things easy for our decolonisers. I am sure that, thanks to his politics, many would think that Fela Anikulapo-Kuti might not be a candidate for decolonising. I have news for them. Fela's music came out of the same place that his older compatriot came from: European classical conservatory education.
8. Sekyi-Otu, 2019, p. 15.
9. Omojola, 1995, p. 40.
10. Ibid., pp. 43–4.
11. Táíwò, 2015, pp. 60–3.
12. Omojola, 1995, p. 45.
13. Kimbanguism is the name given to the social and religious movement

led by Simon Kimbangu (1887–1951). His Church was one of the earliest examples of what later became known as 'African-Instituted Churches', the founding of which was provoked by the racism of both secular and religious authorities in colonial Africa. As Aurélien Mokoko Gampiot puts it: 'An African-initiated church born in the 1920s from the preaching and healing campaign conducted by Simon Kimbangu, a Congolese Baptist catechist, in reaction to the colonial situation in the Belgian Congo, Kimbanguism has cultivated a theology of Black liberation by offering a unique understanding of the Bible'. (Gampiot, 2017, p. 1.)

14. Táíwò, 2010a.
15. For full elaboration see ibid., Chapter 1.
16. See Conklin, 1997 and Macamo (ed.), 2005.
17. See Adéèkó and Adésòkàn (eds), 2017.

1. WHAT, AFTER ALL, IS DECOLONISATION?

1. For details, see Táíwò, 2010a, Chapter 1, entitled 'Colonialism: A Philosophical Profile'.
2. Fanon, 2004, p. 3.
3. Fanon, 2008, pp. xvi, 206.
4. Fanon, 2004, p. 2.
5. Sekyi-Otu, 1996, p. 17.
6. Táíwò, 2018a, 2018b.
7. See, for instance, Ndlovu-Gatsheni, 2013.
8. Cabral, 1980, p. 130.
9. Nkrumah, 1965, p. 239.
10. Awolowo, 1973, p. 358. I would recommend that people read the entire address because it states in one place many of Awolowo's reflections on and analyses of the failure of African countries and their leaders to deliver on the promise of independence.
11. 'We may continue and indeed we will be right to continue to use the power and influence which sovereignty confers, as well as the tactics and manoeuvres which international diplomacy legitimizes, to extract more and more alms from our benefactors. But the inherent evil remains—and it remains with us and with no one else: unless a beggar

shakes off and irrevocably turns his back on, his begging habit, he will forever remain a beggar for, the more he begs the more he develops the beggar characteristics of lack of initiative, courage, drive and self-reliance'. (Awolowo, 1981, p. 30.)

12. Anyone who thinks that the success of decolonisation is to be judged by whether it leads to human emancipation either has no understanding of the very limited nature of decolonisation, wherever in the world it has taken place, or is merely engaging in unhelpful hyperbole.

13. Fanon, 2004, p. 237.

14. Nkrumah, 1957, p. 164.

15. Wiredu, 1980, p. 1.

16. It is important to be clear which colonialism we are dealing with here. We must make a distinction between Latin America and North America and Africa. This is not a distinction without a difference. Under the aegis of modern colonialism, Latin American and North American colonies were overseas provinces of the metropole. What this means is that the anti-colonial struggles in them were intra-family affairs between the *mestizo* descendants of the Spanish and Portuguese conquerors in much of Central and South America, the colonisers in Haiti who, it needs be remarked, wanted no part of the independence that the insurrectionary enslaved people sought, and the European descendants in North America and their respective mother countries. No doubt, the lineaments of the anti-colonial struggles in those places differ qualitatively from the exploitation-driven colonisation that dominated in Africa, outside of the settler colonies of North, East and southern Africa. The place of the First Nations of the Western hemisphere is in a very significant sense different from the concerns of those dominated by the family fights between the European-descended rulers of those territories in situ and in Europe. I am not sure, for example, outside of appropriating phrases from local languages, how many of the 'decolonial' thinkers in our day have facility in the native languages or the culture that they embody. But that is not our focus in this work.

17. What happens with the colonial legacy in the sphere of politics and the relationship of this to the contemporary political fortunes of the ex-colonies is one of the biggest blind spots in the decolonisation lit-

erature. More is made of this in Chapter 4. I leave out here incidences of internal colonialism within former European-dominated colonies. This is also without prejudice to the fact that post-independence, citizens of the erstwhile colonies might find themselves chafing under the burden of rule by governments to which they have not consented. The difference is that in this case the source of illegitimacy is not extraneous to the polity concerned.

18. Again, we need to specify the diverse economic models under colonialism. India was a hybrid model that combined economic exploitation with some economic building, especially in the area of industrial production and railway construction. Agriculture was developed in the Caribbean but here, again, once emancipation happened, ex-enslaved persons there nested in the citizenship of the mother countries and they demanded recognition from the metropolitan administrations. In Africa, it was an exploitation and extraction regime par excellence. The Portuguese and the French at the beginning toyed with the idea of designating their territories as overseas provinces and extending citizenship to their inhabitants. The practice did not last. New designations were invented and the colonised were neither citizens of the metropole nor were they citizens of their erstwhile polities. We see the contrast in boldest relief in South Africa and former Southern and Northern Rhodesia, where settlers were citizens and prosperous economies were built on the backs of native Africans to serve them and the metropole. This was especially so in South Africa, the only really industrial economy on the continent.

19. Nyerere, 1961, p. 33.

20. This is a mistake that is rampant in the decolonisation literature. For further details, see Ashar, 2015 and Ndlovu-Gatsheni, 2013. I shall be flagging this throughout this book.

21. One of them, Sabelo J. Ndlovu-Gatsheni, asserts that I wrote *Africa Must Be Modern* (Táíwò, 2012) because I am 'enchanted with Euromodernity'. He claims: 'Even today, those who are enchanted with Euromodernity continue to push the colonial struggle of completing the "unfinished project of modernity" as a guarantor of human freedom and human flourishing .... This is why one finds such leading

African philosophers as Olufemi Taiwo writing books like *Africa Must Be Modern: A Manifesto* ... in which he posits that "modernity is life," and its key tenet is "the open future"....' (Ndlovu-Gatsheni, 2020, pp. 3–4). It was Walter Kaufmann who once accused Sir Karl R. Popper of deploying what Kaufmann called 'quilt quotations' formed by connecting disparate parts of an author's work to make them say what the critic then slams as their position. Ndlovu-Gatsheni, too, has used quilted quotations from my book to accuse me of saying things I never said. I have a simple answer for him on his main charge. I plead guilty as charged. But, here is the rub. Had our respective home countries and their intellectuals and leaders been enchanted with the same modernity, we would not have to be plying our wares in Babylon, as the Rastafarians might put it. Additionally, I cannot think of a better place to be disenchanted with European modernity than in the bosom of Richard Wagner. But I have refrained from substantive discussion of Ndlovu-Gatsheni's work because he is the foremost disciple of decoloniality in Africa and decoloniality is not my concern in this book.

22. Since I've already made the case for this elsewhere, I am going to take it for granted here. As far as I know, none of our leading decolonisers has shown that the thesis of the book is wrong or even problematic.

23. See Amin, 1973; Phillips, 1989; Rodney, 1972; and Kay, 1976.

24. See Césaire, 2000; Fanon, 2004; and Patterson, 2018.

25. I cannot emphasise this point enough. A recurring theme that informs the case made in this book against decolonisation$_2$ is its singular failure to take seriously the agency of the colonised. It is as if the only colonised the decolonisers are interested in are those who are implacably opposed to anything and everything that has even a marginal element of the colonial in it. This is not a helpful tack to take when part of what we are interested in is the complexity of human choice-making.

26. For a similar view, see Wiredu, 1996, p. 83.

27. See, for further details, Cabral, 2018; Mills, 2015, pp. 1–24; and Mbembe, 2016.

28. Mbembe, 2016, pp. 30–1.

29. See Bewaji, 2015, p. 14.

30. An example is Edwin Etieyibo, for whom decolonisation means 'the

act or practice of ridding the curriculum or an educational system of unworthy (colonial) influences that have some negative and unwelcome bearing on the autochthonous values or ideals of the people of the former colony'. This does not entail the total rejection of 'everything foreign or colonial', only those 'unworthy'. (Etieyibo, 2018, p. 13.) This is why I say that when all is said and done, it is not clear what a decolonised curriculum would look like. The discourse does not often offer a clear direction. See also Matolino, 2020, for another critical take on the idea of decolonisation. He differs from me in his willingness to work with the conflation of decolonisation and decoloniality.

31. A reviewer of this manuscript took issue with this particular criticism. Yes, I agree with the reviewer that 'journals, as institutions of disciplinary practice, belong to a *shared community of practitioners*. What if I want to claim and appropriate this intellectual space as my own? Surely that's also another option'. I do not see anything with which to disagree. What I fail to see is why any particular journal must be the only locus of this intellectual space. My point is that African scholars should take seriously the business of re-establishing the old spaces that their forebears used to own or charter new ones and set the parameters of disciplinary practice in their domain; after all, it is their very narrative that is at stake. Meanwhile, this reaction does not answer my question: are Africans ever responsible for anything that happens in their world? I refuse to believe that anything in our world is inevitable.

32. Mbembe, 2016, p. 36, paraphrasing Ngũgĩ wa Thiong'o.

33. Mills, 2015, p. 8.

34. Branch, 2018, p. 85. I have already done this in my own work on religion, where I have asked that we dispense with the idea of 'African traditional religion' (Táíwò, 2008); the idea of 'the postcolonial state', (Táíwò, 2017); and African political philosophy as a mere instantiation of the genre of 'political philosophy' (Táíwò, 2004a). For philosophy, I made the case for diversifying the philosophy curriculum before the decolonising craze arrived on the scene in 1993. Meanwhile, I would like to draw a distinction between a scholar like Branch asking us to pay attention to what is being done on the continent and another like Raewyn Connell, who calls for 'Decolonizing Sociology' in the following terms: 'correcting the distortions and exclusions pro-

duced by empire and global inequality and reshaping the discipline in a democratic direction on a world scale'. Not only this but she also, in a substantive manner, actually remedies the distortions and exclusions by engaging thinkers like Paulin J. Hountondji and Akínsọlá Akìwọwọ and arguing with them in her own work. See Connell, 2007, 2018.

35. The idea is usually attributed to the medieval English Franciscan friar William of Ockham.

36. Táíwò, 2018a, 2018b.

37. Richards, 2014; Connell, 2018; Uzomah, 2018; Msila (ed.), 2017; Dhawan (ed.), 2014; Tamale, 2020; and Khader, 2019, respectively. See also Jane-Johnstone, 2015; Fayemi and Macaulay-Adeyelure, 2016; Cabral, 2018; Creary (ed.), 2012.

38. Soyinka, 1982.

39. It reminds me of a similar consequence of Thomas Kuhn's introduction of the word 'paradigm' in Kuhn, 1996 (first published in 1962), and how it became a catch-all term that everyone thought they understood only because no-one sat down to probe into its promiscuous deployment, until someone did present a taxonomy derived from the many usages the author gathered from diverse writings. See Masterman, 1970. I am afraid that decolonisation has become like that. I have refrained from cluttering this chapter with instances of these muddles; they are readily available in the literature.

40. Fanon, 2004, Chapter 3.

41. Cabral, 2016, p. 123. See also Táíwò, 2013.

42. Cabral, 2016, p. 84.

43. Fanon, 2004, p. 10.

44. Cabral, 1980, p. 253.

2. DECOLONISATION AND THE POLITICS OF LANGUAGE: AN OVERSOLD PROMISE?

1. Reprinted from *Ousmane Sembeme*. Copyright © 1993 by Five Colleges Inc. Published by the University of Massachusetts Press.

2. See Jeyifo, 2018.

3. Ngũgĩ, 1986, p. 2.

4. Ibid.

5. If you have any doubt that Africans quickly wised up to the possibilities

of this new mode of social living, consider why Lugard had to set the hands of the clock back when it came to the operation of the modern legal system in one jurisdiction, Nigeria. See Adewoye, 1977.

6. Ngũgĩ, 1986, p. 3

7. Ibid.

8. Zeyad El Nabolsy has reminded me, and he thinks it is somehow ironic for Ngũgĩ's case, of Kwame Anthony Appiah's (1992, pp. 50–1) argument in his essay, 'Topologies of Nativism', that the insistence on identifying humans in terms of a national literature carried out in a national language has Herderian antecedents in the late 18th century. Pointing out that Ngũgĩ's discourse shares some assumptions with Herder's project does not diminish his argument. But it does put on him and his supporters the onus of answering some of the strictures that have been placed on the earlier incarnation of this case.

9. Ngũgĩ, 1986, p. 4

10. Ibid., p. 13.

11. Ibid., p. 11.

12. Ibid., p. 4.

13. We can see the continuing impact of this formulation in the writings of various thinkers, such as Bewaji, 2002; Berrington X. S. Ntombela, '"The Double-Edged Sword": African Languages Under Siege', in Msila (ed.), 2017, pp. 161–79; Murungi, 2018; and Mbembe, 2021, although he seems to be dialling down the decolonising meter in this work. But, given that this is a translation of a work originally published in French in 2010, and there is no indication that this represents a rethinking of some of the muddles that we highlighted in the previous chapter, there is no reason to think that there is any revision of the commitment to decolonising.

14. And, of course, it does not seem to bother Ngũgĩ and his fellow decolonisers if neither the English nor the French recognise our production as properly fitting within their identity schemes.

15. Ngũgĩ, 1986, p. 16.

16. Cabral, 2016, pp. 162–3. Emphasis original.

17. Ibid., p. 135.

18. Ibid., pp. 134–5.

19. This is a reality the acknowledgment of which is almost a sign of conceding truth to racism, as far as decolonisers are concerned. Yet, it only takes a keen historical sense to acknowledge that all human societies have developed through stages that are almost synonymous with the evolution of our species itself: remember there was a time when, across the world, we thought that the truth could be bled out of our veins!

20. Cabral, 2016, p. 136.

21. Another important African thinker, Biodun Jeyifo (2018), has also rejoined Ngũgĩ's argument. He also took issue with the idea that how a language such as English came to us makes it impossible for it ever to become or be considered an African language.

22. Ngũgĩ, 1986, p. 3.

23. Bown (ed.), 1973.

24. The Korean example is instructive in this respect. Korea also got its start in modernity through Christian evangelisation.

25. The intellectual productions of Africans from those times represent another fecund source for African philosophy and intellectual history that decolonising renders illegible to scholars. An example is to be found in Adéẹ̀kọ (ed.), 2017.

26. Mphahlele, 'What Price Negritude?', in *The African Image* (London: Faber, 1962), quoted from Bown (ed.), 1973, p. 39.

27. Ibid., p. 39.

28. Ibid.

29. Ibid., pp. 39–40.

30. Ibid., p. 40. My emphasis.

31. Ibid.

32. Ibid, pp. 40–1.

33. Ibid.

34. Appiah, 2006.

35. McConnell, 2013.

36. See Diagne, 2011; Jones, 2010; Thiam, 2014; and Wilder, 2015.

37. Wiredu, 1995, p. 22. My emphasis.

38. Wiredu, 2006, p. 291.

39. Ibid.

40. Wiredu, 1995, p. 22.

41. Wiredu, 2006, p. 291.
42. Personal communication.
43. Wiredu, 1995, p. 23.
44. Ibid.
45. Ibid.
46. Ibid., p. 24.
47. Ibid.
48. Wiredu, 1996, Part IV; Sindima, 1990, pp. 190–209; Kenneth Kaunda, 'The Future of Nationalism,' in Mutiso and Rohio (eds), 1974, p. 468; Julius Nyerere, 'Democracy and the Party System,' *Freedom and Unity/ Uhuru na Umoja*, excerpted in Mutiso and Rohio (eds), 1974, p. 478.
49. Wiredu, 1995, p. 23. My emphasis.
50. Wiredu, 1996, p. 5.
51. Wiredu, 1995, p. 24.
52. On this score, Appiah was simply wrong when he averred that 'Literature, by and large, in sub-Saharan Africa means europhone literature (except in the Swahili culture area, where Swahili and the colonial languages are active together). And what matters in its being europhone is more than its inscription in the languages of the colonizers'. (Appiah, 1992, p. 55.)
53. Bamgbose, 2000, pp. 20–1. Notes omitted.
54. Wiredu, 1996, seems to acknowledge this. 'In Africa we will need to adopt countless new words and symbolic devices in using our languages to domesticate the sciences', p. 85.
55. Bamgbose, 2000, pp. 66–7.
56. Bamgbose (ed.), 1992, p. v.
57. Awóbùlúyì (ed.), 1990.
58. I am glad to find out after I had completed the draft of this work that in a review of the first metalanguage volume cited above, Adéléke Adéèkó had anticipated some of the points that I make here, especially the limits of what I now name equivalence-ism, and the absence of what I call here a discursive tradition that would facilitate cross-, inter-, multi-disciplinary conversations within the context of intellectual work framed by Yorùbá and its motley phenomena. See Adéèkó, 1992. Incidentally, domain-specific dictionaries have been produced over time. See Odétáyò, 1993.

59. See Adéẹ̀kọ́, 1992, p. 199. The quote from Ọlábìyí Yái, at p. 200, is quite apposite (the interventions in square brackets are Adéẹ̀kọ́'s):

As Ọlábìyí Yái has said, we cannot engage in "indigenization" policies [ok?] until we have made certain that the language of investigation is the true focus of our attention. Disturbed by the translation of "oral literature" as "*lítíréṣọ̀ àtẹnudẹnu*" (the mouth-to-mouth literature), Yái says, "a kàn túmọ̀ 'oral literature' sí Yorùbá ni; a kò wo ilé kí a tó sọ ọmọ lórúkọ: ojú, àwọ̀, òórùn, gbogbo nnkan tó n mù tàbí dúró sinsin tí í se èròjà eré ni a ti fi '*àtẹnudẹnu' gbọ̀n dànù*'" [we simplistically turn "oral literature" into Yoruba; we do not look into the house before we name the child: looks, complexion, the smell, all the things that are submerged or apparent that well make up the play environment, we shove into oblivion with "from-mouth-to-mouth"]. This is so because, Yái says, Yorùbá scholars, like most African oral literature critics, have failed to perceive that theoretical engagements are intricately woven into the philosophy of knowledge: "a kò lè dábàá tíọ̀rì *lítíréṣọ̀* tó péye tí a kò bá ní imọ̀ fílọ́sọ́fì imọ̀ Yorùbá tí àwon gẹ̀ẹ̀sì ń pè ní 'epistemology' tàbí 'gnoseology'" [we cannot advance profitable literary theories if we do not understand the Yoruba concept of knowledge, the one called epistemology or gnoseology in English].

60. Akiwọwọ, 1983, 1986, 1988, 1990, 1999; Adéoyè, 1979, 1985; Awoniyi, 1975; Abíọ́dún, 2014; Òjó, 1982; Bamgbose, 1990.

61. I invite scholars, within their respective cultural registers, to join issues with Dismas Masolo in his interpretation of the concept of 'Jok' in Luo; Kwasi Wiredu on the concept of truth in Akan; Alexis Kagame on the concept of 'Ntu' in Kinyarwanda; Moses Makinde on the concept of 'Ori' in Yorùbá; Barry Hallen and John Olubi Sodipo on the twin concepts of 'Mọ̀' and 'Gbàgbọ́' in Yorùbá and Akínṣọlá Akiwọwọ on the concept of 'Àṣùwàdà'. We should have full-blown debates and contestations concerning where they belong in their original languages, what is the limit of their purchase in knowledge production in their respective cultures, how they fare in comparison with other occurrences in other areas of discourse in the same and so on. I need not remind us that none of these examples was written in the original language. I

cite them because they are the ones with which I am familiar where the authors have more than just superficially deployed them as equivalents in discourses that are wholly conducted in English and French. As far as I know, only Akìwọwọ tried to write on the core idea of 'Àṣùwàda' in Yorùbá. Incidentally, they never construed their work in terms of decolonising. They just wanted to do their disciplinary chores and through them share with the world the theoretical insights to be found in their heritages. I do not know a single decoloniser in the same context who has risen to the level attained by these significant thinkers. There is a lesson there.

62. The first doctoral dissertations written entirely in Yorùbá were defended in 1991: S. Adebajo, 1991; A. Akinyemi, 1991. See Isola, 1992, p. 21.

63. See Adéjùmọ̀, 'Ìpò Wo Lobìnrin Wà Nínú Ìtàn Àròṣọ Fágúnwà?', in Adéèkọ́ and Adéṣọ̀kàn (eds), 2017.

64. Adéjùmọ̀, 2001, p. xi.

65. Church Missionary Society Bookshop, 2015, p. 161. Just a note on the complexity of our local languages and our not really engaging with them. Because Yorùbá is a tonal language, it becomes crucial what tones a word carries when we try to establish its many meanings. There may be a problem with the tones supplied in the present case 'aròfò' whereas I think the correct word is 'àròfò'. On this, see the entry in Delano, 1958. This is something to take up with fellow scholars of the language, another indication of why it is important to generate a discursive tradition rather than staying satisfied with equivalence-ism in the name of decolonising.

66. Church Missionary Society Bookshop, 2015, p. 74.

67. Delano, 1958, p. 69.

68. Abraham, 1958, p. 174.

69. Why would a book written in Yorùbá, for an audience of people already working in Yorùbá, need an English concept for part of its elucidation? Why not do a conceptual analysis of èfè, taking care to differentiate it from its kin in Yorùbá theory and practice, and justifying the preference for the adopted meaning—all within a Yorùbá context or discursive tradition?

70. I have guest-edited a special issue of the *Journal of Contemporary African Studies* devoted to a symposium on his works. See Táíwò (ed.), 2021b.

71. Táíwò, 2004b.
72. Ngũgĩ, 1986, p. xi.
73. Ngũgĩ, 1993.
74. Ofeimun, 2012, p. 37.
75. Bamgbose, 2000, p. 46.
76. Ibid., p. 50.
77. Ibid., p. 50.
78. Ibid., p. 51. See especially 'Table 4: Typology of African Language Use in Education', p. 53, for those examples.
79. Ibid., p. 97.
80. Ibid.
81. Ibid., p. 99.
82. Jeyifo, 2018, p. 135. Jeyifo uses a denial of this thesis as the basis for affirming, unapologetically, that English is already an African language even as he celebrates, as do I, Ngũgĩ's sterling contributions to scholarship and the struggle for liberation.
83. See Oyèláràn, 1988; Adewole, 1987.
84. Soyinka, 1983; Adéoyè, 1971.
85. Unlike the editors of the *Oxford English Dictionary* who have no difficulty incorporating new words into the language deriving from, e.g., Yorùbá, the most recent example being in 2019. 'Absolute autochthony' makes it almost impossible to accommodate new words of foreign extraction into our autochthonous languages.
86. A fact well known, theorised and celebrated in Senghor, 1971, but ignored by his detractors.
87. Diagne, 2004, p. 67.
88. Ngũgĩ, 1986, pp. 18–19. For a recent iteration of the same criticism, see Serequeberhan, 'Decolonization and the Practice of Philosophy', in Creary (ed.), 2012, pp. 137–59.
89. Ngũgĩ, 1986, p. 27 and 2016, pp. 50–5. There are some problematic assumptions and identifications in this passage. 'African languages' are synonymous with 'the languages of the African peasantry and working class'. How are we to understand this?
90. I have chosen to take a narrow view of Ngũgĩ's characterisation of 'African language'. This needs be pointed out because when he distinguished between the stooges of imperialism in the 'African neo-colo-

nial bourgeoisie' and the infantry of the 'resistance tradition', I assume that he was not suggesting that the 'patriotic students, intellectuals (academic and non-academic), soldiers and other progressive elements of the petty middle class' only write in 'African languages', or that the fact that they are motivated by resistance, rather than collaboration, is the Africanising element of their language. If protest articulated in English automatically becomes African, then the debate we are having will be completely otiose. By the same token, it cannot be their linguistic choice, per se, that makes their position un-African, but their obsequious stance towards imperialism. This is not a plausible position to take. But that is beyond the ken of this discussion.

91. This probably explains why they never seem interested in what African theorists and proponents of modernity have to say regarding politics and society informed by the philosophical anthropology that undergirds modernity. And when they do, their purview is almost always limited to their 'usual suspects' made up of Fanon; Cabral; Césaire; and, occasionally, Paulin J. Hountondji—and those, never in their embrace of modernity.

92. See Dako, 2019, pp. 230–3.

93. Africans are not alone in this. The Russian Court adopted French as the language of sophistication in the late 18th and early 19th centuries.

94. A fact recently acknowledged and memorialised by the inclusion of so many Nigerian words and usages, around half of them Yorùbá, in the *Oxford English Dictionary*.

95. There lies the reason why Indian scholars end up as leading lights of modernity and African scholars are distancing themselves from the creative legacy of domesticating the same and are dissipating their energies looking for alternatives in 'their own African languages', in which most of them lack basic proficiency, not to mention fluency, to undertake recondite thinking. Worse still, they sometimes think they are decolonising by counterposing Gianni Vattimo to Georg Hegel and substituting Deleuze for Voltaire while execrating the sterling contributions of a Senghor!

96. This last idea came out of a conversation I once had with a colleague who was always hung up on demarcating between philosophy and

pseudo-philosophy. One day, I asked him if he would consider Max Weber a philosopher. After some hemming and hawing, he conceded that Weber is. Then I quickly mentioned another German thinker in the Weberian mould, Niklas Luhmann. Without skipping a beat, my colleague retorted: 'That one is not a philosopher'. Then I made him the offer that I just stated: 'you take the label and I'll take the ideas'.

3. DECOLONISING PHILOSOPHY OR EMBRACING NATIVISM/ ATAVISM? ON THE LIMITS OF PEDIGREE ARGUMENTS

1. Reprinted from Ousmane Sembeme. Copyright © 1993 by Five Colleges Inc. Published by the University of Massachusetts Press.
2. Ibid.
3. I am grateful to Sekyi-Otu (2019, Chapter 3) for taking on this travesty and injecting some sanity into the discussion.
4. Sekyi-Otu, 2019, p. 165.
5. Senghor, 1964, p. 82. Cited in Serequeberhan, in Creary (ed.), 2012, p. 143. My emphasis. There are convergences between Senghor and Cabral on this point concerning privileging the agency of the colonised when it comes to determining what parts of a foreign, including colonial, civilisation to incorporate into their own. (Cabral, 2016, pp. 115–16, 137.) This undermines the repeated attempts in the literature to make it appear as if there is a gulf of difference between thinkers like Senghor and Cabral.
6. Serequeberhan, in Creary (ed.), 2012, p. 143.
7. Ibid., 2012, pp. 142–3.
8. Incidentally, as someone who knows the works of both Senghor and Serequeberhan, I can confidently assert that only one of them is 'grounded in an indigenous history or tradition' and that one definitely is not Serequeberhan, my friend and contemporary!
9. Soyinka, 1999, Chapter 2.
10. Serequeberhan, in Creary (ed.), 2012, p. 145.
11. Bewaji, 2016, p. 50.
12. Serequeberhan, in Creary (ed.), 2012, p. 146.
13. Ibid., p. 147.
14. Although I do not address it in this chapter, the elevation of colonialism to a whole philosophical framework in the discourse of decoloni-

ality is the primary reason I find it unattractive, even disturbing. But I always wonder whether I have a solid understanding of the discourse. What I do know is that there is a distinction between decolonisation and the idea of decoloniality, even though many African scholars—in yet another unfortunate example of our ever jumping on bandwagons—now seem to think either that the two are the same or that they seamlessly connect with each other. I do not see much illumination coming from that conflation. Hence, my decision to not engage it. See Appadurai, 2021.

15. See, in general, Ogundiran, 2012; Ochonu, 2014; and Shelton, 1971.
16. Ajayi, 2000, pp. 165–74.
17. Ibid., p. 165.
18. Ibid., p. 166.
19. Ibid., p. 167. My emphasis.
20. Ibid., p. 167.
21. Ibid., p. 168.
22. Ibid., p. 169. In a recent book that one can only hope our decolonisers read, Hermann L. Bennett made a related point concerning the error of typing the entire relationship between Europe and Africa from early times only in terms of the trans-Atlantic slave trade and the New World slavery it spawned. For those who might think that the sovereignty that Ajayi remarked that African societies lost was something to trifle with, Bennett reminds his readers that prior to the changes that were brought about by the slave trade, Europe and Africa related with one another in terms of mutual recognition of sovereignties, a lot of those relations brokered by the dominance of the Catholic Church which, until the 15th century, was the source of legitimacy for princely power in the Iberian Peninsula—the immediate focus of his work—and points beyond. He explains:

> *African Kings and Black Slaves* delineates how and under what circumstances Catholic dogma, institutions, and law mattered in the European encounter with Africans. This history magnifies a field of politics engendering early modern sovereignty that culminated in a taxonomy of African difference, which in turn rendered the inhabitants of some polities into slaves. Even before the systemization of the slave trade and slavery—which only two centuries later

came to be exclusively linked with people of African descent—we see how Christianity mediated encounters with pagan polities resulting in different outcomes. To say as much calls into question the telos that has long served to absorb the African-European encounter and its immediate history into the story of New World slavery, thereby overlooking the part that Africa and Africans played in the evolution of Iberian sovereignty and imperial expansion before 1492. Though familiar with the Portuguese and Spanish encounters with Africans, scholars rarely reflect on the earliest sequence of events involving Iberians interacting with African polities and how that history might trouble the existing narratives of the West and its emergence [Footnote omitted]. Instead, the emphasis has been on the inauguration of the slave trade and slavery and assigning economic prominence to those institutions in the unfolding histories of the Americas. (Bennett, 2019, p. 5.)

Unfortunately, the dominant timeline in decolonisation discourse does not even extend to the period of the slave trade that Bennett says does not suffice to account for the complexity and complexion of the relationship between Europe and Africa in earlier times. I thank Professor Timothy B. Vasko for bringing this text to my attention.

23. Ajayi, 2000, pp. 170–1.
24. Osaghae, 1991, p. 26.
25. Ibid., p. 25.
26. Ibid., p. 27.
27. See Phillips, 1989; Kay, 1976; Amin, 1973; Rodney, 1972; and Cabral, 1980.
28. Osaghae, 1991, p. 32.
29. Ibid., p. 31.
30. Ibid., p. 34.
31. For the greater period of the slave trade on the West African coast, most slaving forts enjoyed what we now recognise as extra-territoriality, but were subject to the overall authority of the local sovereigns. Only in the late 18th and early 19th centuries did colonial ambitions begin to blossom and become veritable sources of conflict between Europeans and their African hosts. If Osaghae was right, why were African states exchanging envoys with European potentates through-

out the period under reference? Historical accuracy should never be allowed to be trumped by apologies for explanatory models of dubious value. In that respect here is a cautionary tale on the play of African agency that the eagerness to bathe everything in colonialism's ether tends to overlook:

Here I am watching live on AriseTV the coronation of the 21st Olu of Warri. The comperes are both Itsekiri but the entire ceremony is being held in English. The Warri Royal Choir of the Palace of Olu of Warri has been performing songs and hymns accompanied by the Laz Ekwueme Orchestra, all armed with string and wind instruments. The orchestra itself is the brainchild of and is sponsored by a classical-music composer and former professor of music who is now the Eze of his local municipality in Anambra State, Nigeria, Lazarus Ekwueme. I detect no hint of anxiety in all the situations just described. If we were to decolonise this situation, what would it look like? And even if we could, why ought we? What is missing that would be added by such a move? Unfortunately, our decolonisers are disconnected from these granular manifestations of African agency because the audience they are interested in is not the audience that embraces or acquiesces to the practices I just tracked. And if we think that there is anything wrong with this picture, only if we trace its cause to colonialism and insist that colonialism explains their persistence can we reasonably call for the decolonisation. Now the choir, at the request of one of the comperes, is performing 'All Hail the King' in, as he called it, '[o]ur native dialect'. Another just called it 'Itsekiri language'. Meanwhile a top hat is part of the royal regalia, as is the case with most royalty in the Niger delta territory of Nigeria. Now is the turn of 'Praise to the Lord'.

For those of us who know our history and take it seriously, nothing here is amiss. A kingdom that was founded in 1480 is of a clearly modern provenance in the context of world history and Africa's place in it. It is also a kingdom that, we are told by one of the comperes, had one of its early monarchs, the 6th, going to a school in Angola run by the Portuguese who, in turn sent a prince to go and study in Portugal and obtain a degree from the University of Coimbra between 1600 and 1611. How do we pretend to tell the full story of this kingdom without these accretions? Why do we insist on reporting as if these early exchanges were between a subordinate Itsekiri and superordinate European others when we know that Itsekiri did not become subordinated till late in the 19th century? There are many things one can quarrel with in the description I just offered. But I am not even in a position to capture the complexities in this situation. This is the kind of attention to detail that decolonising analysts fail to do. If some of what is presented here is plausible, Itsekiri do not need decolonisers to make them global; they already crossed that bridge before colonisation became their portion. If there are values here, they are not to be newly announced to the world; an attentive world not dominated by prejudice or tending to mischief-making is already aware of them or can discover them if it is so inclined. Decolonising of the second kind is utterly irrelevant. The crown has a cross symbol on it, to boot!

Here is the moral of this story. When you witness pageantry akin to the coronation of the Itsekiri king, inflected with Christian and other alien, especially European, content, the prudent scholar should not be too quick to decide that such is a manifestation on the part of the Itsekiri, elite and commoner alike, of a failure to decolonise their practices. Such a rush to judgement assumes implausibly, I am convinced, and maybe even wrongly, that those practices could not have come into the culture except by colonial imposition. Even if that were the case—and I insist that it is not in the present case—it is something to be established by research, not assumed almost as self-evident or as unproblematic, or even incontrovertible. This must be done in each case and the practice of lumping together cultural areas and traditions pertaining to them, as if Africa is more homogeneous than other continents, should be jettisoned. What we witnessed today can and should not be reduced to the impact of colonial rule in Itsekiri that lasted for less than a hundred years compared with the long history of the Itsekiri that they date, thanks to the Gregorian calendar, to 1480. (Note to self on 5 October 2021). See the account in Kenny, 1983.

32. See, generally, Asiwaju, 2001.
33. Táíwò, 2010a, Chapter 2.
34. Zeyad El Nabolsy, in personal communication, has reminded me that

some might consider this an inapt analogy. There is debate in Spain concerning the place of Islamic colonisation in the history of Spain. For right-wing historians and philosophers, the expulsion of Muslims from Spain in 1492, referred to as *Reconquista* in Spanish historiography, should be emphasised and, as much as possible, Islamic rule should be treated as an aberration that is not worthy of being made into an important pole in the history of the country. Others, however, beg to differ, preferring instead to emphasise the lasting impact on al-Andalus, as it is called, and on the evolution of Spanish history and culture. I dare anyone to point to a similar debate in African—notice the continental referent—history concerning what role to assign to colonialism in its evolution. For the most part, our intellectuals are content to use colonialism as the singular, or at least the most significant, pole for plotting African history. For a good summary of the debate in Spanish history, see García-Sanjuán, 2018, pp. 127–45.

35. Macamo, 'Denying Modernity: The Regulation of Native Labour in Colonial Mozambique and Its Postcolonial Aftermath', in Macamo (ed.), 2005, pp. 68–9.

36. I presented similar views to the current one at a seminar where the most strenuous objection to my account was from an African scholar who was so attached to this periodisation regime that it was not until I asked him to give me titles with the prevalence of 'precolonial' in scholarship on Asia as a single unit of analysis that he somewhat relented. He conceded that he could only recall titles referencing 'precolonial India' and I am sure even that is not a standard manner of articulating periodisation in Indian historiography.

37. Decolonisers just need to become better students of African history to cure themselves of this error. Those of us who study that history know better.

38. Soyinka, 1975, issues a similar caution in his now much-analysed 'Author's Note' in the frontispiece:

> The bane of themes of this genre is that they are no sooner employed creatively than they acquire the facile tag of "clash of cultures," a prejudicial label, which, quite apart from its frequent misapplication, presupposes a potential equality *in every given situation*

of the alien culture and the indigenous, on the actual soil of the latter. ... I find it necessary to caution the would-be producer of this play against a sadly familiar reductionist tendency, and to direct his vision instead to the far more difficult and risky task of eliciting the play's threnodic essence. ... The Colonial Factor is an incident, a catalytic incident merely. ... The confrontation in the play is largely metaphysical.

39. Wiredu, 1995, p. 24.
40. Nwakeze, 1987, p. 105.
41. See Crummell, 1862.
42. 'Problem moderns' refers to the canonical thinkers of modern Euro-American philosophy, e.g., David Hume, Immanuel Kant and G. W. F. Hegel, 'whose legacy continues to raise questions concerning their sincerity and the role that race and racism played in their philosophical formulations. Problem moderns are problematic for how they distorted modernity even as they were principal framers or interpreters of its discourse'. (Táíwò, 2018b, p. 198.) For a full discussion of the problem moderns, see Táíwò, 2018a.
43. Wiredu, 1995, p. 30. As pointed out in note 47 to Chapter 2, above, Kenneth Kaunda and Julius Nyerere pioneered this line of argumentation against multiparty democracy inspired by liberalism in African political thought.
44. Again, there was nothing unusual in their approaches. Similar movements for social transformation motivated by an openness to modernity were taking place in Egypt and Japan during the same period. See Hamed, 1990; and Abu-Lughod, 1963. I would like to thank Zeyad El Nabolsy, my research assistant and graduate student, for bringing both publications to my notice and procuring Hamed's for me.
45. See 'Appendix C, Constitution of the New Fantee Confederacy', in Sarbah, 1968, p. 327.
46. For a discussion of the Fanti and the Egba cases, see Táíwò, 2010a, Chapter 6.
47. See, in addition, Táíwò, 2010b, 2004a, 2017; and Coller, 2015.
48. Three compendious collections come to mind here: Mutiso and Rohio (eds), 1974; Langley (ed.), 1979; and Otite (ed.), 1978.

49. Nkrumah, 1963, p. 66.

50. Awolowo, 1960, p. 255.

51. He cited Fortes and Evans-Pritchard (eds), 1940; and Busia, 1951.

52. Other defenders of consensus democracy include Edward Wamala, 'Government by Consensus: An Analysis of a Traditional Form of Democracy'; Joe Teffo, 'Democracy, Kingship, and Consensus: A South African Perspective', both in Wiredu (ed.), 2004, pp. 435–42, 443–9.

53. For illustration, see Offor, 2006, pp. 265–77; Salami, 2006, pp. 67–78; Bewaji, 2016; Otubanjo, 'Themes in African Traditional Political Thought' and Osaghae, 'The Passage from the Past to the Present in African Political Thought: The Question of Relevance', both in Ayoade and Agbaje (eds.), 1989, pp. 3–17, 53–75; Uroh, 'The Indigenous Igbo Political Philosophy and the Quest for Political Legitimacy', in Vaughan (ed.), 2004, pp. 271–99; Agulanna and Osimiri, 'African Worldview and the Question of Democratic Substance', in Ukpokolo (ed.), 2017, pp. 333–49; Kayange, 2018.

54. See Táíwò, 2019a.

55. Irele, 1992, p. 222.

56. Nkrumah, 1961, p. 159.

57. Solanke, 1931, pp. 18–19.

58. See Abu-Lughod, 1963; and El-Ariss (ed.), 2018.

59. Cabral, 1980, p. 57.

60. Awolowo, 1960, 1968; Irele, 1992; Hountondji, 2002; and Sekyi-Otu, 2019.

61. Irele, 1992, p. 222. For a North African exemplar, see Wahba, 2022.

62. Gardiner, 1966; Mernissi, 2009; An-Na'im, 1990, 2008; Ibrahim, 2004.

63. Mandela, 'Address to Court Before Sentence', in Langley (ed.), 1979, pp. 667–8.

64. Senghor, 1998; Soyinka, 1999. For a recent intervention, see Ilesanmi, 2020.

4. DECOLONISE THIS! TAKING HISTORY AND AGENCY SERIOUSLY

1. Reprinted from Ousmane Sembeme. Copyright © 1993 by Five Colleges Inc. Published by the University of Massachusetts Press.

2. In many Igbo and some Yorùbá communities, there are so-called 'age grades': cohorts of individuals of the same age group organised for the purposes of community and individual improvement, and membership of which is not voluntary. You are born into your age grade and the relevant society expects you to perform your role in it as your community decrees. In some of them, refusing membership attracts sanctions that effectively render you a non-entity in the society concerned.

3. See Bewaji, 2015; and Ndlovu-Gatsheni, 2020.

4. For a full discussion of this see, Grovogui, 2006, especially Chapters 3, 4 and 5.

5. Táíwò, 2011.

6. Awolowo, 1960, p. 255.

7. I have adapted the last three paragraphs from Táíwò, 2011.

8. See Connor, 1973.

9. I am surprised that decolonisers who are otherwise preoccupied with the legacy of colonialism do not turn their minds to this and ask, as one of the tasks of decolonisation, that future boundaries reflect the atavistic cultural boundaries of their decolonised imagination.

10. For a discussion of the contrast between 'racialising' and 'historicising' modernity, see Táíwò, 2018b.

11. See Táíwò, 2010b.

12. I have argued for the essential incompatibility between liberal representative democracy and chieftaincy in a different work. See Táíwò, 2021a.

13. Of course, there are exceptions. The point here is that one does not routinely witness the same level of outrage at the denigration of the humanity of ordinary folk in many of our countries. See Táíwò, 2016, for a commentary on a Nigerian parliamentarian slapped by another parliamentarian, with nothing ever happening to the slapper. Another case is making its way through the courts of a Nigerian senator caught on video physically assaulting a shop assistant in Abuja, the federal capital. Nothing has so far happened to him. Finally, for a more scholarly treatment, see Táíwò, 2006.

14. Back in the eighties of the last century, when I started thinking about these issues relating to law and Marxism, the late scholar E. P. Thompson

245

was excoriated for calling the rule of law 'an unqualified human good'. Now we have Africans talking about the rule of law in polities dominated by absolute monarchies that wielded powers and applied laws from the binding of which they were exempted.

15. Bewaji, 2015.

16. See James, 2012. The careers of Sylvestre Mathurin Williams, Alexander Crummell, Edward Wilmot Blyden and Martin R. Delany, all pioneer pan-Africanist thinkers and activists, are instructive in this respect.

17. I have called attention to this in my Introduction to the North American edition of Táíwò, 2014, where I warned against complacency on the part of those who take their modern life for granted and are not mindful of the challenges posed by those seized with pre-modern sensibilities.

BIBLIOGRAPHY

Abíọ́dún, Rowland (2014) *Yorùbá Art and Language: Seeking the African in African Art*. Cambridge: Cambridge University Press.

Abraham, Roy C. (1958) *Dictionary of Modern Yorùbá*. London: University of London Press.

Abu-Lughod, Ibrahim (1963) *The Arab Rediscovery of Europe: A Study in Cultural Encounters*. Princeton, NJ: Princeton University Press.

Adebajo, S. (1991) 'Àwọn Onkọwe Yorùbá Isaaju' [Earliest Yorùbá Writers]. Doctoral Dissertation, Department of African Languages and Literatures, Obafemi Awolowo University, Ile-Ife.

Adéẹ̀kọ́, Adélékè (1992) '"The Language of Head-Calling": A Review Essay on Yoruba Metalanguage: Èdè Ìperí Yorùbá', *Research in African Literatures*, vol. 23, no. 1: 197–201.

———— (ed.) (2017) *Philip Quaque's Letters to London, 1765–1811*. Pretoria: UNISA Press.

———— and Akin Adéṣọ̀kàn (eds) (2017) *Celebrating D.O. Fágúnwà: Aspects of African and World Literary History*. Ibadan: Bookcraft.

Adéjùmọ̀, Àrìnpé (2001) *Ìṣẹ̀fẹ̀ Nínú Àwọn Eré-Onítàn Yorùbá*. Cape Town: Centre for Advanced Studies of African Society (CASAS).

Adéoyè, C. L. (1971) *Ẹ̀dá Ọmọ Oòd'uà*. 2nd ed. Ibadan: Oxford University Press.

———— (1979) *Àṣà àti Ìṣe Yorùbá*. Ibadan: University Press.

———— (1985) *Ìgbàgbọ́ àti Ẹ̀sìn Yorùbá*. Ibadan: Evans.

Adewole, L. A. (1987) *The Yoruba Language: Published Works and Doctoral*

BIBLIOGRAPHY

Dissertations, 1843–1986, African Linguistic Bibliographies 3, Eds. Franz Rottland and Rainer Vossen. Hamburg: Helmut Buske Verlag.

Adewoye, Omoniyi (1977) *The Judicial System in Southern Nigeria, 1854–1954*. Atlantic Highlands, NJ: Humanities Press.

Ajayi, J. F. Ade (2000) 'Colonialism: An Episode in African History', in Toyin Falola (ed.), *Tradition and Change in Africa: The Essays of J.F. Ade Ajayi*. Trenton, NJ: Africa World Press.

Akinyemi, A. (1991) 'Ìlò Oríkì Ní Àwùjọ Ìlú Ọyọ́' [The Uses of Oríkì in Ọyọ́ Community]. Doctoral Dissertation, Department of African Languages and Literatures, Obafemi Awolowo University, Ile-Ife.

Akiwọwọ, Akínṣọlá (1983) *Ajobi and Ajogbe: Variations on the Theme of Sociation*. Ile-Ife: University of Ife Press.

———— (1986) 'Àṣùwàdà Èniyàn', *IFÈ: Annals of the Institute of Cultural Studies*, no. 1: 113–23.

———— (1988) 'Universalism and Indigenisation in Sociological Theory: Introduction', *International Sociology*, vol. 3, no. 2: 155–60.

———— (1990) 'Contributions to the Sociology of Knowledge from an African Oral Poetry'. Reprinted in Martin Albrow and Elizabeth King (eds), *Globalization, Knowledge and Society*. London: Sage Publications.

———— (1999) 'Indigenous Sociologies: Extending the Scope of the Argument', *International Sociology*, vol. 14, no. 2: 115–38.

Amin, Samir (1973) *Neocolonialism in West Africa*. London: Penguin.

An-Na'im, Abdullahi Ahmed (1990) *Toward an Islamic Reformation: Civil Liberties, Human Rights and International Law*. Syracuse, NY: Syracuse University Press.

———— (2008) *Islam and the Secular State: Negotiating the Future of Sharia*. Cambridge, MA: Harvard University Press.

Appadurai, Arjun (2021) 'Beyond Domination: The Future and Past of Decolonization', *The Nation*, 9 March.

Appiah, Kwame Anthony (1992) *In My Father's House*. New York: Oxford University Press.

———— (2006) 'The Case for Contamination', *The New York Times Magazine*, 1 January.

Ashar, Meera (2015) 'Decolonizing What? Categories, Concepts and the Enduring "Not Yet"', *Cultural Dynamics*, vol. 27, no. 2: 253–65.

BIBLIOGRAPHY

Asiwaju, A. I. (2001) *West African Transformations: Comparative Impacts of French and British Colonialism*. Lagos: Malthouse Press.

Awóbùlúyì, Oládélé (ed.) (1990) *Yorùbá Metalanguage (Èdè-Ìperí Yorùbá)*. Vol. 2. Ibadan: University Press.

Awolowo, Obafemi (1960) *AWO: The Autobiography of Chief Obafemi Awolowo*. Cambridge: Cambridge University Press.

———— (1968) *The People's Republic*. Ibadan: Oxford University Press.

———— (1973) 'Address at the University of Ibadan Alumni Association Dinner Party, 17 November 1973', in Tekena Tamuno (ed.), *Ibadan Voices*. Ibadan: University of Ibadan Press.

———— (1981) *The Voice of Courage: Selected Speeches of Obafemi Awolowo*, ed. Olaiya Fagbamigbe. Vol. 1. Akure: Fagbamigbe Publishers.

Awoniyi, Timothy A. (1975) 'Ọmọlúwàbí: The Fundamental Basis of Yorùbá Education', in Wande Abimbola (ed.), *Oral Tradition*. Ile-Ife: Dept. of African Languages and Literatures.

Ayoade, John A. A. and Adigun A. B. Agbaje (eds) (1989) *African Traditional Political Thought and Institutions*. Lagos: Centre for Black and African Arts and Civilization.

Bamgbose, Ayo (1990) *Fonoloji àti gírámà Yorùbá*. Ibadan: Ibadan University Press.

———— (ed.) (1992) *Yorùbá Metalanguage (Èdè-Ìperí Yorùbá)*. Vol. 1. Ibadan: University Press.

———— (2000) *Language and Exclusion: The Consequences of Language Policies in Africa*. Hamburg: Lit Verlag.

Bennett, Herman L. (2019) *African Kings and Black Slaves*. Philadelphia: University of Pennsylvania Press.

Bewaji, John Ayotunde Isola (2002) 'African Languages and Critical Discourse', in Olusegun Oladipo (ed.), *The Third Way in African Philosophy: Essays in Honour of Kwasi Wiredu*. Ibadan: Hope Publications.

———— (2015) 'Liberation Humanities for Africa and the Diaspora: An Inaugural Professorial Lecture', Faculty of the Humanities and Education, University of the West Indies, Mona, Kingston, Jamaica.

———— (2016) *The Rule of Law and Governance in Indigenous Yoruba Society: a Study in African Philosophy of Law*. Lanham, MD: Lexington Books.

BIBLIOGRAPHY

Bown, Lalage (ed.) (1973) *Two Centuries of African English: A Survey and Anthology of Non-Fictional English Prose by African Writers since 1769.* London: Heinemann.

Branch, Adam (2018) 'Decolonizing the African Studies Centre', *Cambridge Journal of Anthropology*, vol. 36, no. 2.

Busia, K. A (1951) *The Position of the Chief in the Modern Political System of Ashanti.* London: Frank Cass.

Cabral, Amílcar (1980) *Unity and Struggle.* Trans. by Michael Wolfers. London: Heinemann.

———— (2016) *Resistance and Decolonization.* Trans. by Dan Wood. London: Rowman & Littlefield.

———— (2018) 'Canon Fire: Decolonizing the Curriculum', a special issue of the *Cambridge Journal of Anthropology*, vol. 36, issue 2: Autumn.

Césaire, Aimé (2000) *Discourse on Colonialism.* Trans. by Joan Pinkham. New York: Monthly Review Press.

Chinweizu, Ihechukwu Madubuike and Onwuchekwa Jemie (1984) *Toward the Decolonization of African Literature.* Enugu: Fourth Dimension Publishers.

Church Missionary Society Bookshop (2015) *A Dictionary of the Yorùbá Language.* Ibadan: University Press.

Coller, Ian (2015) 'African Liberalism in the Age of Empire? Hassuna D'Ghies and Liberal Constitutionalism in North Africa, 1822–1835', *Modern Intellectual History*, vol. 12, no. 3: 529–53.

Conklin, Alice L. (1997) *A Mission to Civilize: The Republican Idea of Empire in France and West Africa, 1895–1930.* Stanford, CA: Stanford University Press.

Connell, Raewyn (2007) *Southern Theory: The Global Dynamics of Knowledge in Social Science.* Malden, MA: Polity Press.

———— (2018) 'Decolonizing Sociology', *Contemporary Sociology*, vol. 47, no. 4: 399–407.

Connor, Walker (1973) 'The Politics of Ethnonationalism', *Journal of International Affairs*, vol. 27, no. 1.

Creary, Nicholas M. (ed.) (2012) *African Intellectuals and Decolonization.* Athens: Ohio University Press.

Crummell, Alexander (1862) *The Future of Africa! Being Addresses, Sermons, etc., etc. Delivered in the Republic of Liberia.* New York: Charles Scribner.

BIBLIOGRAPHY

Dako, Kari (2019) 'About the English Language in Ghana Today and about Ghanaian English and Language in Ghana', in Helen Yitah and Helen Lauer (eds), *Philosophical Foundations of the African Humanities through Postcolonial Perspectives*. Leiden: Brill Rodopi.

Delano, Isaac O. (1958) *Àtúmọ̀ Èdè Yorùbá*. Oxford: Oxford University Press.

Dhawan, Nikita (ed.) (2014) *Decolonizing Enlightenment: Transnational Justice, Human Rights and Democracy in a Postcolonial World*. Opladen: Barbara Budrich Publishers.

Diagne, Souleymane Bachir (2004) 'Precolonial African Philosophy in Arabic', in Kwasi Wiredu (ed.), *A Companion to African Philosophy*. Malden, MA: Blackwell.

——— (2011) *African Art as Philosophy: Senghor, Bergson, and the Idea of Negritude*. Calcutta, London and New York: Seagull Books.

El-Ariss, Tarek (ed.) (2018) *The Arab Renaissance: A Bilingual Anthology*. New York: Modern Language Association of America.

Etieyibo, Edwin (2018) 'Afri-decolonisation, Decolonisation, Africanisation and the Task of Africanising the Philosophy Curriculum', in Edwin Etieyibo (ed.), *Decolonisation, Africanisation and the Philosophy Curriculum*. London: Routledge.

Fanon, Frantz (2004) *The Wretched of the Earth*. Trans. by Richard Philcox. New York: Grove Press.

——— (2008) *Black Skin, White Masks*. Trans. by Richard Philcox. New York: Grove Press.

Fayemi, Ademola Kazeem and O. C. Macaulay-Adeyelure (2016) 'Decolonizing Bioethics in Africa', *Bioethics Online*, vol. 3, no. 4: 68–90.

Fortes, M. and E. E. Evans-Pritchard (eds) (1940) *African Political Systems*. Oxford: Oxford University Press.

Gampiot, Aurélien Mokoko (2017) *Kimbanguism: An African Understanding of the Bible*. Trans. by Cécile Coquet-Mokoko. Philadelphia: Pennsylvania State University Press.

García-Sanjuán, Alejandro (2018) 'Rejecting al-Andalus, exalting Reconquista: historical memory in contemporary Spain', *Journal of Medieval Iberian Studies*, vol. 10, no. 1.

Gardiner, Robert (1966) *A World of Peoples: the Reith Lectures, 1965*. London: British Broadcasting Corporation.

BIBLIOGRAPHY

Grovogui, Siba N. (2006) *Beyond Eurocentrism and Anarchy: Memories of International Order and Institutions*. New York: Palgrave.

Hamed, Raouf Abbas (1990) *The Japanese and Egyptian Enlightenment: A Comparative Study of Fukuzawa Yukichi and Rif'ā'ah al-Tahtāwī*, Studia Culturae Islamicae 41. Tokyo: Institute for the Study of Languages and Cultures of Asia and Africa.

Hountondji, Paulin (2002) *The Struggle for Meaning: Reflections on Philosophy, Culture, and Democracy in Africa*. Trans. by John Conteh-Morgan. Athens: Ohio University Center for International Studies.

Ibrahim, Saad Eddin (2004) 'An Open Door', *Wilson Quarterly*, vol. 28, no. 2: 36–46.

Ilesanmi, Simeon (2020) 'Political Atrocities, Moral Indignation, and Forgiveness in African Religious Ethics', *Religions*, vol. 11, no. 620.

Irele, Abiola (1992) 'In Praise of Alienation', in V. Y. Mudimbe (ed.), *The Surreptitious Speech*. Chicago, IL: University of Chicago Press.

Isola, Akinwunmi (1992) 'The African Writer's Tongue', *Research in African Literatures*, vol. 23, no. 1.

James, C. L. R. (2012) *The Pan-African Revolt*. Oakland, CA: PM Press.

Jane-Johnstone, Megan (2015) 'Decolonizing Nursing Ethics', *Nursing and Health Policy Perspectives*, vol. 62, no. 2: 141–2.

Jeyifo, Biodun (2018) 'English is an African language—Ka Dupe! (for and against Ngũgĩ)', *Journal of African Cultural Studies*, vol. 30, no. 2: 133–47.

Jones, Donna V. (2010) *The Racial Discourse of Life Philosophy: Negritude, Vitalism, and Modernity*. New York: Columbia University Press.

Kay, Geoffrey (1976) *Development and Underdevelopment: A Marxist Analysis*. London: Macmillan.

Kayange, Grivas M. (2018) 'African Traditional Deliberative and Agonistic Democracy: A Maravi Perspective', *Utafiti*, vol. 13, no. 2: 23–44.

Kenny, Joseph (1983) *The Catholic Church in Tropical Africa, 1445–1850*. Ibadan: University of Ibadan Press.

Khader, Serene J. (2019) *Decolonizing Universalism: A Transnational Feminist Ethic*. Oxford: Oxford University Press.

Kuhn, Thomas (1996 [1962]) *The Structure of Scientific Revolutions*, 3rd ed. Chicago, IL: University of Chicago Press.

BIBLIOGRAPHY

Langley, J. Ayodele (ed.) (1979) *Ideologies of Liberation in Black Africa, 1856–1970*. London: Rex Collings.

Macamo, Elísio Salvado (ed.) (2005) *Negotiating Modernity: Africa's Ambivalent Experience*. Dakar: CODESRIA.

Masterman, Margaret (1970) 'The Nature of a Paradigm', in Imre Lakatos and Alan Musgrave (eds), *Criticism and the Growth of Knowledge*. Cambridge: Cambridge University Press.

Matolino, Bernard (2020) 'Whither Epistemic Decolonization', *Philosophical Papers*, vol. 49, no. 2: 213–31.

Mbembe, Achille (2016) 'Decolonizing the University: New Directions', *Arts and Humanities in Higher Education*, vol. 15, no. 1: 29–45.

―――― (2021) *Out of the Dark Night: Essays on Decolonization*. New York: Columbia University Press.

McConnell, Justine (2013) *Black Odysseys: The Homeric Odyssey in the African Diaspora Since 1939*. Oxford: Oxford University Press.

Mernissi, Fatima (2009) *Islam and Democracy: The Fear of the Modern West*. Trans. by Mary Jo Lakeland. New York: Basic Books.

Mills, Charles (2015) 'Decolonizing Western Political Philosophy', *New Political Science*, vol. 37, no. 1: 1–24.

Msila, Vuyisile (ed.) (2017) *Decolonising Knowledge for Africa's Renewal: Examining African Perspectives and Philosophies*. Bryanston: Kr Publishing.

Murungi, John (2018) *African Philosophical Currents*. London and New York: Routledge.

Mutiso, Gideon-Cyrus M. and S. W. Rohio (eds) (1974) *Readings in African Political Thought*. London: Heinemann.

Ndlovu-Gatsheni, Sabelo J. (2013) *Coloniality of Power in Postcolonial Africa: Myths of Decolonization*. Dakar: CODESRIA.

―――― (2020) *Decolonization, Development and Knowledge in Africa: Turning Over a New Leaf*. London and New York: Routledge.

Ngũgĩ wa Thiong'o (1986) *Decolonising the Mind: The Politics of Language in African Literature*. Nairobi: East African Educational Publishers.

―――― (1993) *Moving the Centre: The Struggle for Cultural Freedoms*. London: James Currey; Nairobi: EAPH; Portsmouth, NH: Heinemann.

―――― (2016) *Secure the Base: Making Africa Visible in the Globe*. London: Seagull Books.

BIBLIOGRAPHY

Nkrumah, Kwame (1957) *Ghana: The Autobiography of Kwame Nkrumah*. New York: International Publishers.

—— (1961) *Selected Speeches of Kwame Nkrumah*. Compiled by Samuel Obeng. Accra: Afram Publications.

—— (1963) *Africa Must Unite*. New York: Praeger.

—— (1965) *Neo-Colonialism: The Last Stage of Imperialism*. London: Panaf.

Nwakeze, P. C. (1987) 'A Critique of Olufemi Taiwo's Criticism of "Legal Positivism and African Legal Tradition"', *International Philosophical Quarterly*, vol. XXVII, no. 1, issue no. 105.

Nyerere, Julius (1961) 'The African and Democracy', in James Duffy and Robert A. Manners (eds), *Africa Speaks*. Princeton, NJ: D. Van Nostrand.

Ochonu, Moses E. (2014) *Colonialism by Proxy: Hausa Imperial Agents and Middle Belt Consciousness in Nigeria*. Bloomington: Indiana University Press.

Ọdẹ́táyọ̀, J. A. (1993) *Ìwé Ìtumọ̀ Ọ̀rọ̀ Ìmọ̀ Ẹ̀dá-Àrígbéwọ̀n: Yorùbá Dictionary of Engineering Physics*. Lagos: n.p.

Ofeimun, Odia (2012) *A House of Many Mansions*. Lagos: Hornbill Press.

Offor, Francis (2006) 'The Quest for Good Governance in Africa: What Form of Democracy is Most Suitable?', *Journal of Social, Political and Economic Studies*, vol. 31, no. 3: pp. 265–77.

Ogundiran, Akinwumi (2012) 'The Formation of an Oyo Imperial Colony during the Atlantic Age', in J. Cameron Monroe and Akinwumi Ogundiran (eds), *Power and Landscape in Atlantic West Africa*. Cambridge: Cambridge University Press.

Òjó, Afolábí (1982) 'Ìwà Ọmọlúàbí', in Olúdáre Ọlájubù (ed.), *Ìwé Àṣà Ìbílẹ̀ Yorùbá*, 2nd ed. Ikeja: Longman.

Olátúndé Olátúnjí, *Ìdàgbàsókè Ẹ̀kọ́ Ìmọ̀ Ìjìnlẹ̀ Yorùbá*, J. F. Odunjo Memorial Lecture Series. Ori Kinni. Lagos: J. F. Odunjo Memorial Lectures Organising Committee.

Omojola, Bode (1995) *Nigerian Art Music*. Ibadan: IFRA.

Osaghae, Eghosa (1991) 'Colonialism and African Political Thought', *Ufahamu: a Journal of African Studies*, vol. 19, nos 2 & 3.

Otite, Onigu (1978) *Themes in African Social and Political Thought*. Enugu: Fourth Dimension Publishers.

BIBLIOGRAPHY

Oyèláràn, Olásópe (1988) 'Ìdàgbàsókè Ẹ̀kọ́ Ìmọ̀ Ìjìnlẹ̀ Yorùbá Láti Ìbẹ̀rẹ̀ Pẹ̀pẹ̀', in Olátúndé O. Olátúnjí, *Ìdàgbàsókè Ẹ̀kọ́ Ìmọ̀ Ìjìnlẹ̀ Yorùbá*, J. F. Odunjo Memorial Lecture Series. Lagos: J. F. Odunjo Memorial Lectures Organising Committee.

Patterson, Orlando (2018) *Slavery and Social Death: A Comparative Study*, 2nd ed. Cambridge, MA: Harvard University Press.

Phillips, Anne (1989) *The Enigma of Colonialism: British Policy in West Africa*. London and Bloomington: James Currey and Indiana University Press.

Richards, Patricia (2014) 'Decolonizing Globalization Studies', *The Global South*, vol. 82, no. 2: 139–54.

Rodney, Walter (1972) *How Europe Underdeveloped Africa*. London: Bogle L'Ouverture.

Salami, Yunusa Kehinde (2006) 'The Democratic Structure of Yoruba Political-Cultural Heritage', *Journal of Pan African Studies*, vol. 1, no. 6: 67–78.

Sarbah, John Mensah (1968) *Fanti National Constitution*, 2nd ed., intro. by Hollis R. Lynch. London: Frank Cass & Co.

Sekyi-Otu, Ato (1996) *Fanon's Dialectic of Experience*. Cambridge, MA: Harvard University Press.

———— (2019) *Left Universalism, Africacentric Essays*. New York: Routledge.

Senghor, Léopold Sédar (1964) *On African Socialism*. Trans. by Mercer Cook. New York: Praeger.

———— (1971) *The Foundations of 'Africanité' or 'Négritude' and 'Arabité'*. Trans. by Mercer Cook. Paris: Présence Africaine.

———— (1998) 'Prayer for Peace', in *The Collected Poetry*. Trans. by Melville Dixon. Charlottesville: University of Virginia Press.

Shelton, Austin J. (1971) *The Igbo-Igala Borderland: Religion and Social Control in Indigenous African Colonialism*. Albany: State University of New York Press.

Sindima, Harvey (1990) 'Liberalism and African Culture', *Journal of Black Studies*, vol. 21, no. 2.

Solanke, Ladipo (1931) *Yoruba Problems and How to Solve Them*. Ibadan: n.p.

BIBLIOGRAPHY

Soyinka, Wole (1975) *Death and the King's Horseman*. London: Methuen.

———— (1982) *The Critic and Society: Barthes, Leftocracy and Other Mythologies*, Inaugural Lecture Series 49. Ile-Ife: University of Ife Press.

———— (1983) *The Forest of a Thousand Daemons*, being a translation of D. O. Fagunwa, *Ògbójú Ọdẹ Nínú Igbó Irúnmalẹ̀*, rev. ed. Surrey: Nelson.

———— (1999) *The Burden of Memory and the Muse of Forgiveness*. New York: Oxford University Press.

Táíwò, Olúfẹ́mi (1993) 'On Diversifying the Philosophy Curriculum', *Teaching Philosophy*, vol. 16, no. 4: 287–99.

———— (2004a) 'Post-Independence African Political Philosophy', in Kwasi Wiredu (ed.), *Companion to African Philosophy*. Oxford: Blackwell.

———— (2004b) 'Of Intellectuals, Politics, and Policy-making in Nigeria', *West Africa Review*, issue 5.

———— (2006) 'The Legal Subject in Modern African Law: a Nigerian Report', *Human Rights Review*, vol. 7, no. 2: 17–34.

———— (2008) 'Òrìṣà; A Prolegomenon to a Philosophy of Yorùbá Religion', in Jacob K. Olupona and Terry Rey (eds), *Òrìsà Devotion as World Religion: The Globalization of Yorùbá Religious Culture*. Madison: University of Wisconsin Press.

———— (2010a) *How Colonialism Preempted Modernity in Africa*. Bloomington: Indiana University Press.

———— (2010b) '"The Love of Freedom Brought Us Here": an Introduction to Modern African Political Philosophy', *South Atlantic Quarterly*, vol. 109, no. 2: 391–410.

———— (2011) 'Africa's Second Struggle for Freedom'. *NEXT* (Nigeria). 19 June (online newspaper now defunct).

———— (2012) *Africa Must be Modern: A Manifesto*. Ibadan: Bookcraft Books.

———— (2013) 'Cabral, Culture, Progress and the Metaphysics of Difference', in Firoze Manji and Bill Fletcher Jr. (eds), *Claim No Easy Victories: The Legacy of Amilcar Cabral*. Dakar: CODESRIA; Ottawa: Daraja Press.

———— (2014) *Africa Must be Modern: A Manifesto*. Bloomington: Indiana University Press.

BIBLIOGRAPHY

———— (2015) 'Looking Back, Facing Forward: (Re)-Imagining a Global Africa', *Black Scholar*, vol. 45, no. 1: 50–68.

———— (2016) 'The slap heard around the world; the shame watched around the world', *TheNews* (Nigeria), 5 May. https://thenewsnigeria.com.ng/2016/05/05/the-slap-heard-around-the-world-the-shame-watched-around-the-world/

———— (2017) 'Philosophy and the State in Postcolonial Africa', in Tejumola Olaniyan (ed.), *State and Culture in Postcolonial Africa*. Bloomington: Indiana University Press.

———— (2018a) 'Of Problem Moderns and Excluded Moderns: On the Essential Hybridity of Modernity', in Paul C. Taylor, Linda Martin Alcoff and Luvell Anderson (eds), *The Routledge Companion to Philosophy of Race*. New York: Routledge.

———— (2018b) 'Excluded Moderns and Race/Racism in Euro-American Philosophy: James Africanus Beale Horton', *CLR James Journal*, vol. 24, no. 1/2: 177–204.

———— (2019a) 'African Intellectuals: Occident Anxiety', *Africa in Fact*, issue 49: 23–7.

———— (2019b) 'Rethinking the Decolonization Trope in Philosophy', *The Southern Journal of Philosophy*, vol. 57, Spindel Supplement: 135–59.

———— (2021a) *Can a Liberal Be a Chief? Can a Chief Be a Liberal? On an Unfinished Business of Colonialism*. Chicago, IL: Prickly Paradigm Press.

———— (ed.) (2021b) 'Doing Sociology in Africa'. Special Issue. *Journal of Contemporary African Studies*, vol. 39, issue 3.

Tamale, Sylvia (2020) *Decolonization and Afro-Feminism*. Ottawa: Daraja Press.

Thiam, Cheikh (2014) *Return to the Kingdom of Childhood: Re-envisioning the Legacy and Philosophical Relevance of Negritude*. Columbus: Ohio State University Press.

Ukpokolo, Isaac E. (ed.) (2017) *Themes, Issues and Problems in African Philosophy*. Cham, Switzerland: Palgrave Macmillan.

Uzomah, Hyginus Onyeaghala (2018) 'Decolonizing African Educational System as a Panacea for Africa's Educational Advancement in the 21st Century', *African Renaissance*, vol. 15, no. 1: 29–43.

BIBLIOGRAPHY

Vaughan, Olufemi (ed.) (2004) *Indigenous Political Structures and Governance in Nigeria.* Ibadan: Bookcraft.

Wahba, Mourad (2022) *Fundamentalism and Secularization.* Trans. by Robert K. Beshara. London: Bloomsbury.

Waterman, Christopher (1990) *Jùjú: a Social History and Ethnography of an African Popular Music.* Chicago, IL: University of Chicago Press.

Wilder, Gary (2015) *Freedom Time: Negritude, Decolonization, and the Future of the World.* Durham, NC: Duke University Press.

Wiredu, Kwasi (1980) *Philosophy and an African Culture.* New York: Cambridge University Press.

——— (1995) *Conceptual Decolonization in African Philosophy: Four Essays.* Selected and introduced by Olusegun Oladipo. Ibadan: Hope Publications.

——— (1996) *Cultural Universals and Particulars.* Bloomington: Indiana University Press.

——— (ed.) (2004) *A Companion to African Philosophy.* Malden, MA: Blackwell.

——— (2006) 'Toward Decolonizing African Philosophy and Religion', in Edward P. Antonio (ed.), *Inculturation and Postcolonial Discourse in African Theology.* New York: Peter Lang.

INDEX

INDEX

INDEX

INDEX

INDEX

INDEX

INDEX

INDEX

Mernissi, Fatima, 56, 171, 178
metaphysics of difference, 13
Mill, John Stuart, 39, 138
Mills, John Attah, 215
Minneapolis Police Department, 203
missionary school of modernity, 163
modern legal system, 73
modern state, 184, 192, 193, 202, 205, 206, 208, 215, 220
modernity and colonialism, 59, 64, 136
modernity, 26, 59, 71, 72, 75, 89, 90, 100, 153, 163, 177, 179, 191, 198, 199, 200, 201, 206, 207, 208, 209, 210, 212, 214, 220, 221, 236n91, 236n95
Modi, Narendra, 39
Montaigne, Michel de, 127
Moorish rule, 149
Morocco, 77, 153, 171, 185, 197
morphology, 110, 122
Moving the Centre: The Struggle for Cultural Freedoms (Ngũgĩ wa Thiong'o), 116
Mozambique, 149, 150
Mphahlele, Ezekiel (Es'kia), 85–91, 126, 149, 178, 204
multilingualism, 119
multiparty democracy, 161, 162
Myanmar, 39, 199, 207

national liberation, 27, 61
native agency, 37, 29, 38, 147

Ndebele, Njabulo, *The Cry of Winnie Mandela*, 90
Négritude, 85
neocolonialism, 29–30, 31, 40. *See also*: Kwame Nkrumah, Obafemi Awolowo
neoliberalism, 51, 52; in United Kingdom, South Korea, Indonesia, Argentina, Italy, Spain, Ireland, Greece, 52–53
Ngũgĩ wa Thiong'o, 2, 14, 54, 59, 67–71, 87, 88, 94, 95, 96, 100, 101, 115, 116, 117, 120, 121, 124, 129, 130, 138, 154, 155; on linguistic decolonisation, 74–85; language policies, 115
Niger, 118
Nigeria Police Force, 203
Nigeria, 1, 2, 9, 10, 11, 30, 37, 46, 59, 71, 73, 75, 110, 118, 141, 147, 164, 166, 196, 203, 204, 205, 206, 208, 219
Nigerian Art Music, 13
Nketia, Joseph, 14
Nkrumah, Kwame, 27–29, 56, 65, 138, 165, 167, 171, 172, 173, 177, 186, 194 *See also*: neo-colonialism
Northern Ireland, 52
Nupe, 84, 122, 124
Nwapa, Flora, 90
Nyerere, Julius, 39, 65, 135, 138, 165, 171, 177, 186, 243n43

Obafemi, Olu, 101

INDEX

INDEX

returnees, 84, 134, 156

Roman, Byzantine and Ottoman colonialisms, 153

Rotimi, Ọla, 18

Rousseau, Jean-Jacques, 108

rule of law, 169, 171, 181, 185 201, 208, 216, 220, 221, 246n14

Russia, 69, 77, 199, 236n93

Sahrawi, 181

Sarbah, John Mensah, 165, 173

satire, 111, 112

scientific revolution, 89

second struggle for freedom, 48, 72, 73, 182, 193, 204

Segun, Mabel, 90

Sekoto, Gerard, 87

Sekyi, William Essuman Gwira, 160, 165

Sekyi-Otu, Ato, 8, 13, 25–26, 36, 41, 53, 131–132

selective vision, 85

self-determination, 34, 40, 174

self-government, 27, 163

self-ownership, 16, 45

semantics, 110, 122

Sembène, Ousmane, 67, 129

Senegal, 49, 118, 129, 141, 217

Senghor, Léopold Sédar, 11, 39, 56, 76, 86, 90, 124, 127, 132, 133, 134, 137, 172, 180, 181, 217, 237n5

Serequeberhan, Tsenay, 15, 43, 132–135, 136, 138, 178, 237n8

Serer, 180

settler colonialism, 16, 17, 21, 49

Sierra Leone, 141, 215

Singapore, 41

Sithole, Ndabaningi, 171

slave-owners, 42–43

Smith, Patricia Olubunmi, 101

Society of African Culture, 85, 87

sociocryonics, 148, 212

Solanke, Ladipo, 173–176

South Africa, 36, 41, 49, 51, 75, 77, 87, 88, 149, 171, 179, 209, 226n18; multiple colonialisms, 52;

South Korea, 39, 52, 69, 151, 188, 199

South Sudan, 196

sovereignty of the subject, 72, 201

Sowande, Fela, 10–13

Soyinka, Wole, 11, 18, 59–60, 76, 83, 90, 101, 127, 134, 180, 181, 242n38

Spain, 48, 53, 149, 150, 187, 242n34

Spanish, 84, 121, 153, 200, 225n16, 239n22, 242n34

Special Anti-Robbery Squad (SARS), 231

Sudan, 39, 48, 147, 195, 196, 210, 214, 218

supernaturalism, 32

syntax, 12, 13, 44, 92, 93, 96, 97, 105, 110, 122, 124, 125, 127

Syria, 181

Tanzania, 47, 115, 135, 215

INDEX

INDEX